Anne Willan's
BASIC FRENCH COOKERY

ANOTHER BEST SELLING COOKERY VOLUME FROM H.P. BOOKS

Publisher: Helen Fisher; Editors: Veronica Durie, Carlene Tejada; Art Director: Don Burton; Book Assembly: Tom Jakeway; Typography: Cindy Coatsworth, Joanne Nociti; Food Stylist: Mable Hoffman; Photography: George deGennaro Studios.

LA VARENNE—Editor: Faye Levy; Editorial Assistant: Berneil Juhnke; Recipe Testing: Linda Collister

Published by H.P. Books, P.O. Box 5367, Tucson, AZ 85703   602/888-2150
ISBN 0-89586-056-2; ISBN 0-89586-086-4 (cloth)
Library of Congress Catalog Card No. 80-83186
©1980 Fisher Publishing, Inc. Printed in U.S.A.

Cover Photo: Roast Chicken Fermière, page 78

A dinner typical of the Burgundy region is shown on the following pages. Left to right: assorted cheeses; Parslied Ham, page 25; Veal Chops Dijonnaise, page 102; Leek Gratin, page 116; Chocolate Truffles, page 167.

What is French Cooking?

What's so special about French cooking? Why is it considered the finest in the West, the envy of less fortunate nations? Is its reputation founded on ingredients, or on recipes, or on the cooks themselves? Or is it a grand con game, invented by the French and perpetuated by the efforts of journalists and restaurateurs?

One outstanding quality of French cuisine is its range. Contrary to popular belief, food need not be fancy to be French. A plain green salad, dressed with oil and vinegar, is just as typical and much more common than a galantine in aspic. Steak with *frites* is a standard lunch, the Gallic equivalent of the U.S. hamburger and French fries. More often than not, dessert is fresh fruit and cheese. The French vary their meals in the number of courses. Helpings are small, so as many different flavors as possible can be enjoyed. Service is leisurely.

Certain features of French cuisine are easy to identify. The sauces provide an example. Escoffier, author of the bible of classic French cooking, said that sauces are the capital ingredient in cooking. They form an integral part of hundreds of recipes from Norman Sole Fillets, page 62, to Chicken in Wine, page 82, to the raspberry sauce in Peach Melba, page 183. Eggs Benedict, page 58, could not exist without Hollandaise Sauce, page 45, nor Tournedos Rossini, page 94, without a Truffle Sauce.

Almost as important as the sauces are the garnishes. These are not just decorations of lemon or parsley. In France, a garnish is an essential part of a dish, endowing it with its character as well as its name. Thus Roast Chicken Fermière, page 78 and pictured on the cover, means chicken with mushrooms, bacon, onions and potatoes. Stuffed Squabs Véronique, page 80, has green grapes, and *indienne* refers to a flavoring of curry. Sole Véronique is yours for the asking simply by changing the main ingredient, and so, for that matter, is Pork Chops Fermière.

There's no doubt that French ingredients are second to none. The variety of fish, meat and produce available is unrivalled anywhere and cooks treat it with due respect. To ensure freshness, they shop often. They make a point of mastering techniques such as whipping egg whites or trussing a bird. They keep an eye on dishes during cooking, turning a pastry that is browning too much on one side, or basting a roast that looks dry. They taste constantly to adjust seasoning and spend that extra five minutes on presentation which transforms a dish from the ordinary to the special.

And this care is appreciated because the French spend time, not only in cooking, but in eating. For centuries French cuisine has prospered both as a science and an art. As a science with a logical structure, it is the basis of so much other cooking. As an art, it is part of the heritage of France.

To me, this is the key to French cooking: an attitude of mind. From the care with which vegetables are selected and the time lavished on the simplest salad, to the passion with which diners discuss everything put before them, the French devote more attention, more love, to cooking than anyone else. They argue about it, enter competitions for it, even award their chefs with the *légion d'honneur*. They revel in every aspect of cooking. You will never go far wrong if you do the same.

Preparing Ahead

Advance preparations are possible at different points for many recipes in this book. To make it easier for you to plan ahead, these advance preparations are shown in italics.

Ingredients You Use

French cooks make the most of fresh foods and flavorings that are at hand and you should do the same. Very few of the ingredients in these La Varenne recipes are hard to obtain, but if you have problems, here are a few guidelines:

Alcohols & liqueurs are in many cases interchangeable. The French use *Cognac* brandy, from a carefully defined area of France, but any good brandy will do. *Kirsch* is cherry eau-de-vie, made domestically as well as imported from Europe. For *Grand Marnier* you can use any orange liqueur and for Calvados, any apple brandy.

Arrowroot is a starch similar to potato starch; both are used to thicken sauces at the end of cooking. Cornstarch can be substituted but it will give a heavier result. Allow two teaspoons cornstarch for every one teaspoon arrowroot or potato starch in the recipe.

Bacon for French dishes should be lean. Try to find a brand that is lightly smoked.

Breadcrumbs are best if you make your own. For *fresh* breadcrumbs, trim the crusts from sliced fresh white bread and cut the bread in cubes. Work them in the blender or food processor, a few at a time. For *dry* breadcrumbs, bake slices of white bread in a 300°F (150°C) oven until golden brown and let cool before working in the blender or processor.

Butter is essential for authentic French flavor. Margarine of similar consistency can be substituted, but recipes, particularly pastry, will not taste the same. The French even use butter to grease their baking pans. Unless otherwise stated, *butter* refers to lightly salted butter.

Cheese for grating can be Gruyère or Parmesan, but remember that Parmesan has a much stronger flavor, so you need about half the quantity. Cheeses which are labeled *Swiss* can sometimes cause problems in cooking because of their high fat content.

Chocolate that is used for cooking in France has an excellent flavor, so use imported chocolate if available. Otherwise you can substitute semisweet chocolate.

Cream should be heavy or whipping cream. Sterilized cream has less flavor than cream that is only pasteurized. In France the cream has a high butterfat content and contains lactic acids that make it as thick as dairy sour cream, with a characteristic tart flavor. For a real French touch to savory dishes, particularly soups and fish sauces, use *crème fraîche.* You can easily make it at home: stir together 2 cups heavy cream and 1 cup of either buttermilk, dairy sour cream or plain yogurt in a saucepan. Heat gently until the mixture is no longer cold, but still below body temperature. Pour into a container and partly cover. Leave at room temperature for six to eight hours or overnight until the cream is thick and tastes slightly acidic. Stir, cover and refrigerate.

Eggs should be 2 ounces in weight, or graded *large.* Eggs of a different size can greatly alter delicate cake batters, pastries or soufflés. However, for simple egg recipes, size is not important.

Flour in this book is regular all-purpose flour, unless otherwise stated. Measure it *before* sifting.

Garlic is used often in French meat and vegetable recipes. The flavor of garlic should always blend with the other ingredients, rather than dominate them. Exceptions are dishes such as Snails with Garlic Butter, page 71, and Provençal Frogs' Legs, page 72.

Herbs should be fresh whenever possible. When one kind is not available, experiment with others, taking care to add strong flavors like rosemary a little at a time. If substituting dried herbs, use one third the quantity.

Milk which is whole, not skimmed, is best for cooking.

Mustard is often added to sauces, both hot and cold. Use ready-prepared Dijon-style mustard. Adjust the quantity to your taste, as some mustards are stronger than others. Do not use hot prepared or dry mustard.

Nutmeg is a favorite spice for dishes containing milk or cream and for many vegetables, especially spinach. There is a great difference between freshly grated and ready-ground nutmeg, so buy whole nutmegs if you can and grate what you need into each dish.

Oil for general cooking should be unflavored vegetable oil unless some other type is specified. For salads, use whatever oil you prefer. For deep-frying, only shortening, lard and certain vegetable oils are suitable as many fats burn at too low a temperature to fry foods satisfactorily.

Parsley is the most common herb. The stems can be added to a bouquet garni for flavoring, while the sprigs are used whole for decoration or chopped for sprinkling. Curly-leaf parsley is the most attractive for sprigs, while flat-leaf Italian parsley has a stronger flavor for sprinkling. For most purposes they are interchangeable.

Pepper is used in nearly all savory dishes and comes in several forms. The most common is whole peppercorns and ground black or white pepper. *Peppercorns* are added to dishes that are cooked a long time, when ground pepper would turn bitter. *Ground white pepper* is made of black peppercorns stripped of their skin, then ground. Use it in light-colored dishes where specks of black pepper would show. Freshly ground black pepper, which has a more aromatic flavor, should be used for everything else.

Potato starch is used just like arrowroot.

Salt is the most important seasoning and comes as rock salt or kosher salt, and fine salt. Kosher salt is easier to use in large quantities of liquid, such as water for cooking vegetables. Fine salt is needed for careful seasoning, when it is added a little at a time or when there is little liquid to dissolve it.

Shallots belong to the onion family. They are used in many fish and meat dishes. If you can't get them, substitute the white part of a green onion, or a fourth of a medium onion.

Sugar refers to the fine white granulated variety, unless otherwise stated in the recipe.

Truffles are widely available canned whole and, at a lower price, in pieces. Fresh truffles are an expensive rarity, even in large cities. If you cannot find canned truffles or they are too costly, omit them.

Vanilla can be bought in the form of extract made from vanilla beans, or as the bean itself. Beans should be split to expose the seeds and soaked in liquid to extract the full flavor. After using, rinse the bean, dry it and use again two or three times. Vanilla extract should be added to a cool mixture; if heated it will evaporate.

Vegetables should be fresh, but frozen ones are better than canned. One exception is tomatoes. If fresh tomatoes are not vine-ripened, canned Italian-style tomatoes often have more flavor for adding to cooked dishes.

Vinegar should be a mild red or white wine vinegar. Herb-flavored vinegars can also be used. Avoid harsh malt or alcohol vinegars.

Wine for cooking need not be expensive but should be good enough to drink. White wines are best when dry but not acidic, and red wines full-bodied but not fruity. Rosé wines are generally not used. During cooking, both red and white wines should be thoroughly reduced to remove their alcohol and some of their acidity. An exception is fortified wines such as Madeira, which should not be cooked for very long because they lose flavor. Port or sweet sherry can be substituted for Madeira.

Anne Willan

Anne Willan, an American citizen, was born in Yorkshire, England. She completed formal education at Cambridge University with a Masters degree in Economics. Anne then studied and taught cooking in London and Paris, gaining the *Grand Diplôme* of the French Cordon Bleu school. In 1965, she moved to the United States, soon joining the editorial staff of the magazine *Gourmet*. The following year Anne married Mark Cherniavsky, a British economist working for the World Bank in Washington, D.C. They have two children, Simon and Emma.

Anne was food editor of the *Washington Star* for two years. She began to develop her own career as a cookery writer, achieving distinction as the editor-in-chief of the 20-volume *Grand Diplôme Cooking Course*. Her first book was *Entertaining Menus*. Her second book, *Great Cooks and Their Recipes* won a Tastemaker award as a notable historical work, and has been translated into German and Italian.

Having moved back to Europe with her family, Anne opened *Ecole de Cuisine La Varenne* in November 1975. The cooking school, which is in Paris, now has an international reputation. Besides serving as its President, Anne directs La Varenne's publishing program. The school has published its own *Tour Book*, featuring recipes used by visiting La Varenne chefs in the U.S.A.

Anne is a regular visitor to the U.S.A. for cookery demonstrations and media appearances.

Techniques to Make It Easy

You will find the following techniques useful in many different dishes.

How to Make a Bouquet Garni

A Bouquet Garni or bunch of herbs, is one of the key flavorings in French cooking, adding a subtle spice to sauces, soups, braises and stews. It consists of a small bay leaf, a sprig of fresh thyme and three to four stems of parsley. The parsley leaves are kept for chopping. Fold the parsley stems in half to enclose the thyme and bay leaf, then tie with string in a tight bundle. If fresh thyme is not available, use 1/4 teaspoon dried leaf thyme, and tie everything together in a piece of cheesecloth. The Bouquet Garni is immersed in liquid during cooking, then discarded before serving. To make a large Bouquet Garni, double the ingredients.

How to Clarify Butter

Clarifying eliminates the milky residue in butter, leaving only the pure fat. Clarified butter is ideal for frying because it does not burn easily. It is also needed for some butter sauces.

Melt the butter in a saucepan over low heat. With a spoon, skim and discard the froth from the surface of the butter. Carefully pour the clear melted butter into a bowl. Stop pouring the butter when you reach the milky residue in the bottom of the pan. Discard the milky residue. The butter is now clarified.

How to Make Egg Glaze

To color pastries golden brown, brush them with Egg Glaze before baking: beat 1 egg with 1/2 teaspoon salt until well mixed. Salt breaks down egg white, so the glaze will become liquid. Just before baking, brush pastry with a light coating of glaze, taking care it does not drip down the sides and seal the pastry to the baking sheet. After glazing, score patterns in the pastry with the point of a knife, if desired.

Egg Glaze is also used to seal two layers of dough together, as in Patty Shells, page 22.

How to Whip Egg Whites to Stiff Peaks

Egg whites are whipped until stiff but not dry. They help cakes and soufflés to rise in the oven and give lightness to cold desserts. For desserts, some of the sugar in the recipe is often set aside for beating into the whites. This makes them glossy and smooth—in effect a light meringue—which is easier to fold into other ingredients.

Whipping egg whites to stiff peaks.

In order for the egg whites to whip properly, the whites, bowl and whisk must be completely free of any trace of water, grease or egg yolk. The French prefer to whip egg whites in a copper bowl because they acquire a greater volume and density than by any other method. The best alternative is to use an electric beater with a metal bowl.

A copper bowl must be cleaned every time it is used. Clean it by rubbing the surface with 1 to 2 tablespoons salt and 1 to 2 tablespoons vinegar, or use salt and the cut surface of a lemon. Rinse and dry thoroughly. The surface of the copper will be shining and almost pink in color.

Begin whipping the whites at low speed. When they become foamy and white, gradually increase the speed to maximum. The whites are beaten enough when they form a stiff peak when the whisk is lifted. The whites gather in the whisk and stick to it without falling. If overbeaten, the egg whites become dry and lumpy and cannot be folded easily with other ingredients.

How to Make Lemon Decorations

Lemons make a charming and functional decoration, particularly for fish. Other citrus fruits can be prepared in the same way for serving with any citrus-flavored dish.

Lemon baskets: Cut a thin slice from the bottom of the lemon so the basket will stand level. With a small sharp knife, remove nearly a quarter section from the top half. Remove the other quarter section from the top half of the lemon, leaving a center strip wide enough to form the basket handle. Cut away the flesh under the handle. Either leave the bottom half of the lemon for squeezing, or remove all the flesh, leaving a basket. Fill with sauce, cut vegetables or fruit.

Making wolf's teeth and lemon baskets.

Wolf's teeth: Cut a thin slice from the top and bottom of the lemon, so the two halves will stand level. With a small pointed knife, cut a zig-zag line all around the lemon cutting to the center of the fruit. Pull the two lemon halves apart. If you like, set a small sprig of parsley in the center or sprinkle with chopped parsley.

Fluted lemon slices: Use a citrus stripper or zester to cut lengthwise grooves down the lemon. Try to space the grooves evenly. Cut the lemon across in thin slices. For fluted half-slices, halve the grooved lemon lengthwise. Lay it flat-side down and cut in thin crosswise slices.

Cutting lemons into fluted slices.

How to Make Croûtes

Allow one slice of white bread for each person. Trim the crusts and cut each slice diagonally into two triangles.

For heart shapes, cut off one small end of each triangle and round the bread into a heart shape.

Heat enough oil, butter or a mixture of both easily to cover the bottom of a skillet. Oil makes very crisp Croûtes and butter gives a good flavor. When the fat is very hot, add the bread in one layer and fry until golden brown on both sides.

Drain the Croûtes immediately on paper towels so they won't be greasy. If you like, rub the fried Croûtes with a cut clove of garlic. They can be fried up to three hours ahead and kept uncovered at room temperature.

How to Use Gelatin

When using gelatin, pay special attention to temperature. First, gelatin must be sprinkled over a small quantity of cold liquid, usually water, to soften. Leave it at least five minutes until it swells and is spongy. Then the gelatin must be dissolved, either by heating it in a water bath, below, or by adding it to a hot mixture. In both cases, stir the mixture thoroughly when adding the gelatin so it is distributed evenly.

Continue stirring the mixture from time to time as it cools. This serves the dual purpose of preventing the gelatin separating and also tells you when it starts to thicken. Gelatin sets at around the freezing point of water, and it sets suddenly. So watch the mixture carefully once it is cool: As you stir, you will feel it getting stiffer. This is the moment when any other ingredients should be added, such as whipped cream or egg whites. Work fast, as the gelatin mixture will set quickly. Do not, however, be tempted to get ahead by adding the cream too soon, as a warm gelatin mixture will cause it to melt and liquify. Quickly pour the finished mixture into a prepared mold. It will take two to four hours to set firmly in the refrigerator.

To unmold gelatin desserts: run a knife around the edge of the dessert and pull it away from the mold with a finger to release the airlock. Dip the bottom of the mold in a bowl of hot water for a few seconds. Set a platter upside down on top and invert the mold and platter. Give a sharp shake so the dessert falls onto the platter.

Gelatin molds or mousses can be kept one to two days in the refrigerator. Their texture will stiffen, so let them come to room temperature before serving. Mixtures containing gelatin cannot be frozen as they separate on thawing.

How to Cook in a Water Bath

A water bath is used for pâtés, terrines and vegetable molds which need slow cooking so heat reaches the center of the food without overcooking the outside. Egg custards, which curdle when overheated, also are cooked in a water bath.

Set the cooking dish in a large shallow pan, such as a roasting pan, and fill the pan with hot water to within one inch of the rim of the dish. Bring the water to a boil on top of the stove, then transfer the dish in the water bath to the oven. Start counting cooking time from the moment when the bath is put in the oven. Water keeps food in the mold at a constant temperature so it cannot get too hot, and makes steam which moistens the food.

A water bath can be used on top of the stove for melting gelatin and chocolate, for cooking sauces like Hollandaise and for keeping food hot.

Another even safer way of keeping delicate sauces warm is to put the container of sauce on a rack set on top of a pan of simmering water.

Placing Petits Pots de Crème, page 176, in a water bath.

How to Blanch & Peel Nuts

Bring a saucepan of water to a boil. If you are using chestnuts, pierce a hole in the shells with a pointed knife. Add the almonds, pistachios or prepared chestnuts, bring back to a boil and remove the pan from the heat. Let the nuts stand in the water one to two minutes. Remove almonds and pistachios. When the nuts are cool enough to handle, peel them.

Almonds: Press the almonds one by one between your thumb and index finger; they will slip out of the skins.

Pistachios: Remove the skins, using a small knife if necessary.

Chestnuts: Remove a few chestnuts at a time from the hot water; pull off peel and inner skin with a knife.

Walnuts and pecans: Do not need peeling.

How to Grind Nuts

Nuts should be ground as finely as possible, especially when they are going to be used in a cake batter. They have a high oil content, so it is not easy to grind the nuts without crushing them and extracting the oil. If crushed, the nuts will be pasty instead of fluffy and light.

Grind nuts, except chestnuts, a few at a time in a special nut mill, a rotary cheese grater, a blender or a food processor. If using a blender or food processor, whirl them as quickly and briefly as possible, checking each time to see if they are fine enough before continuing. If using them for a sweet dish, you can grind them with part of the sugar, or with flour if the dish is savory.

How to Peel, Seed & Chop Tomatoes

Tomatoes must often be peeled and seeded because the skin and seeds would spoil the smooth texture of a sauce or stew.

Peeling: Bring a large saucepan of water to a boil. Fill a bowl with cold water. Using a small knife, remove the core of each tomato. Cut a cross in the opposite end of the tomato, making a shallow cut to slit only the skin but not the flesh. Plunge the tomatoes into the boiling water and leave them 10 to 15 seconds; the skin will begin to pull away from the slit. Do not leave them for too long, or they will start to cook. With a slotted spoon, transfer the tomatoes immediately to the bowl of cold water. When cool, drain them and peel off the skin with a small knife; it will come away easily.

Seeding: Halve each tomato horizontally. Hold each half over a bowl and squeeze the seeds and juice into the bowl without crushing the pulp.

Chopping: Using a large knife, slice each half tomato, then turn the tomato around and slice it crosswise. The tomato flesh will now be in chunks. If needed, chop them smaller.

How to Fold Mixtures Together

To preserve the lightness of the ingredients, many mixtures are folded together rather than stirred or beaten. Whipped egg whites are folded into soufflé bases and batters, so they don't lose the air that makes the mixtures rise. In gelatin desserts, whipped cream is folded into the basic mixture so the cream does not separate due to overbeating. Flour and melted butter are folded into *génoise* batter so they do not cause the delicate egg mixture to lose its volume.

Peeling and seeding tomatoes.

Folding one mixture into another.

Two mixtures fold together most easily if their consistency is similar. If one ingredient is much lighter than the other, stir a little of it thoroughly into the heavier mixture. This procedure is especially helpful for folding egg whites into a base mixture to make soufflés. Then add the heavier mixture to the lighter one, so the heavier mixture does not sit at the bottom of the bowl.

Use a wooden spatula or a large metal spoon for folding. Cut the spoon across the center of the mixture, scraping the bottom of the bowl, and scooping the spoon under the mixture towards the left side of the bowl. At the same time, with the left hand, turn the bowl counterclockwise. Reverse the directions if you are left-handed. This should be a synchronized movement: cut and scoop the spoon with one hand, turn the bowl with the other. In this way, the spoon reaches as great a volume of mixture as possible in one movement, so the mixture is folded quickly and the ingredients mixed easily, losing a minimum of air.

How to Flame Foods

Flaming is not just for spectacular show. At the same time as it burns off the alcohol, the flame toasts the dish and, if it contains sugar, helps to caramelize it. When the flame goes out, only the essence of the liquor will remain. Dishes must be flamed with a liquor that contains a high proportion of alcohol, such as rum or brandy. Liqueurs such as Grand Marnier are either used alone or mixed with a higher-proof liquor for flaming.

Be sure the food you want to flame is very hot. Heat the liquor in a very small saucepan until hot but not boiling. **Stand back and turn your face from the flames,** then light the liquor with a long match or by tipping the pan towards a gas flame. Pour the flaming alcohol over the food and baste the dish rapidly. If the dish was not hot enough, the flames will die at once. They should be left to go out naturally, but if the food starts to scorch, blow out the flame. Crepes are especially inclined to burn at the edges.

Alternatively, the liquor can be heated with the food, but sometimes it is absorbed before it is hot enough to light. Heating the liquor and food separately gives a more certain flame.

How to Make Caramel

Caramel is the last stage reached when boiling a sugar syrup. The syrup browns to a deep golden caramel just before it burns. Caramel is not only a flavoring for desserts, it can also be used in sweet-sour sauces.

To make caramel: Use a heavy saucepan or the syrup will cook unevenly, burning in some spots before it browns in others. Heat sugar and water over low heat, shaking the pan occasionally, until the sugar is dissolved. Sugar syrup should never be stirred during cooking as it may crystallize before it cooks to the stage you want. When the sugar is dissolved, boil the syrup over high heat. At first it will boil rapidly, then the bubbles will break more slowly until the syrup turns golden at the edges of the pan. This is the start of caramelization. When caramel is golden brown it is mild and sweet. The darker it turns, the better the flavor of the caramel, until it starts to burn and become bitter. The caramel has reached this stage when it smokes. Caramel syrup changes color fast, so watch it carefully, lifting it off the heat from time to time to control cooking. When it is deep golden, dip the base of the pan in cold water to stop cooking immediately.

> **Caramel reaches a VERY high temperature, so take care when working with it. Use an oven glove to protect your hand from splashes and, when adding warm water to make a caramel sauce, stand back as the mixture will splatter.**

Making caramel.

How to Caramelize Ingredients

Fruits and vegetables, especially apples and root vegetables like carrots, are often cooked with a little sugar until caramelized or glazed.

Cooking should be done over high heat. This is so the sugar, which is usually mixed with oil or butter, or a spoonful or two of water, coats the food in a shiny, even layer, called a *glaze*. Cooking is often continued until the coating browns and the food is caramelized. For an even finish, always use a wide pan so all the ingredients are in contact with the base. If necessary, cook them in two batches.

How to Taste for Seasoning

Knowing how to *taste for seasoning* is one of the most important skills of a good cook. Even a well-cooked dish with the best ingredients will be disappointing if it is not seasoned carefully.

Seasoning normally refers to salt and pepper. If any others such as nutmeg or lemon juice are to be used, the recipe will say so. The exact amount of seasoning cannot be predicted because it depends on the type of ingredients used and how long they are cooked. The mild or pungent flavors of additions like bacon and cheese must also be considered. It will also vary with the kind of salt and pepper you like to use.

At the beginning of cooking, you should season a mixture lightly, especially if the dish will cook a long time. Liquid will evaporate and flavors mellow, concentrating the seasoning. Taste at least once during cooking and always check flavor before serving. Sauces and stuffings should be highly flavored to highlight the ingredients they accompany. However, soups and other dishes that are served on their own should be more subtly flavored.

The seasoning of some dishes, like terrines or potato cakes, cannot be adjusted once they are cooked. These are the most difficult recipes to season and adding salt and pepper is a matter of experience. If you are in doubt, sauté a small amount of the mixture to be cooked and taste to check flavor. Add more seasoning if necessary.

How to Make a Sauce of Coating Consistency

Coating consistency is the desired thickness of a sauce that is neither gluey nor runny but adheres lightly to food.

If too thick, a sauce will taste unpleasant; if too thin, it will run off the food instead of coating it.

Making a sauce of coating consistency.

Judging the correct consistency for a sauce is a matter of experience. One test is to dip a spoon into the sauce, lift it out and hold it rounded-side up. If the sauce just clings to the spoon, it is of light coating consistency and is fine for sauces that will be served apart from the rest of the dish. For a thicker sauce to coat food, draw a finger across the back of the spoon; your finger should leave a clear trail.

How to Reduce a Cooking Liquid or Sauce

Often when a dish is done, the cooked meat, poultry or vegetables are removed to a serving dish, and the cooking liquid is boiled, uncovered, to the right flavor and consistency. This process, called *reduction*, is vital to French cuisine. As the liquid boils, its flavor becomes more concentrated. If it contains flour, its consistency thickens. When you are reducing a liquid, bear in mind that it will evaporate more quickly in a wide pan. You can leave unthickened liquids to reduce without attention, but thickened sauces will stick if not stirred from time to time.

How to Thicken a Sauce with Potato Starch or Kneaded Butter

If a sauce tastes good but is too thin, it should be thickened with potato starch, arrowroot or kneaded butter instead of by reduction. All three thicken a mixture quickly and easily. Potato starch and arrowroot give a lighter result while kneaded butter is richer.

Potato starch or arrowroot: Stir the starch into a small quantity of cold water or other liquid until dissolved. Pour it gradually into the boiling sauce, whisking constantly. Add enough for the sauce to thicken to the desired consistency. Bring sauce just back to a boil.

Kneaded butter: Kneaded butter is a mixture of approximately equal quantities of butter and flour. Soften the butter on a plate with a fork and work in the flour. Whisk the kneaded butter, piece by piece, into the boiling sauce until thickened to the desired consistency. Simmer one minute and remove from the heat.

How to Make Gravy

The principle of making gravy for roast and pan-fried meats and poultry is simple. The meat juices which congeal and slightly caramelize in the bottom of a roasting pan or skillet, are dissolved with hot liquid. The liquid used can be a mixture of wine and stock or water.

Gravy for red meats should be dark brown. A lighter colored gravy is desirable for white meats and poultry. To add flavor to gravy from roasts, cook a quartered onion and carrot, plus any bones, in the pan with the meat. If juices start to burn on the bottom of the pan before roasting is finished, add stock or water, using only a little at a time so the meat does not steam and lose its seared crust.

At the end of cooking, pour excess fat from the pan. The French like to leave some fat in their gravy particularly for dry meats like veal and chicken, but this is a matter of taste. Usually you'll find the juices remaining in the pan are sufficiently browned because of the high heat used in pan-frying and in roasting by the French method. However, if they are still pale, you can continue cooking them on top of the stove.

Next add about 1/2 cup of liquid per person. This can be water, stock, red or white wine, or a mixture depending on the recipe and your own preference. Boil hard, stirring with a metal spoon to dissolve all the juices congealed on the bottom and sides of the pan, until the liquid is reduced by half. This will give about 1/4 cup of gravy per person. Strain the gravy into a saucepan, skim off excess fat, season and taste. If the gravy is still thin, continue boiling until it is concentrated.

The French prefer gravy to have the natural meat flavor, so no thickening and few extra ingredients such as a little Madeira or chopped herbs, are added sometimes just before serving.

How to Prevent Skin Forming on Flour-Based Sauces & Creams

When flour-based mixtures such as white and velouté sauces, cream puff pastry, pastry cream and soufflé mixtures, are prepared in advance, a skin may form on top. To prevent this, as soon as the mixture is cooked, rub the surface with butter to seal it from the air: Take a small piece of cold butter on a fork or knife and dab it quickly over the surface of the warm mixture. It will gradually melt. Because the mixture will be whisked when it is reheated, the butter will be absorbed.

Rubbing the surface of sauce with butter to prevent a skin forming.

How to Use a Pastry Bag

A pastry bag is almost indispensable for shaping many pastries such as Ladyfingers, page 163, Eclairs, page 161, and Cream Puffs, page 160. It can also be used for decorations made with Duchess Potatoes, page 124, Butter Cream, page 141, Chantilly Cream, page 157, and meringue.

Filling a pastry bag with mixture.

Pressing mixture through pastry bag.

Meringue, Cream Puff Pastry and Chantilly Cream require a fairly large tube of 3/8- to 5/8-inch diameter; when working with Butter Cream a 1/4- to 3/8-inch pipe is best. As a general rule, plain tubes are used for shaping pastries and star tubes for piping decorations.

Filling a pastry bag: Put the tube in the bag. Hold the bag, tip downwards, in your left hand and fold an inch or two of the bag over your open hand. Gently spoon in the mixture; then unfold the top of the bag and twist it to close, pushing the mixture down toward the tube.

Piping: Hold the bag in your right hand, keeping the twisted top between the thumb and first finger. Use the remaining fingers of your right hand to press the mixture in the bag. With the left hand, support the bag without squeezing it. While piping, hold the bag slightly above the surface to be decorated so the tube does not touch it.

Reverse these directions if you are left-handed.

Remember that simple designs are often the most effective.

How to Line Tartlet or Boat Molds

Butter the molds and arrange them close together near the working surface.

Place the ball of dough on the floured working surface. Pound it lightly with the rolling pin to flatten it. Roll out the dough, working from the center of the ball to the edges, to obtain an even rectangle. It should be about 1/4 inch thick and large enough to allow two inches from the edge of the outside mold to the edge of the dough.

Wrap the dough around the rolling pin, lift it and gently lay it on top of the molds, being careful not to stretch it. Press dough into the base of the molds with a small ball of dough dipped in flour.

Roll the rolling pin over the tops of the molds to trim the pastry. Using your forefinger and thumb, press the dough evenly up the sides from the bottom to increase the height of the edge. Neaten the edges with your finger and thumb. Do not let dough overlap the edges of the molds.

Prick the bottoms of the shells thoroughly to prevent air bubbles forming during cooking.

Chill the shells thoroughly before baking, then set them on a baking sheet.

How to Line a Pie Pan

If possible, use a pie pan with a removable base so the pie can be unmolded. Butter the pie pan.

Place the ball of dough on a floured working surface. Pound it lightly with the rolling pin to

1/Wrap rolled-out dough around rolling pin and unroll over pie pan.

2/Roll the rolling pin over top of pie pan to cut off excess dough.

How to Line a Pie Pan

3/With your thumb and forefinger, press dough up sides of pie pan.

flatten it. Roll out the dough, working from the center of the ball to the edges, and turning the dough after each stroke to obtain an even round. The round should be about 1/4 inch thick and two inches larger than the pie pan.

Wrap the dough around the rolling pin, lift it over the pie pan and unroll it. Let the dough rest over the edge of the pan, overlapping it slightly inside. Be careful not to stretch it. Gently lift the edges of the dough with one hand and press it well into the bottom corners of the pan with the other, using a small ball of dough which has been dipped in flour.

Roll the rolling pin over the top of the pan to cut off the excess dough. If the edges of the pan are not sharp enough to cut dough, trim it with a knife. Using your forefinger and thumb, press the dough evenly up the sides from the bottom to increase the height of the edge. Neaten the edge with your finger and thumb and flute it if you are making a sweet pie. Do not let the dough overlap the edge of the pan.

Prick the base of the shell thoroughly to prevent air bubbles forming during cooking.

Chill the shell thoroughly before baking.

How to Bake Pie or Tartlet Shells Blind

Preheat the oven to 400°F (205°C). Roll out the dough and line the pie pans or tartlet molds. Chill thoroughly.

For a pie, cut a round of waxed or parchment paper two inches larger than the diameter of the pie. For tartlets, crumple small pieces of the paper. Line the pie or tartlet shells with the paper, pressing it well into the bottom corners. Fill pie shell three-fourths full with uncooked beans or rice—this holds the dough in shape. The beans or rice can be used again for the same purpose. For tartlets, you can place a smaller tartlet mold, lightly buttered on the underside, in the lined pan instead of using paper and beans.

Bake a large pie shell in the preheated oven 15 minutes and tartlet shells six to ten minutes or until the pastry is set and lightly browned. Lift out the paper and beans and continue baking a pie shell six to eight minutes and tartlet shells about five minutes or until the pastry is golden brown. Let the shells cool slightly. Then unmold and transfer to a rack to cool completely.

Using dried beans in paper to bake blind.

DECORATIONS FOR SAVORY DISHES		
Ingredient	**What to Do**	**Where to Use**
capers	Drain	Sprinkle on cold fish or meat dishes
croûtes	Fry (pages 8 and 29)	Arrange around or under poultry or meats in a rich sauce
hard-cooked eggs	Chop, or separate white from yolk and chop separately	Sprinkle on salads, on cold fish or egg dishes or on hot vegetables
lemons	Make lemon decorations (page 8)	Arrange on platters of fish or cooked salads
lettuce leaves	Use whole or halved	Arrange underneath cold meat, fish or poultry, or around salads
parsley	Chop Separate in fresh sprigs Deep-fry in bunch, then use sprigs	Sprinkle on food mixed with sauce Arrange on platters of appetizer pastries or cold meat Decorate fried foods
pickles, olives	Drain and use whole or sliced	Add to platters of sliced terrines or cold meats
raw vegetables	Leave whole (radishes, cherry tomatoes) Prepare simple salads (page 133)	Add to platters of sliced cold meats
watercress	Use bunches of the leafy part	Arrange on platters of roast or pan-fried meats

Appetizers

French cookbooks rarely devote much space to appetizers—they leave them to the cook's imagination. And, once you know a few basic pastries and sauces, you can create countless new appetizers just by varying the fillings and flavors.

Appetizers can be divided into two categories: hors d'oeuvre, served at a cocktail party or with drinks before a meal; and appetizers that form the first course of the meal. Vegetable and meat appetizers are usually first courses. Filled pastries double as both. Make hors d'oeuvre bite-size so they can be handled easily.

How to Plan Appetizers

When planning appetizers, keep one rule in mind: make them light and in small portions so your guests have room for the rest of the meal. This is the ideal place to stretch ingredients. An expensive ingredient like *foie gras* (goose liver) will be shown to best advantage, so you can buy just a small amount. This is also the time to use up bits of fish, meat or vegetables that would not be enough for a main course.

Don't think you need to spend hours on preparation. Some of the best appetizers take so little time there are no recipes to describe them. For instance, you can serve thinly sliced raw or cooked ham with gherkin pickles, green or black olives, sliced rye bread and a crock of butter. Smoked fish, whether salmon, trout, mackerel or eel, is a favorite accompanied by buttered whole-wheat bread and lemon wedges. Leftover cooked fish or chicken can be mixed with mayonnaise and served on lettuce leaves. Simplest of all are clams or oysters on the half shell, or caviar. All three should be served with lemon halves and buttered whole-wheat or rye bread.

How to Prepare Appetizers Ahead

Because so many meat and vegetable appetizers are served cold, they can be prepared ahead. Many are improved if the flavors have time to blend and mature, particularly pâtés and terrines.

Pastries and crepes, which are best when made the same day, have the advantage of needing ingredients that are generally at hand—flour, butter, eggs and milk. Fillings can range from simple scrambled eggs to luxuries like lobster, shrimp, oysters or asparagus. Because they are invariably mixed with mayonnaise (if cold) or white sauce (if hot), a little goes a long way.

How to Serve Appetizers

Appetizers should be an invitation, but must not overwhelm the dishes to follow. So go lightly on the seasoning, and take time on presentation. For cocktails, make pastries all the same size and arrange them in a grand display on a platter. A touch here and there of black olive, red tomato or paprika, and green parsley can make all the difference. Add color to cold appetizers with lettuce leaves and lemon decorations.

Some appetizers, such as Mushroom Crepes or Country Terrine, become a light main course when served in large portions. Conversely, many recipes in other chapters of this book make good appetizers, such as Fish Croquettes, page 64, Mussels in White Wine, page 70, and Snails in Garlic Butter, page 71. Alternatives include many of the egg and cheese dishes, Spinach Soufflé, page 117, and any of the salads with the exception of Green Salad.

Mushroom Crepes
Crêpes aux Champignons

Always let crepe batter stand 1 to 2 hours before cooking so your crepes will be light and tender.

16 Crepes, see below	**Pinch of nutmeg**
Water	**1/2 cup milk**
3/4 lb. large mushrooms, diced	**1/2 cup whipping cream**
3 tablespoons butter	**1/2 cup grated Gruyère cheese or**
Juice of 1/2 lemon	**1/4 cup grated Parmesan cheese**
Salt and pepper to taste	
Thick Basic White Sauce, page 40,	
made with 2-1/2 cups milk	

Crepes:

1 cup all-purpose flour	**2 tablespoons melted butter or**
1/4 teaspoon salt	**vegetable oil**
1 cup milk	**1/3 cup clarified butter, page 7, or**
3 eggs	**vegetable oil**

Prepare Crepes. Grease a shallow 2-quart baking dish. In a medium saucepan, place 1/4 inch of water, mushrooms, 2 tablespoons butter, lemon juice, salt and pepper. Cover and cook over high heat 5 minutes or until liquid boils to top of pan and mushrooms are tender. Cool. Preheat broiler. Prepare Thick Basic White Sauce and stir in cooking liquid from mushrooms. Season with salt, pepper and nutmeg. Stir half the sauce into mushrooms. Spoon a tablespoon of mushroom mixture onto each crepe; roll into cigar shapes. Arrange rolled crepes diagonally in prepared baking dish. Stir milk and cream into remaining sauce. Reheat and taste for seasoning. Pour sauce over crepes, covering them completely. Sprinkle with grated cheese. Melt remaining 1 tablespoon butter and sprinkle over grated cheese. Heat under broiler until bubbling and browned. *Mushroom Crepes with the sauce can be made 3 days ahead, covered and refrigerated or frozen. Reheat chilled crepes in a 350°F (175°C) oven 20 to 30 minutes until bubbling and browned.* Makes 7 servings or 16 crepes.

Crepes:
Sift flour into a large bowl. Make a well in center of flour and add salt and half the milk. Gradually whisk in flour to make a smooth batter. Whisk in eggs; do not overbeat as batter will become elastic and crepes will be tough. Stir in melted butter or oil with half the remaining milk. Cover and let batter stand 1 to 2 hours; it will thicken slightly. *Batter can be made 24 hours ahead, covered and refrigerated.* Just before using, stir in enough remaining milk to make batter the consistency of thin cream. Brush a 7-inch crepe pan with clarified butter or oil. Heat until a drop of batter sprinkled in pan sizzles. Pour 2 to 3 tablespoons batter into pan, turning pan quickly to coat bottom evenly. Cook over medium-high heat until crepe is browned on bottom; turn with a metal spatula. Brown other side and turn out onto a plate. Continue with remaining batter, greasing pan only when crepes start to stick. Pile cooked crepes on top of each other to keep bottom ones moist and warm. *If making crepes ahead, layer with waxed paper, cover and refrigerate up to 3 days or freeze.* Makes 14 or 16 crepes.

How to Clean Mushrooms

Put the mushrooms into a bowl of water and rub them between your fingers to dislodge any sand. Lift the mushrooms from the water. Check whether there is sand on the bottom of the bowl. Discard the water. If there was sand on the bottom of the bowl, rinse out the bowl and wash the mushrooms again using the same method. Dry the mushrooms on paper towels or with a cloth.

Eggplant Charlotte
Charlotte d'Aubergines

Yogurt's tart flavor perfectly balances the richness of eggplant in this mold.

3 to 4 small eggplants (about 2 lbs.)
Salt
1 cup olive oil
1 medium onion, finely chopped
1 clove garlic, crushed

10 tomatoes (2 lbs.), peeled, seeded, chopped, page 10
Salt and pepper to taste
1 cup plain yogurt
1 cup stock

Wipe eggplants and trim stems; do not peel. Cut into 3/8-inch slices. Sprinkle with salt and let stand 30 minutes. Drain, rinse with cold water and dry on paper towels. Heat 2 tablespoons olive oil in a large skillet. Add onion. Sauté until lightly browned, stirring often. Add garlic, tomatoes, salt and pepper. Cook tomato mixture over medium heat, stirring often, 20 to 25 minutes until mixture is thick and pulpy. Taste for seasoning. Reserve about a third of the tomato mixture for sauce. Heat some of the remaining olive oil in a large skillet and brown eggplant slices on both sides in several batches, adding oil as needed. Arrange a layer of overlapping eggplant slices in a 1-quart charlotte mold or 8-inch, round cake pan. Spread with a little tomato mixture and yogurt. Continue layers until all eggplant slices and yogurt are used, ending with an eggplant layer. *Eggplant Charlotte can be prepared to this point 24 hours ahead, covered and refrigerated.* Mix reserved tomato mixture with stock. Preheat oven to 350°F (175°C). Cover mold with foil. Bake 40 to 50 minutes until a skewer inserted in center is hot to the touch when withdrawn after 30 seconds. To serve hot, cool charlotte slightly, then unmold onto a platter. Bring tomato mixture to a boil in a medium saucepan. Taste for seasoning and spoon around base of mold. To serve at room temperature, let charlotte cool and unmold a short time before serving; spoon cool sauce around base. Makes 6 servings.

How to Make Eggplant Charlotte

1/Overlap browned eggplant slices in a charlotte mold.

2/Serve hot or at room temperature.

Cocktail Tartlets & Boats

Tartelettes et Barquettes de Cocktail

Hot or cold, round or boat-shaped, the more you vary these tartlets, the prettier your platter will be.

Pie Pastry, pages 148-149, made with
  1-1/2 cups flour

Shrimp, Ham & Cheese, or
  Smoked Salmon Filling, see below

Shrimp Filling:
1-1/2 cups cooked shrimp, finely chopped
1/3 cup Mayonnaise, page 50

1 tablespoon tomato paste
Paprika

Ham & Cheese Filling:
1/2 cup cooked ham, finely diced
1/2 cup Gruyère cheese,
  finely diced
2 to 3 tablespoons Mayonnaise, page 50

1 teaspoon Dijon-style mustard
1/2 slice canned pimiento, drained,
  cut in thin strips

Smoked Salmon Filling:
1 (3-oz.) pkg. cream cheese
4 to 6 tablespoons whipping cream
1/4 lb. smoked salmon, finely chopped

Pepper
2 tablespoons capers, drained, chopped

Refrigerate Pie Pastry at least 30 minutes. Prepare desired filling. Preheat oven to 400°F (205°C). Grease twenty 1-1/2-inch tartlet molds or 2-1/2-inch boat molds. Roll out dough 1/4 inch thick and use to line molds, page 14. Refrigerate until dough is firm, then bake blind, page 16. Cool shells in molds. Remove cooled shells from molds and spoon in desired filling. Makes about 20 tartlets or boats.

Shrimp Filling:

In a medium bowl, mix shrimp with Mayonnaise and tomato paste, adding more or less of each to taste. Generously sprinkle half of each boat with paprika.

Ham & Cheese Filling:

In a medium bowl, combine ham, cheese, Mayonnaise and mustard. Spoon into baked pastry shells. Smooth tops with a spoon. Decorate with 2 crossed strips of pimiento.

Smoked Salmon Filling:

In a medium bowl, beat cream cheese with enough cream to soften. Stir in smoked salmon with a little more cream, if needed, to make a soft mixture. Add pepper to taste. Mound in tartlet shells. Sprinkle with capers.

Chilling helps dough hold its shape during baking and reduces shrinkage.

Quiche Lorraine
Quiche Lorraine

For a filling that is not quite so rich, use half milk and half cream.

Pie Pastry, pages 148-149, made with	**Pinch of nutmeg**
1-1/2 cups flour	**1 tablespoon butter**
3 eggs	**4 to 5 slices bacon, diced**
1-1/2 cups whipping cream	**1/3 cup diced Gruyère cheese**
Salt and pepper to taste	

Refrigerate Pie Pastry at least 30 minutes. Preheat oven to 400°F (205°C). Roll out chilled dough 1/4 inch thick and use to line a 9- to 10-inch pie pan, pages 14 and 15. Refrigerate until dough is firm, then bake blind, page 16, 15 minutes or until set but not completely browned. Cool shell slightly in pie pan. Reduce oven temperature to 375°F (190°C) and place a baking sheet in oven to heat. Beat eggs with cream, salt, pepper and nutmeg. Melt butter in a small skillet. Sauté bacon in butter until browned. Sprinkle bacon and cheese over bottom of pie shell. Place pie pan on hot baking sheet. Pour egg filling over bacon and cheese. Bake 35 to 40 minutes until filling is set and golden brown. Do not overcook or filling will curdle. The quiche will puff while baking and shrink slightly when taken from oven. Cool slightly. Serve hot or at room temperature. *Quiche Lorraine can be made 1 day ahead, but not more because pastry becomes soggy; cover tightly and refrigerate. Reheat chilled quiche in a 350°F (175°C) oven.* Makes 6 to 8 servings.

Variation

Onion Quiche (Quiche à l'Oignon): Omit bacon and cheese. Thinly slice 4 large (1-1/2 lbs.) Bermuda or other mild onions. Melt 2 tablespoons butter in a medium, heavy saucepan. Stir in onions and salt and pepper. Press a piece of buttered foil on top of onions. Cover saucepan. Cook over low heat, stirring occasionally, 20 to 30 minutes until onions are very soft. Do not brown. Cool slightly. Spread in baked pie shell. Pour egg filling over onions and continue as above.

Sausage Rolls
Rouleaux aux Saucisses

These tidbits can be frozen, but do not refrigerate because they become soggy.

Puff Pastry, pages 154-155,	**Egg Glaze, page 7**
made with 2/3 cup butter or	**30 cocktail sausages**
1 lb. Puff Pastry Trimmings	

Prepare Puff Pastry, completing all 6 turns. Refrigerate at least 1 hour. Preheat oven to 425°F (220°C). Sprinkle water on 2 baking sheets. Roll out Puff Pastry dough 1/4 inch thick. Trim edges with a knife. Brush entire surface with Egg Glaze. Cut in 6-inch wide strips. Place cocktail sausages lengthwise along one edge of each strip; roll up. Gently press seam to seal. Cut roll between each sausage. Place each Sausage Roll seam-side down on prepared baking sheets. Brush with Egg Glaze. Use the back of a knife to decorate tops with a lattice pattern without cutting through dough to sausage. Refrigerate 15 minutes or until dough is firm. Bake 8 to 12 minutes until puffed and browned. Transfer to a rack to cool. *Sausage Rolls can be frozen unbaked or baked.* Makes about 30 rolls.

Smoked Oyster Bouchées
Bouchées de Cocktail aux Huîtres Fumées

This hot filling can also be used in Cocktail Tartlets & Boats, page 20.

Puff Pastry, pages 154-155, made with
  2/3 cup butter

Egg Glaze, page 7
Curried Smoked Oyster Filling, see below

Curried Smoked Oyster Filling:
Medium Basic White Sauce, page 40,
  made with 1 cup milk
1 teaspoon curry powder
1 (3-1/2-oz.) can smoked oysters,
  drained, chopped

1 hard-cooked egg, page 52, chopped
Salt and pepper, if desired

Prepare Puff Pastry, completing all 6 turns. Refrigerate at least 1 hour. Preheat oven to 425°F (220°C). Sprinkle water on 2 baking sheets. Roll dough out to between 1/8 and 1/4 inch thick. Cut out 1-1/2-inch rounds with a fluted cookie cutter. Place half the rounds on prepared baking sheets. Cut a 1/2-inch circle from the center of each remaining round with a plain cookie cutter to make rings. Brush Egg Glaze on rounds on baking sheets. Immediately place rings on top of glazed rounds and press gently to seal. Refrigerate 15 minutes. Brush top of rings with Egg Glaze, taking care none spills down the sides. Bake 12 to 15 minutes until puffed and browned. Transfer to a rack to cool. While pastry is still warm, remove center "hat" and reserve. Scoop out any uncooked dough with a teaspoon. *Cocktail Patty Shells can be made 3 to 4 days ahead and kept in an airtight container. They can also be frozen unbaked or baked.* Prepare Curried Smoked Oyster Filling. Not more than 2 hours before serving, generously fill shells with filling. Heat filled shells uncovered on a baking sheet 10 to 15 minutes in a 325°F (165°C) oven. Replace "hats" on top just before serving. Makes about 50 patty shells.

Curried Smoked Oyster Filling:
Prepare Medium Basic White Sauce, using all optional ingredients and whisking curry powder with flour into melted butter. Simmer 3 to 5 minutes. Stir in oysters and chopped egg. Taste for seasoning. Add salt and pepper, if desired.

Cheese Fingers
Allumettes au Fromage

Puff Pastry is a challenge, but the results make the effort worthwhile.

Puff Pastry, pages 154-155,
  made with 2/3 cup butter, or
1 lb. Puff Pastry trimmings

Egg Glaze, page 7
1-1/2 cups grated Parmesan cheese

Prepare Puff Pastry, completing all 6 turns. Refrigerate at least 1 hour. Preheat oven to 425°F (220°C). Sprinkle water on 2 baking sheets. Roll out Puff Pastry dough 1/4 inch thick. Trim edges with a knife. Brush entire surface with Egg Glaze. Sprinkle generously with grated cheese. Cut in 6-inch wide strips. Cut strips in half lengthwise, making strips 3 inches wide. Cut crosswise to make 3" x 1" strips. Place on prepared baking sheets. Refrigerate 15 minutes or until dough is firm. Bake 8 to 12 minutes until puffed and browned. Transfer to a rack to cool. *Cheese Fingers can be made 2 days ahead and stored in an airtight container. They can also be frozen unbaked or baked.* Makes about 80 fingers.

1/Cut out rounds and rings from Puff Pastry.

2/Fill patty shells with curried smoked oysters.

How to Make Smoked Oyster Bouchées

Mushrooms à la Grecque

Champignons à la Grecque

This highly seasoned appetizer can be made with a variety of vegetables.

1 tablespoon peppercorns
4 tablespoons coriander seeds
3 bay leaves
4 thyme sprigs
3 to 4 parsley sprigs
2 tablespoons tomato paste
1-1/2 to 2 cups White Veal Stock, page 31,
  Chicken Stock, page 32, or water
1/4 cup white wine

Juice of 1 lemon
1/4 cup vegetable oil
1/4 cup olive oil
20 to 25 baby onions
2 lbs. mushrooms
4 tomatoes, peeled, seeded, chopped,
  page 10
Salt to taste

Tie peppercorns, coriander seeds, bay leaves, thyme and parsley in a piece of cheesecloth. In a medium bowl, mix tomato paste, stock or water, wine and lemon juice. In a large saucepan, heat vegetable oil and olive oil. Stir in baby onions. Sauté 3 minutes or until lightly browned. Add mushrooms, tomatoes, spice bag, tomato-paste mixture and salt. Liquid should just cover mushrooms; add more stock if needed. Bring to a fast boil. Boil uncovered 20 minutes or until mushrooms and onions are tender. Cook over high heat at a rolling boil the entire cooking time so oil and liquid emulsify and thicken the sauce. Let cool. Taste for seasoning. Remove spice bag. The flavor of this dish mellows on standing. Serve at room temperature. *Mushrooms à la Grecque can be prepared 2 days ahead, covered and refrigerated.* Makes 6 to 8 servings.

Country Terrine Photo on page 27.
Terrine de Campagne

Made with cream, this terrine will be moist, but won't keep more than one week.

1/2 lb. bacon, sliced
1 tablespoon butter
1 onion, chopped
1 lb. pork (half fat, half lean), ground
1/2 lb. veal, ground
1/2 lb. chicken livers, finely chopped
2 garlic cloves, finely chopped
1/4 teaspoon ground allspice
Pinch of ground cloves
Pinch of nutmeg
2 small eggs, slightly beaten
1/2 cup whipping cream, if desired

2 tablespoons brandy
Salt and pepper to taste
1/2 cup shelled pistachios, blanched,
    peeled, page 9, if desired
1 thick slice cooked ham (about 1/2 lb.),
    cut in strips
1 bay leaf
1 sprig fresh thyme or
    1/2 teaspoon dried leaf thyme
2 to 3 tablespoons water
1/3 cup all-purpose flour

Line a 2-quart terrine mold or deep casserole with bacon, reserving a few slices for top. Preheat oven to 350°F (175°C). Melt butter in a small saucepan. Stir in onion. Sauté until soft but not browned. Cool. In a large bowl, mix sautéed onion with pork, veal, chicken livers, garlic, allspice, cloves, nutmeg, eggs, cream, if desired, brandy, salt and pepper. Beat until seasoning is evenly blended. Sauté a small piece of mixture and taste for seasoning; it should be very spicy. Beat in pistachios, if desired. Spread a third of the mixture in prepared mold. Place half the ham strips lengthwise over mixture in mold. Top with another third of the mixture. Arrange remaining ham strips on top. Add remaining meat mixture. Cover with reserved bacon. Place bay leaf and thyme on top of bacon; cover with a lid. In a small bowl, gently mix water and flour to make a paste; do not beat or paste will become elastic. Spread flour paste around edge of lid to seal terrine. Place terrine in a water bath, page 9. Bring water to a boil on top of stove, then transfer terrine in water bath to oven. Bake 1-1/2 hours or until a skewer inserted in center is hot to the touch when withdrawn after 30 seconds. Remove cooked terrine from oven and cool to warm. Remove cooked flour paste and lid. Press terrine with a board or plate weighted with a 2-pound weight until terrine is completely cool. Refrigerate terrine up to 7 days before serving; the flavor will improve after a few days. Serve in mold or unmolded; cut in 1/2-inch slices. *Country Terrine can be frozen.* Makes 8 servings.

Chicken Liver Pâté
Pâté de Foies de Volailles

A delicious hors d'oeuvre to be served on toast triangles, bread or crackers.

3/4 cup butter
1 onion, chopped
1/2 lb. chicken livers
2 shallots, finely chopped
1 garlic clove, crushed

Salt and pepper to taste
2 tablespoons brandy
1/3 cup clarified butter, page 7,
   if desired

Melt 3 tablespoons butter in a medium skillet. Stir in onion. Cook over low heat until soft but not browned. Stir in chicken livers. Cook over medium heat 2 to 3 minutes until browned on all sides but still pink in center. Stir in shallots, garlic, salt and pepper. Reduce heat to low and continue cooking 1 minute. Remove from heat; cool slightly. Puree mixture in food processor or blender or press it through a sieve. Let cool to lukewarm. Beat in remaining butter and brandy. Taste for seasoning. Spoon pâté into 4 custard cups or ramekins. *Chicken Liver Pâté can be made 4 days ahead and refrigerated. To extend storage time to 1 week, smooth top and spoon clarified butter over top to prevent a crust from forming.* Makes 4 to 6 servings.

Parslied Ham   Photo on pages 2 and 3.
Jambon Persillé

Mild cooked country ham is perfect for this dish, but processed ham works, too.

Shank half of a ham with bone (7 to 8 lbs.)
2 calf's feet or pig's feet, split
1 lb. veal bones
1 large bouquet garni, page 7
12 peppercorns, tied in cheesecloth

1 bottle dry white wine
About 3 qts. water
1 tablespoon white wine vinegar
1/2 cup chopped parsley
Salt and pepper, if desired

Cut ham into 2-inch chunks, reserving bone; set meat aside. Blanch calf's feet or pig's feet by covering with cold water and bringing to a boil. Reduce heat and simmer 5 minutes. Drain. In a large pot, place reserved ham bone, blanched calf's feet or pig's feet, veal bones, bouquet garni, bag of peppercorns and wine. Add water barely to cover. Cover with lid. Bring slowly to a boil. Reduce heat and simmer 3 hours or until feet are tender and meat pulls from bone. Add chunked ham to pot. Simmer 1 hour longer or until ham is tender enough to pull apart with a fork; skim often while simmering to remove fat that rises to surface. Remove from heat; cool slightly. Place warm ham and pig's feet in a large bowl, reserve. Simmer cooking liquid with bones uncovered until reduced to 1-1/2 quarts. Strain through a cheesecloth into a large bowl. Stir in vinegar. Add parsley while liquid is hot for a bright green color. Taste for seasoning. Add salt and pepper, if desired. Skim off fat as it rises to surface. Use 2 forks to pull meat from feet, discarding bones. Pull apart ham chunks to make smaller chunks of meat. Pile meat loosely in a deep 2-1/2-quart bowl. Spoon parsley liquid over and around pieces of meat to completely cover. Cover and refrigerate 3 to 4 hours until firmly set. *Parslied Ham can be made 7 to 10 days ahead, covered and refrigerated. The flavor will improve after a few days.* To unmold, run a knife around edge of aspic; dip bottom of bowl in hot water a few seconds. Place a serving plate over bowl and invert plate and bowl. Give bowl and plate a firm shake so Parslied Ham falls onto plate. Remove bowl. Let ham come to room temperature before serving. Cut in wedges. Makes 15 to 20 servings.

Sausage in Brioche
Saucisson en Brioche

If you prefer more meat, increase the number of sausages to four.

Brioche, pages 166-167
2 French garlic or Polish kielbasa
   sausages, (about 1-1/2 lbs.)

Egg Glaze, page 7

Prepare Brioche dough and let rise at room temperature. Refrigerate 30 minutes before rolling out. If sausage is already cooked, remove skin. If raw, place in boiling water in a medium saucepan. Bring water almost to a boil again. Reduce heat and poach 18 to 20 minutes. Do not let water temperature rise above 175°F (80°C). Drain and cool. Remove skin. Grease two 9" x 5" x 4" loaf pans. Preheat oven to 400°F (205°C). Roll out dough to an 18" x 7" rectangle. Place sausages lengthwise along center of dough; wrap dough around sausages. Pinch edges to seal. Turn seam-side down. Cut roll between sausages. Pinch ends of each roll to seal and place in prepared pans. Cover with a damp cloth towel. Let rise at room temperature 25 to 30 minutes until pans are almost full. Do not let dough become too warm while rising or butter will melt from dough. *Unbaked Sausage in Brioche can be frozen in the loaf pan before rising. It should be thawed and left to rise before baking.* Brush Egg Glaze over loaves. Bake 40 to 45 minutes until Brioche is browned well and starts to pull away from sides of pan. Turn out of pan onto a rack to cool. Serve the same day or freeze. To serve, cut cooled loaf in 3/4-inch slices, discarding ends. Makes 2 loaves or 12 to 20 servings.

Artichokes Vinaigrette
Artichauts Vinaigrette

Fingerbowls will be needed for rinsing your hands after eating these artichokes.

4 large artichokes
Salt and pepper to taste
2 tablespoons wine vinegar
6 tablespoons vegetable oil

2 tablespoons chopped fresh herbs such as
   parsley, tarragon, chives or chervil

Break stems from artichokes to remove tough fibers. Cut 1 inch off top with a knife. Snip off sharp points of each leaf with scissors. Wash artichokes. In a large pot, bring to a boil enough salted water to cover artichokes. Put artichokes into boiling water and place a wet cloth towel on water surface to keep artichokes submerged; reduce heat. Simmer uncovered 30 to 40 minutes until a leaf can easily be pulled out. Drain artichokes. If serving at room temperature, rinse with cold water. Gently squeeze excess water from each artichoke and drain upside-down 5 minutes. Artichokes can be soggy if not drained well. Firmly grasp the tender, purple leaves in center of artichoke and pull out in 1 piece to retain cup shape. Scoop out hairy choke with a teaspoon; discard. Place clump of purple leaves upside-down in center of artichoke, pressing sharp points into artichoke bottom. *Artichokes can be prepared to this point 12 hours ahead, covered and refrigerated.* Serve hot or at room temperature. Whisk vinegar with salt and pepper. Gradually beat in oil so dressing emulsifies. Taste for seasoning. Whisk in chopped herbs. Pour a little dressing into cup in center of artichoke. Serve remaining dressing separately. Makes 4 servings.

Sausage in Brioche is on the cutting board. Country Terrine, page 24, is in the crock.

Stocks & Soups

Simmer a few bones and vegetables in water and you'll have *stock,* a basic ingredient in many French soups, sauces and main dishes. Stock is simple and inexpensive to make at home. Don't regard it as just a tiresome intermediate preparation that leads nowhere. If you add a simple garnish like chopped fresh herbs or sliced mushrooms, you'll have a clear soup. For something more substantial, cook a few vegetables in the stock, as in French Onion Soup. More sophisticated is Consommé which is made of stock clarified with egg whites and simmered with beef and vegetables so it becomes sparkling clear and aromatic.

For a soup of completely different character, simmer chopped vegetables in stock, puree them and enrich the soup with milk, cream or butter to make a thickened soup. Bisque is a variation made with shellfish. Rice or potatoes often give body to this type of soup, though its consistency should never approach the thickness of a sauce. Both clear and thickened soups can be made out of almost any ingredient—in fact you can serve a clear vegetable soup one day and turn it into a thickened soup the next by pureeing it and adding cream. You will hardly recognize it!

How to Make Stock

Stock depends on bones for most of its flavor and body—particularly veal bones which contain a good deal of gelatin. Chicken and other poultry bones have some gelatin also, as do fish bones. There are only two requirements for making good stock: the liquid must be skimmed often to remove grease and foam, particularly while coming to a boil, and it must be cooked at a low simmer—never boiled. If stock does boil, it becomes cloudy and acquires an unpleasant acrid taste.

Vegetables, notably onion and carrot, add flavor to all kinds of stock. Some benefit from the addition of a stick of celery, a bouquet garni and even a clove of garlic. In general, avoid strong ingredients like cabbage or turnip. Stock is never seasoned at the beginning of cooking. This is because the liquid is boiled to reduce it to half or less of its original volume and strong flavors—especially salt—can become overpowering. If you season stock at the end of cooking, or when adding it to a dish, you can adjust the taste to suit the other ingredients.

Stocks require little work, though some must be simmered for several hours to extract all the flavor and gelatin from the bones. Veal and beef take longest—four to five hours—while an hour or two is enough for poultry and 20 minutes for a fish stock. At the end of cooking, you can discard vegetables and bones for they have yielded all their flavor.

How to Prepare Stock Ahead

Stock is easy to prepare ahead. Once the liquid has come to a boil and simmered an hour, you can interrupt cooking, cool the stock by placing the pot in a sink of cold running water and refrigerate it up to a day before continuing. After stock is cooked completely, strain it and cool quickly for it turns sour within a few hours at room temperature. Refrigerate it as soon as possible and never leave it in a warm kitchen. If stored in an aluminum pot, it can also turn sour. Stock freezes perfectly or it can be stored one to two days (for fish stock) or two to three days (for poultry and meat stock) in the refrigerator. To keep poultry and meat stock longer still, bring it to a boil and simmer 10 minutes before refrigerating again for a day or two.

How to Use Stock

As a general rule, white stock goes with light meats such as poultry, veal and pork. Brown stock is mainly for beef and lamb dishes. Uses of the other types are equally logical: fish stock for seafood, and chicken stock for poultry. But even if you have only one or two kinds of stock on hand, some substituting is still possible. Beef stock doubles for Brown Veal Stock and chicken for White Veal Stock. Only Fish Stock has no substitute and even then a simple version can be made with clam juice.

Soup Garnishes

Fried Croutons, are the most common garnish for thickened soups. In France they are passed in a separate bowl to preserve their crispness. However, do not serve them with Consommé because their fat clouds the soup. Ideal for serving with Consommé are small poached eggs or shreds of leftover crepes. Miniature Cheese Puffs can be served separately. Most other garnishes suit either type of soup, so choose what you like.

Croûtes of sliced bread that are toasted rather than fried can be topped with grated cheese before browning. Grated cheese can also be served separately, a favorite accompaniment to fish and mixed vegetable soups. One way to garnish a thickened soup is with its main ingredient. Shrimp Bisque is topped with a few shrimp and Fresh Pea Soup with a few peas, thus giving the key to what is within.

Miniature Cheese Puffs *Photo on page 63.*
Petits Choux au Fromage

Cream Puff Pastry, page 160, made with 1/2 cup flour

1/4 cup grated Parmesan cheese

Preheat oven to 400°F (205°C). Lightly grease a baking sheet. Prepare Cream Puff Pastry, beating in cheese after adding eggs. Spoon mixture into a pastry bag fitted with an 1/8-inch plain tube. Pipe thimble-size mounds onto prepared baking sheet. Bake 12 to 15 minutes until crisp and browned. Serve hot or at room temperature. Makes about 30 puffs.

Croûtes
Croûtes

1/2 cup olive oil
1 (1/2-lb.) long loaf French bread, cut in 20 diagonal slices

1 garlic clove

Heat olive oil in a medium skillet until very hot. Add half the bread slices. Toss until Croûtes are evenly browned. Remove and drain on paper towels. Repeat with remaining bread slices. Rub each Croûte with the cut side of a half clove of garlic. Makes 20 Croûtes.

Croutons
Croûtons

3 slices white bread
3 tablespoons vegetable oil

3 tablespoons butter

Trim crusts from bread. Cut bread into small cubes. In a medium skillet, heat oil and butter until very hot. Add bread cubes and shake skillet over heat until Croutons are evenly browned. Remove Croutons and drain on paper towels. Makes about 2 cups of Croutons.

Brown Veal Stock
Fond Brun de Veau

Browning the bones adds flavor and gives this stock its rich color.

4 to 5 lbs. veal bones, cracked or
  cut in 2 or 3 pieces
2 onions, quartered
2 carrots, quartered
2 celery stalks, cut in 2-inch pieces
1 large bouquet garni, page 7

10 peppercorns
1 garlic clove
1 tablespoon tomato paste
3 to 4 qts. water
1/2 onion, if desired

Preheat oven to 450°F (230°C). If you don't have a heavy cleaver, ask a butcher to crack or cut bones. Place bones in a roasting pan and roast, stirring occasionally, 30 to 40 minutes until browned. Stir in quartered onions, carrots and celery. Continue roasting until vegetables are browned. Transfer bones and vegetables from pan to a large pot, leaving fat in roasting pan. Add bouquet garni, peppercorns, garlic, tomato paste and water to bones and vegetables. Slowly bring to a boil, taking 20 to 30 minutes and skimming often. To add more color, singe the cut part of half an onion over an electric or gas stove burner until black. Add to the stock. Reduce heat and simmer uncovered 4 to 5 hours, skimming occasionally. Add more water during cooking to keep bones covered. Stock should reduce very slowly to about 2 quarts. Strain and taste. If not well-flavored, boil to reduce and concentrate the flavor. Cool quickly by placing pot in a sink of cold running water. Refrigerate. When cold, skim solidified fat off top. *Brown Veal Stock can be made 2 to 3 days ahead, covered and refrigerated or frozen. After 3 days of refrigeration, boil stock 10 minutes and cool. Stock can then be refrigerated another 1 or 2 days.* Makes about 2 quarts of stock.

Variation

Brown Beef Stock (Fond Brun de Boeuf): Substitute beef bones for veal bones. Brown Beef Stock has a milder flavor than Brown Veal Stock. It also has less body because it contains less gelatin. It is often used to make rich sauces for beef and game.

Stock is not seasoned with salt and pepper because it will be used to make soups, sauces, stews, etc. of varying degrees of saltiness. Adjust seasoning when finishing a dish.

1/Use roasted veal bones and cut up vegetables. 2/Skim fat and foam from stock occasionally.

How to Make Brown Veal Stock

White Veal Stock
Fond Blanc de Veau

Try to get veal knuckle bones. They contain the most gelatin.

**4 to 5 lbs. veal bones, cracked or
    cut in 2 or 3 pieces**
2 onions, quartered
2 carrots, quartered
2 celery stalks, cut in 2-inch pieces

1 large bouquet garni, page 7
10 peppercorns
1 garlic clove
3 to 4 qts. water

If you don't have a heavy cleaver, ask a butcher to crack or cut bones. Place all ingredients in a large pot. Slowly bring to a boil, taking 20 to 30 minutes and skimming often. Reduce heat and simmer uncovered 4 to 5 hours, skimming occasionally. Add more water during cooking to keep bones covered. Stock should reduce very slowly to about 2 quarts. Strain stock and taste. If not well-flavored, boil to reduce and concentrate the flavor. Cool stock quickly by placing pot in a sink of cold running water. Refrigerate. When cold, skim solidified fat off top. *White Veal Stock can be made 2 to 3 days ahead, covered and refrigerated or frozen. After 3 days of refrigeration, boil 10 minutes and cool. Stock can be refrigerated another 1 or 2 days.* Makes about 2 quarts of stock.

Chicken Stock
Fond de Volaille

Make light stock by poaching a whole chicken. Use the chicken meat for another recipe.

**3 lbs. raw chicken backs and necks or
 1 whole chicken**
2 onions, quartered
2 carrots, quartered
2 celery stalks, cut in 2-inch pieces

1 large bouquet garni, page 7
10 peppercorns
1 garlic clove
1-1/2 to 2 qts. water

Place all ingredients in a large pot. Chicken should be covered with water. Slowly bring to a boil, taking 20 to 30 minutes and skimming often. Reduce heat and simmer backs and necks uncovered 3 to 4 hours, skimming occasionally. If using a whole chicken, remove chicken after 1-1/2 hours or when thigh is tender when pierced with a skewer. Add more water during cooking to keep bones covered. Strain stock and taste. If not well-flavored, boil to reduce and concentrate the flavor. Cool stock quickly by placing pot in a sink of cold running water. Refrigerate. When cold, skim solidified fat off top. *Chicken Stock can be made 2 to 3 days ahead, covered and refrigerated or frozen. After 3 days of refrigeration, boil stock 10 minutes and cool. Stock can then be refrigerated another 1 or 2 days.* Makes about 1-1/2 quarts of stock.

Variation

Turkey Stock (Fond de Dinde): Substitute 3 pounds raw turkey wings, backs and necks for the chicken pieces.

Fish Stock
Fumet de Poisson

Do not let fish stock boil, or it will be bitter.

1 tablespoon butter
1 medium onion, sliced
**1-1/2 lbs. fish bones, broken into
 medium pieces**
1 qt. water

10 peppercorns
1 bouquet garni, page 7
**1 cup dry white wine or the juice of
 1/2 lemon, if desired**

Melt butter in a large pot. Stir in onion. Cook over medium heat until onion is soft but not browned. Add fish bones, water, peppercorns, bouquet garni and wine or lemon juice. Liquid should almost cover bones. Do not add fish skins or stock will darken. Slowly bring to a boil, skimming often. Reduce heat and simmer uncovered 20 minutes. Strain. Cool before refrigerating. *Fish Stock can be made 1 to 2 days ahead, covered and refrigerated or frozen.* Makes about 1 quart of stock.

Variation

Fish Stock with Clam Juice (Fumet de Poisson au Jus de Palourdes): Omit fish bones. Add 2 cups bottled clam juice with 3 cups water, 1/2 cup dry white wine and a bouquet garni. Proceed as above. If finished stock is too salty, add a little more water before using.

Consommé
Consommé

Good consommé is sparkling clear. Egg whites cook to filter out any cloudiness.

1-1/2 qts. Brown Beef Stock, page 30, or
   Chicken Stock, page 32
1 envelope gelatin, if desired
Salt and pepper to taste
3/4 lb. very lean beef, chopped
2 carrots, chopped
Green tops of 2 leeks, chopped

2 celery stalks, chopped
2 tomatoes, quartered
3 egg whites
1/4 cup Madeira or sherry
Julienne, Brunoise, Madrilène or
   Niçoise Garnish, see below

Refrigerate stock until partially set. Skim fat from surface. If stock doesn't set, reserve 1/2 cup stock to soften gelatin. Softened gelatin will be added later. In a large pot, melt remaining stock and remove any remaining fat by quickly running strips of paper towel over surface. Remove from heat; cool. Add salt and pepper. Stir in beef, carrots, leeks, celery and tomatoes. Beat egg whites until frothy. Stir into cool stock. Bring slowly to a boil, stirring constantly 10 to 15 minutes. Stop stirring as soon as stock looks milky which means egg whites are cooked. With pot over medium heat, let cooked egg-white particles rise undisturbed to surface, forming a filter. Reduce heat to low. Use a ladle to make a small hole in egg-white filter so broth can bubble through. Don't make more than 1 hole or filter may break. Simmer gently 1 hour to extract flavor from beef and vegetables. Be careful not to move saucepan or filter may break. If stock did not partially set when chilled, sprinkle gelatin over 1/2 cup reserved stock. Let stand 5 minutes or until spongy. Carefully spoon spongy gelatin through hole in filter. Simmer 2 to 3 minutes to dissolve. Remove Consommé from heat. Add Madeira or sherry through hole in filter. More seasoning added at this point may cloud Consommé. Place a scalded dish towel over a colander. Place colander over a large bowl. Ladle half the Consommé over dish towel, then slide in filter with remaining Consommé. Let drain slowly without pressing. Colander should not touch the liquid so there is room for liquid to drain. If Consommé is not sparkling clear, strain again. Prepare garnish. For hot Consommé, bring almost to a boil and add garnish just before serving. Do not cook garnishes in Consommé as they will cloud it. For cold Consommé, refrigerate until slightly jelled. Just before serving, stir with a fork; spoon into chilled bowls and top with garnish. *Consommé can be made 2 to 3 days ahead, covered and refrigerated or frozen.* Makes 4 servings.

Garnishes

Julienne Garnish for Beef Consommé (Garniture pour Consommé Julienne): Cut 1 small carrot, 1 celery stalk, 1 small white turnip and white part of 1 small leek into very thin strips. Simmer in 1 cup Consommé 5 to 8 minutes until tender. Drain and add to Consommé.
Brunoise Garnish for Beef Consommé (Garniture pour Consommé Brunoise): Use the same vegetables as for Julienne Garnish, above, and cut into tiny dice. Simmer in 1 cup Consommé 5 to 8 minutes until tender. Drain and add to Consommé.
Niçoise Garnish for Beef or Chicken Consommé (Garniture pour Consommé Niçoise): Cut 1 small potato and 4 green beans into 1/8-inch dice. Simmer in 1 cup Consommé 4 to 5 minutes or until tender. Drain. Peel, seed and dice 1 tomato, page 10. Add vegetables to Consommé just before serving.
Madrilène Garnish for Beef or Chicken Consommé (Garniture pour Consommé Madrilène): Just before serving, peel, seed and cut 2 tomatoes in thin strips. Add to Consommé.

Shrimp Bisque
Bisque de Crevettes

Every part of the shrimp is used in this rich, satisfying soup.

2 tablespoons butter
1/2 carrot, diced
1/2 onion, diced
1 bouquet garni, page 7
1-1/2 lbs. medium unpeeled raw shrimp
1/2 cup white wine
1 tablespoon brandy
5 cups White Veal Stock, page 31,
  Chicken Stock, page 32, or
  Fish Stock, page 32

2 tablespoons uncooked rice
Salt and pepper to taste
Croutons, below
1 tablespoon sherry or Madeira
4 tablespoons whipping cream
Pinch red (cayenne) pepper

Melt 1 tablespoon butter in a large saucepan. Stir in carrot, onion and bouquet garni. Cover and cook over low heat 5 to 7 minutes until vegetables are soft but not brown. Stir in shrimp. Cook 1 to 2 minutes longer, stirring occasionally. Pour in wine and brandy. Boil 1 minute to reduce liquid. Stir in 2 cups stock. Simmer 2 to 3 minutes until shrimp is just tender. Remove from heat; cool slightly. Lift out 12 shrimp; peel, discarding intestinal vein. Set peeled shrimp aside. Return shells to saucepan. Add remaining 3 cups stock. Grind shrimp and vegetable mixture with liquid in a food processor or blender, removing bouquet garni. Return mixture to pan with bouquet garni, stir in rice and salt and pepper. Cover and simmer 15 to 20 minutes. Discard bouquet garni. Puree in blender, then press soup through a fine strainer. Coarsely chop reserved shrimp. Prepare Croutons. Bring soup to a boil. Add sherry or Madeira and cream. Simmer 2 minutes. Remove soup from heat. Add red pepper and remaining 1 tablespoon butter in pieces. Taste for seasoning. Serve in soup bowls with a spoonful of chopped shrimp on top. Serve Croutons separately. Makes 6 servings.

Rouille Sauce
Sauce Rouille

A spicy sauce to spread on fried bread and serve with fish soup.

1 slice bread, crusts discarded
2 tablespoons water
1 small hot pepper, chopped
3 to 4 garlic cloves, crushed

1 egg yolk
Salt and pepper
1/2 cup olive oil

Soak bread in water. Squeeze dry. Puree bread, small hot pepper, garlic, egg yolk and salt to taste with 2 tablespoons olive oil in blender. With blender on medium speed, gradually add remaining 6 tablespoons olive oil. Taste for seasoning and add pepper and more salt if needed.

Mediterranean Fish Soup
Bouillabaisse

The more kinds of fish used, the more interesting the flavor, so use at least five different varieties.

3 lbs. white fish such as whiting, bass,
   red snapper, perch, haddock,
   flounder or monkfish
2 lbs. rich fish such as eel or mackerel
2 qts. Simple Fish Stock, see below
2 large Dungeness crabs or
   8 to 10 small blue crabs
1 large spiny lobster or
   8 to 10 small lobster tails
3/4 cup olive oil
2 medium onions, sliced
White part of 2 leeks, sliced
2 celery stalks, sliced
3 tomatoes, peeled, seeded, chopped,
   page 10

3 to 4 garlic cloves, crushed
1 bouquet garni, page 7
Thin strip of orange peel
2 sprigs fresh fennel or
   1 teaspoon dried fennel
1/4 teaspoon saffron
Salt and pepper to taste
Croûtes, page 29
Rouille Sauce, if desired, opposite
1 tablespoon tomato paste
1 tablespoon anise liqueur such as
   Pernod or Pastis
1/4 cup chopped parsley

Simple Fish Stock:
Reserved fish heads and tails
2 to 2-1/2 qts. water

Cut fish in 2- to 3-inch chunks, reserving heads and tails for Simple Fish Stock. Prepare Simple Fish Stock. With a cleaver, chop large crabs and spiny lobster in pieces, shells included. Discard head sac and intestinal veins of lobster and spongy finger-like gills of crabs. Heat olive oil in a large pot. Stir in onions, leeks and celery. Sauté until soft but not browned. Add Simple Fish Stock, tomatoes, garlic, bouquet garni, orange peel and fennel. Sprinkle saffron, salt and pepper over mixture. Bring to a boil; reduce heat and simmer 30 to 45 minutes. *Mediterranean Fish Soup can be prepared to this point 8 hours ahead, covered and refrigerated.* Prepare Croûtes and Rouille Sauce, if desired. Bring uncovered soup broth to a boil 20 minutes before serving. Add rich fish and shellfish. Boil hard 7 minutes. Do not stir, but shake pot occasionally to prevent sticking. Lay white fish on top of mixture and boil 5 to 8 minutes longer until fish begins to flake easily. If necessary, add water to just cover fish. Keep liquid at a rolling boil during entire cooking time so oil emulsifies with broth and does not float on surface. Remove from heat. Transfer fish to a warm platter, arranging each kind separately. Cover with foil; keep warm. Whisk tomato paste and anise liqueur into hot broth. Taste for seasoning. Pour into a tureen. Sprinkle broth and fish pieces with parsley. Serve immediately. Let each guest take fish and spoon broth over it. Serve Croûtes and Rouille Sauce separately so guests can spread sauce on Croûtes. Mediterranean Fish Soup can also be served as 2 separate courses of soup and fish. Makes 8 to 10 servings.

Simple Fish Stock:
Place reserved fish heads and tails in a large saucepan. Barely cover with water. Bring to a boil. Reduce heat and simmer 15 minutes. Strain.

Fresh Pea Soup
Potage St. Germain

Like dill with cucumber, mint with peas is a classic combination.

2 cups shelled fresh peas or
  1 (10-oz.) pkg. frozen peas
2 to 3 sprigs fresh mint
1 qt. Chicken Stock, page 32

Salt and pepper to taste
1/2 cup whipping cream
1 teaspoon sugar, if desired
2 tablespoons butter, cut in small pieces

In a small saucepan, bring 1-1/2 cups salted water to a boil. Add 1/4 cup peas. Cook 5 to 10 minutes until just tender. Drain and rinse with cold water; set aside. Finely chop the leaves of 1 sprig of mint; set aside. In a large saucepan, bring stock, remaining mint and salt and pepper to a boil. Add remaining peas. Simmer uncovered 15 to 20 minutes until peas are very tender. Fresh peas may take longer than frozen, depending on their size. Discard cooked mint. Puree pea mixture in blender. Strain to remove any skins. Stir in 1/4 cup cream. Bring soup to a boil. Taste for seasoning. Add sugar, if desired. Pour hot water over 1/4 cup cooked peas to warm them. Remove soup from heat. Stir in butter until melted. Spoon soup into bowls. Add a spoonful of cream to each serving and stir for a marbled effect. Sprinkle each serving with drained warmed peas and chopped mint. Serve immediately. Makes 4 servings.

French Onion Soup
Soupe à l'Oignon

Strong-flavored, long yellow onions are best for onion soup.

1/4 cup butter
6 yellow onions, thinly sliced
1 whole onion, peeled
1 teaspoon sugar
5 cups White Veal Stock, page 31, or
  Brown Beef Stock, page 30

Salt and pepper to taste
1 loaf French bread or 2 to 3 long
  crisp rolls, cut in 1/2-inch slices
1/4 cup grated Parmesan cheese
3/4 cup grated Gruyère cheese
2 tablespoons melted butter

Melt 3 tablespoons butter in a large pot. Add sliced onions. Sauté over low heat, stirring often, 15 to 20 minutes until onions are deep golden brown. Be careful not to scorch them. Cut a thin slice off top and bottom of whole onion. Dip cut ends in sugar. Melt remaining 1 tablespoon butter in a small saucepan. Add whole onion. Cook over low heat until onion browns and caramelizes on both ends. Add whole onion to sliced onions. Continue to cook over low heat until sliced onions are dark brown. Add stock, salt and pepper. Simmer 10 to 15 minutes. Discard whole onion. Taste soup for seasoning. *French Onion Soup can be made to this point 2 to 3 days ahead, covered and refrigerated.* Just before serving, preheat broiler. Place bread slices on a baking sheet and broil until lightly browned. Place 2 to 3 slices of toasted bread in individual heatproof bowls; spoon in soup. Mix Parmesan and Gruyère cheeses. Sprinkle a thick layer of cheese over each serving. Pour melted butter over each serving. Broil until browned. Serve very hot. Makes 4 servings.

Sauces

Most cooks would agree that sauces are the greatest challenge of French cuisine. *Liquid gold,* they have been called, but you can easily be your own alchemist. There are five basic sauces that form a logical structure: White Sauce, Velouté, Brown Sauce, Hollandaise and Mayonnaise. From these five, hundreds of other classic sauces can be developed.

When making any of them, there are three things to remember. First, the ingredients must be combined properly so they do not form lumps or separate. Second, the sauce must be the right consistency, neither too thick nor too runny. And third, the seasoning is vital.

Sauces can be divided into two types: flour-based sauces and emulsified sauces.

Flour-Based Sauces

Basic White Sauce, Velouté and Basic Brown Sauce are all defined as *flour-based*, because they are thickened either with flour (for White and Velouté) or with potato (for Brown). In White and Velouté sauces the flour is first cooked with melted butter to form a *roux*, then milk is added to make White Sauce, or stock to make Velouté Sauce. For Brown Sauce, potato starch is mixed with a little stock to form a thin paste and whisked into the remaining stock.

For a smooth texture, all of these sauces must be whisked continuously as they come to a boil. After that they should be stirred now and again to prevent sticking during cooking.

Cooking time for flour-based sauces depends on their consistency. If a sauce is thin, both in consistency and flavor, it must be boiled for 15 minutes or even half an hour so it evaporates and becomes thicker and more concentrated. This process is called *reduction* and applies most often to sauces based on stock, as milk scorches easily during long cooking. In any case, all flour-based sauces must be cooked at least three minutes to get rid of any taste of uncooked flour.

Emulsified Sauces

Emulsified sauces are more tricky than flour-based ones because their ingredients combine properly only at certain temperatures. The hot emulsified sauces, Hollandaise and Béarnaise, that are made with egg yolks and butter, should never be more than warm. Their cold cousin, Mayonnaise, which is based on egg yolks and oil, should be cool but not chilled.

Add the butter or oil to the egg yolks slowly, particularly at first when the emulsion is forming. Constant whisking is essential to prevent *curdling*, when fat separates from the egg yolks, giving a granular appearance. You'll know if a sauce is curdling because the consistency will change suddenly, becoming thin, with oily drops on the surface. If this happens, immediately stop adding the butter or oil and whisk furiously. Most sauces can be rescued even if they do curdle. For methods, see recipes.

Thickness & Seasoning

For most uses, the right thickness for a sauce is *coating consistency.* A sauce should never be so thick that you cannot see the shape and color of the food it covers. On the other hand, too thin a sauce is unpleasantly watery. For how to judge the right consistency of a sauce, see page 12.

Brown and Velouté sauces are often served when they have the consistency of thin cream, particularly if they accompany roast or broiled meats instead of gravy. White Sauce should always have body, and when it is used as a base for soufflés or croquettes or to coat foods for browning in the oven, it should be quite thick. If in doubt, make a sauce too thick rather than too thin, as it can easily be diluted.

Careful seasoning is important no matter what you cook, but in sauces it is critical. Add seasoning at the beginning of cooking and taste often, adding salt and pepper little by little. The flavor of a finished sauce should be well-balanced. As it must enhance the flavor of the food it accompanies, it should be too concentrated to eat alone. A sauce should not be too strong. Its role is to highlight but never to overwhelm.

Menu Planning

The three basic flour sauces—White, Velouté and Brown—are rarely used alone, so think of them as foundations to which at least one more ingredient must be added to make the finished sauce. For White Sauce and Velouté Sauce this can be simply a few spoonfuls of cream, which turn them into Cream Sauce or Creamy Velouté. Wine, vinegar, mustard and onion transform Basic Brown Sauce into Mustard-Flavored Brown Sauce. So use your imagination in creating new variations. Mushrooms, shallots, onions, tomatoes, fresh herbs and mustard can be added separately or in combination to most sauces. Try flavoring White Sauce or Mayonnaise with curry powder and you'll be amazed how they brighten egg, fish or chicken dishes.

More delicate sauces—White, Velouté and Hollandaise—are usually served with vegetables, poultry, fish and veal. Brown sauces are kept for beef and lamb. Mayonnaise goes with almost anything and its ingredients can be adjusted so the flavor is delicate or robust, depending on the food it accompanies. So when planning a meal, first decide on the meat, fish or fowl, and then choose an appropriate sauce. Do not, however, add a sauce to every course. One or two sauces in any menu is enough.

How to Prepare Sauces Ahead

Flour-based sauces can be made ahead and refrigerated or frozen, so you can save time by making these basics in large quantities for storage. However, to avoid curdling, add egg yolks or butter only when reheating the sauce. Flavorings such as liquor or herbs also taste better if added at the last minute.

Emulsified sauces cannot be made far ahead. Mayonnaise can be kept two or three days, but any of the hot emulsified sauces should be served as soon as possible. If necessary they can be kept warm for about half an hour in a water bath, or on a rack above hot water, page 9, but they must be whisked often and carefully watched.

How to Serve Sauces

Flour-based sauces may be mixed with food, spooned over it as a coating or served separately, depending on the individual recipe. Emulsified sauces are so delicate that they separate on contact with hot food, so they are almost always served in a sauceboat.

Basic White Sauce   Photo on page 49.
Sauce Béchamel

This sauce can be used on its own, or form the base for other sauces such as Cheese Sauce, opposite.

Use these Ingredients	To Make			
	1 cup	**1-1/2 cups**	**2 cups**	**2-1/2 cups**
milk	1 cup	1-1/2 cups	2 cups	2-1/2 cups
slices onion (optional)	1	1	2	2
bay leaf (optional)	1	1	1	1
peppercorns (optional)	6	9	12	18
salt and white pepper	to taste	to taste	to taste	to taste
nutmeg	pinch	pinch	pinch	pinch
Thick Sauce				
butter	2 tablespoons	3 tablespoons	4 tablespoons	5 tablespoons
all-purpose flour	2 tablespoons	3 tablespoons	4 tablespoons	5 tablespoons
Medium Sauce				
butter	1-1/2 tablespoons	2-1/4 tablespoons	3 tablespoons	3-3/4 tablespoons
all-purpose flour	1-1/2 tablespoons	2-1/4 tablespoons	3 tablespoons	3-3/4 tablespoons
Thin Sauce				
butter	1 tablespoon	1-1/2 tablespoons	2 tablespoons	2-1/2 tablespoons
all-purpose flour	1 tablespoon	1-1/2 tablespoons	2 tablespoons	2-1/2 tablespoons

In a small saucepan, scald milk by bringing it just to a boil. Add onion, bayleaf and peppercorns, if desired. Remove from heat. Cover and let stand 5 to 10 minutes. Melt butter in a medium, heavy saucepan. Whisk in flour. Cook over low heat, whisking constantly, 1 to 2 minutes until foaming but not brown. Cool. Strain hot milk. Pour into butter mixture, whisking constantly. Bring sauce to a boil, still whisking constantly. Season with salt, white pepper and nutmeg. Simmer 3 to 5 minutes, whisking constantly. Remove from heat and rub surface with butter, page 13, to prevent a skin from forming. *Basic White Sauce can be made 2 to 3 days ahead, covered and refrigerated or frozen.*

Cream Sauce
Sauce Crème

A rich version of Basic White Sauce to serve with fish, eggs, vegetables and poultry.

Medium Basic White Sauce, above, made with 1 cup milk

1/4 cup whipping cream
Salt and white pepper to taste

Combine Basic White Sauce and cream in a small saucepan. Simmer until sauce has desired consistency. Season with salt and white pepper. *Cream Sauce can be made 2 to 3 days ahead, covered and refrigerated.* Makes about 1-1/4 cups of sauce.

Cheese Sauce
Sauce Mornay

Classic French cheese sauce goes with eggs, fish, poultry, white meats and vegetables.

**Thin Basic White Sauce, opposite,
   made with 1 cup milk
1 egg yolk
1/4 cup grated Gruyère, or 1-1/2
   tablespoons grated Parmesan cheese,
   or a combination of the two**

**Salt and white pepper to taste
1 teaspoon Dijon-style mustard, if desired**

Prepare Basic White Sauce and remove from heat. Beat egg yolk and cheese into hot sauce. Season with salt and white pepper. Add mustard, if desired. Do not reheat or cheese will become stringy. Makes about 1-1/4 cups of sauce.

Velouté Sauce
Sauce Velouté

One of the five basic sauces. Cream is usually added if it is to be served with veal, poultry or fish.

**1-1/4 to 2 cups White Veal Stock, page 31,
   Chicken Stock, page 32, or
   Fish Stock, page 32**

**1-1/2 tablespoons butter
1-1/2 tablespoons all-purpose flour
Salt and white pepper**

If the stock you have is not very flavorful, boil 2 cups stock in a medium saucepan until reduced to 1-1/4 cups, concentrating the flavor. Bring stock to a boil. Melt butter in a medium, heavy saucepan. Whisk in flour. Cook over low heat 1 to 2 minutes until mixture foams but doesn't brown. Cool. Gradually whisk in hot stock. Bring sauce to a boil, whisking constantly. Season lightly; flavor will concentrate as sauce simmers. Reduce heat. Simmer 5 to 10 minutes, skimming and whisking occasionally, until sauce has desired consistency. Taste for seasoning. Add salt and white pepper, if desired. *Velouté Sauce can be made 2 to 3 days ahead, covered and refrigerated or frozen.* Makes about 1 cup of sauce.

Variations

Creamy Velouté (Velouté à la Crème): Gradually stir 2 to 3 tablespoons whipping cream into simmering sauce.

Chicken & Mushroom Sauce (Sauce Suprême): Add 1/4 cup chopped mushroom stems to butter mixture with stock. After simmering to desired consistency, strain sauce. Gradually stir in 1/4 cup whipping cream. Return to heat and simmer again to desired consistency. Remove from heat. Lightly season with salt and white pepper. Stir in 1 tablespoon butter. Serve with poultry. *Chicken & Mushroom Sauce can be made 2 to 3 days ahead and refrigerated. It can be frozen before butter is added. Add butter to reheated sauce just before serving.*

If a sauce starts to scorch on the bottom of the pan, at once pour it into a clean pan without stirring. Burnt bits will be left behind.

Basic Brown Sauce   Photo on page 49.
Fond de Veau Lié

Use as a base for Brown Mushroom Sauce, below, Madeira Sauce and Piquant Sauce, page 44.

3 to 4 cups Brown Veal Stock, pages 30-31
2 tablespoons potato starch

4 tablespoons Madeira or water
Salt and pepper to taste

If the stock you have is not very flavorful, boil about 4 cups stock in a medium saucepan until reduced to 3 cups, concentrating the flavor. Bring stock to a boil. In a cup or small bowl, mix potato starch with Madeira or water to make a paste. Gradually whisk paste into hot stock. Bring back to a boil, whisking constantly, then simmer until thick enough to coat a spoon lightly, page 12. Season with salt and pepper. Strain through a fine strainer. *Basic Brown Sauce can be made 4 days ahead, covered and refrigerated or frozen.* Makes about 3 cups of sauce.

How to Make Basic Brown Sauce

Brown Mushroom Sauce
Sauce Chasseur

This sauce can be served with all meats, broiled or roast chicken, and rabbit.

4 tablespoons butter
2 shallots, finely chopped
1/4 lb. mushrooms, thinly sliced
1 cup white wine
1 cup Basic Brown Sauce, see above
1/2 cup Tomato Sauce, page 48, or
  2 tablespoons tomato paste

1 tablespoon finely chopped parsley
2 teaspoons finely chopped fresh tarragon
  or 3/4 teaspoon dried tarragon,
  if desired
Salt and pepper to taste

Melt 2 tablespoons butter in a medium saucepan. Cut remaining 2 tablespoons butter in pieces; set aside. Stir shallots into melted butter. Sauté until soft but not brown. Stir in mushrooms. Cook over high heat 2 to 3 minutes until tender. Pour in wine. Boil until liquid is reduced to about 1/3 cup. Stir in Basic Brown Sauce and Tomato Sauce or tomato paste. Bring to a boil, stirring often. Immediately remove from heat and whisk in butter pieces, parsley and tarragon, if desired. Season lightly with salt and pepper. Sauce should not be boiled after last addition of butter. *Brown Mushroom Sauce can be made 2 to 3 days ahead, covered and refrigerated. It can be frozen before last addition of butter. Add butter to reheated sauce just before serving.* Makes about 1-1/2 cups of sauce.

1/Thicken sauce by whisking in potato starch paste.

2/Strain sauce through a fine strainer.

Mustard-Flavored Brown Sauce

Sauce Robert

One of the oldest of all sauces, it dates from the Middle Ages and is traditionally served with pork chops.

1 tablespoon butter
1/2 onion, finely chopped
3/4 cup white wine
1/4 cup white wine vinegar

2 cups Basic Brown Sauce, see above
2 to 3 tablespoons Dijon-style mustard
Salt and pepper to taste

Melt butter in a medium saucepan. Stir in onion. Sauté until soft but not brown. Pour in wine and vinegar. Boil until liquid is reduced to 1/4 cup. Stir in Basic Brown Sauce. Bring to a boil. Remove from heat and stir in mustard. Season with salt and pepper. *Mustard-Flavored Brown Sauce can be made 4 days ahead, covered and refrigerated or frozen.* Makes about 2 cups of sauce.

Piquant Sauce
Sauce Piquante

An enhancing sauce for pork, boiled beef and broiled chicken.

1/2 cup white wine
1/2 cup white wine vinegar
2 shallots, finely chopped
2 cups Basic Brown Sauce, pages 42-43
2 tablespoons gherkin pickles,
   coarsely chopped

1 tablespoon finely chopped parsley
2 teaspoons finely chopped fresh tarragon
   or 3/4 teaspoon dried tarragon
2 teaspoons finely chopped fresh chervil
   or 3/4 teaspoon dried chervil
Salt and pepper to taste

Combine wine, vinegar and shallots in a medium saucepan. Boil until liquid reduces to 1 tablespoon. Stir in Basic Brown Sauce and simmer 5 more minutes. Just before serving, stir in pickles, parsley, tarragon and chervil. Season with salt and pepper. *Piquant Sauce can be made 4 days ahead, covered and refrigerated or frozen.* Makes about 2 cups of sauce.

Madeira Sauce
Sauce Madère

Excellent with beef fillet, veal, ham and variety meats such as liver.

6 tablespoons Madeira
2 cups Basic Brown Sauce, pages 42-43

Salt and pepper to taste

Combine 3 tablespoons Madeira and Basic Brown Sauce in a medium saucepan. Simmer 8 to 10 minutes. Stir in remaining 3 tablespoons Madeira and bring sauce just to a boil. Season lightly with salt and pepper. *Madeira Sauce can be made 4 days ahead, covered and refrigerated or frozen.* Makes about 2 cups of sauce.

Truffle Sauce
Sauce Périgueux

Truffle Sauce is a luxury, so use it for beef fillet, ham or veal roast.

1 small can truffles
3 tablespoons Madeira

2 cups Basic Brown Sauce, pages 42-43
Salt and pepper to taste

Drain truffles, reserving juice. Dice truffles and set aside. Mix Madeira, truffle juice and Basic Brown Sauce in a medium saucepan. Simmer 8 to 10 minutes. Stir in diced truffles. Season lightly with salt and pepper. *Truffle Sauce can be made 4 days ahead, covered and refrigerated or frozen.* Makes about 1-3/4 cups of sauce.

Allow about 1/4 cup of White, Velouté or Brown sauce per person and slightly less of rich emulsified sauces like Hollandaise or Mayonnaise.

Hollandaise Sauce
Sauce Hollandaise

A favorite with eggs, vegetables and poached fish.

3/4 cup butter	**Salt and white pepper to taste**
3 tablespoons water	**Juice of 1/2 lemon or to taste**
3 egg yolks	**1 tablespoon lukewarm water, if desired**

Clarify butter, page 7, and cool to lukewarm. In a small heavy saucepan, whisk 3 tablespoons water with egg yolks and a little salt and pepper 30 seconds or until pale. Place pan over low heat or in a water bath, page 9, and whisk constantly until mixture is creamy and thick enough for whisk to leave a trail on the base of pan, page 46. The pan should be hot but never burning to the touch. Remove from heat and whisk in clarified butter, a few drops at a time. Do not add butter too fast or sauce may curdle. When sauce starts to thicken, butter can be added a little faster. After all butter has been added, stir in salt, white pepper and lemon juice to taste. Hollandaise Sauce is served warm, not hot. It can be kept warm in a water bath up to 1 hour but is best served immediately. If sauce is too thick to pour, stir in 1 tablespoon lukewarm water just before serving. Remedies for curdling or overcooking are below. Makes about 1 cup of sauce.

Remedies for Curdling

If Hollandaise or Béarnaise Sauces curdle, it is almost always because they are too hot. Remove curdled sauce from heat and whisk in an ice cube. If this is not successful, start sauce again by whisking 1 egg yolk and 1 tablespoon of water in a small saucepan over low heat until creamy. Remove from heat. Gradually whisk curdled sauce drop by drop into creamy egg yolk mixture. If sauce is badly curdled, it must be discarded.

Occasionally the sauces separate because they are undercooked and do not thicken properly. In this case, whisk in 1 tablespoon of boiling water.

If Mayonnaise curdles, beat in 1 tablespoon of boiling water. If this is not successful, start again by beating a fresh egg yolk with salt and pepper. Whisk in the curdled mixture drop by drop. Or, if mustard is used, beat curdled Mayonnaise into 1 teaspoon of Dijon-style mustard.

1/Mix vinegar, wine, peppercorns, shallots and tarragon in a saucepan.

2/Cooked mixture is thick enough when a whisk leaves a trail in the pan. If mixture is overcooked, eggs will become scrambled!

Béarnaise Sauce
Sauce Béarnaise

Serve this sauce with steak or with broiled or sautéed rich fish such as salmon.

3/4 cup butter
3 tablespoons vinegar
3 tablespoons white wine
10 peppercorns
3 shallots, finely chopped
1 tablespoon coarsely chopped fresh
   tarragon, or tarragon leaves
   preserved in vinegar

3 egg yolks
Salt and white pepper or
   red (cayenne) pepper to taste
1 to 2 tablespoons finely chopped fresh
   tarragon leaves or tarragon leaves
   preserved in vinegar
1 tablespoon finely chopped chervil or
   parsley

Clarify butter, page 7, and cool to lukewarm. In a small heavy saucepan, combine vinegar, wine, peppercorns, shallots and 1 tablespoon coarsely chopped tarragon. Boil until reduced to 2 tablespoons. Cool. Whisk in egg yolks, salt and white or red pepper. Whisk 30 seconds or until pale. Place pan over low heat or in a water bath, page 9, and whisk constantly until mixture is creamy and thick enough for whisk to leave a trail on base of pan. It should be slightly thicker than for Hollandaise Sauce. The pan should be hot but never burning to the touch. Remove from heat and whisk in clarified butter drop by drop. When sauce starts to thicken, clarified butter can be added a little faster. After all butter is added, strain sauce. Stir in finely chopped tarragon leaves and chervil or parsley. Taste for seasoning. Add more salt and pepper or red pepper, if desired. Béarnaise Sauce should have a peppery taste. It is served warm, not hot. It can be kept warm in a water bath, page 9, up to 1 hour, but is best served immediately. Remedies for curdling or overcooking are on page 45. Makes about 1 cup of sauce.

How to Make Béarnaise Sauce

3/First whisk clarified butter into sauce drop by drop,
then in a thin stream.

Light Tomato Sauce
Sauce Aurore

Aurore *refers to the dawn and this sauce has a rosy tint—attractive with eggs, fish and vegetables.*

1/4 cup strained Stewed Tomatoes, see
  below, or 2 teaspoons tomato paste
1 cup Velouté Sauce, page 41

Salt and pepper, if desired
2 tablespoons butter

Stewed Tomatoes:
1-1/2 teaspoons vegetable oil
1/2 shallot or 1/2 small onion,
  finely chopped
1/2 lb. fresh tomatoes, peeled, seeded,
  chopped, page 10

1 small bouquet garni, page 7
Salt and pepper to taste

Prepare Stewed Tomatoes if using. If you substitute tomato paste for Stewed Tomatoes, the sauce will have a less delicate flavor. Whisk Stewed Tomatoes or tomato paste into Velouté Sauce. Simmer until hot. Taste for seasoning. Add salt and pepper, if desired. Remove from heat and stir in butter. *Light Tomato Sauce can be made 2 to 3 days ahead, covered and refrigerated or frozen before butter is added. Add butter to reheated sauce just before serving.* Makes about 1-1/4 cups of sauce.

Stewed Tomatoes:
Heat oil in a medium skillet. Add shallot or onion. Cook over medium heat, stirring often, until soft but not browned. Add remaining ingredients. Cook over medium heat, stirring often, 20 to 30 minutes until nearly all moisture has evaporated. Taste for seasoning.

White Butter Sauce
Sauce Beurre Blanc

Thickened with butter only, Beurre Blanc is extremely delicate. It's delicious with poached fish.

3 tablespoons white wine vinegar
2 shallots, very finely chopped
3 tablespoons dry white wine
1 tablespoon whipping cream

1 cup butter cut in small pieces,
  refrigerated
Salt and white pepper to taste

In a small heavy saucepan, boil vinegar and shallots until liquid is reduced to 1 tablespoon. Add wine. Boil 5 minutes or until reduced to 1 to 2 tablespoons. Stir in cream and reduce again to 1 to 2 tablespoons. Place pan over low heat and gradually whisk in butter, piece by piece. Butter must be very cold to achieve a smooth, creamy sauce. Remove from heat occasionally, whisking constantly, so butter softens and thickens sauce without melting. Season with salt and pepper. Serve immediately. Sauce can be kept warm in a water bath, page 9, for a few minutes but the butter tends to melt and make the sauce oily. If sauce does separate, it cannot be remedied. Makes about 1 cup of sauce.

Tomato Sauce
Sauce Tomate

Enjoy this sauce with veal, poultry, eggs, fish and pasta.

2 tablespoons butter
1 onion, chopped
2 tablespoons all-purpose flour
1-1/2 cups stock or stock mixed with
  juice from canned tomatoes
3 cups canned Italian-style tomatoes
  (1-1/2 lbs.), drained, chopped, or
  2 lbs. fresh ripe tomatoes, quartered

1 garlic clove, crushed
1 bouquet garni, page 7
1/2 teaspoon sugar
Salt and pepper to taste
2 tablespoons tomato paste, if desired

Melt butter in a medium saucepan. Stir in onion. Sauté until soft but not brown. Remove from heat; stir in flour. Pour in stock and bring to a boil, stirring occasionally. Stir in tomatoes, garlic, bouquet garni, sugar, salt and pepper. Simmer uncovered 30 to 40 minutes for canned tomatoes and 45 to 60 minutes for fresh tomatoes until tomatoes are very soft and sauce is slightly thickened; stir often. Press sauce through a strainer to extract all tomato puree. Return liquid to saucepan. Simmer until thick enough to coat a spoon, page 12. If fresh tomatoes are used, add tomato paste for a darker color. Taste for seasoning. Makes about 2-1/2 cups of sauce.

From top to bottom: Basic White Sauce, page 40; Basic Brown Sauce, page 42, and White Butter Sauce.

Mayonnaise
Mayonnaise

Vary the flavor by substituting lemon juice for vinegar and olive oil for some of the salad oil.

2 egg yolks
2 tablespoons white wine vinegar or
  1 tablespoon lemon juice
1 to 2 teaspoons dry or Dijon-style
  mustard, if desired

Salt and white pepper to taste
1-1/2 cups vegetable oil
Warm water, if desired

All ingredients must be at room temperature. If egg yolks are too cold, mixture will not emulsify. If oil is too cool, heat the bowl or oil just to lukewarm. On a cold day, warm bowl and whisk in hot water. In a small bowl, beat egg yolks with 1 tablespoon vinegar or 1/2 tablespoon lemon juice, 1 teaspoon mustard, if desired, and salt and pepper until thick. Add oil drop by drop, whisking constantly; if oil is added too fast, mixture will curdle. Mixture should be very thick after 2 tablespoons oil have been added. Remaining oil can be added 1 tablespoon at a time, beating well between each addition, or in a thin steady stream if using an electric mixer. After all oil has been added, stir in remaining vinegar or lemon juice. If desired, add more mustard, salt and pepper. The amount of seasoning depends on the oil and vinegar used and what is served with the Mayonnaise. If desired, thin Mayonnaise with a little warm water. Store in a covered container at room temperature. *Mayonnaise can be made 2 to 3 days ahead, covered and refrigerated. If it is refrigerated, bring it to room temperature before stirring or it may curdle.* For remedies for curdling, see page 45. Makes about 1-1/2 cups of Mayonnaise.

Variations

Green Mayonnaise (Mayonnaise Verte): Boil 2 cups water in a medium saucepan. Add 6 spinach leaves, 1/4 cup parsley sprigs and 2 tablespoons fresh tarragon or chervil leaves. Boil 3 minutes. Remove from heat, drain and rinse with cold water. Drain thoroughly. Puree in a food processor. Stir 2 tablespoons of puree into 1 cup Mayonnaise. Season with salt and pepper. Serve with fish, eggs and vegetables.
Rémoulade Sauce (Sauce Rémoulade): Stir 1 teaspoon Dijon-style mustard, 2 tablespoons chopped capers, 3 tablespoons chopped gherkin pickles, 1 tablespoon chopped parsley, 2 teaspoons chopped fresh chervil or 3/4 teaspoon dried chervil, 2 teaspoons chopped fresh tarragon or 3/4 teaspoon dried tarragon, and 1/2 teaspoon anchovy paste or 1 teaspoon crushed anchovy fillets into 1 cup Mayonnaise. Season with salt and pepper. Serve with fish, eggs and vegetables.
Chantilly Mayonnaise (Mayonnaise Chantilly): Whip 1/4 cup whipping cream until stiff. Stir in 1 cup Mayonnaise. Season with salt and pepper. Serve with vegetable salads and asparagus.
Tomato Mayonnaise (Mayonnaise Tomatée): Stir 1 to 2 tablespoons tomato paste into 1 cup Mayonnaise. Serve with eggs and fish.

Eggs

Eggs are the most versatile of all ingredients. They can be boiled, poached, fried, shirred, scrambled or cooked as an omelet. They can be served plain or garnished. Their mild flavor makes them the perfect partner for flavors ranging from ham to chicken, fish, shellfish and cooked vegetables—not to mention their role in desserts. Besides hundreds of savory egg dishes, many cakes, pastries, custards and soufflés depend on eggs as a raising or binding agent.

Hundreds of egg dishes can be developed from these ideas. So think of recipes as basic outlines to be varied as you wish, adding extra ingredients at the appropriate time. For example, omelets are usually filled just before they are folded, but when the omelet is to be served flat, like Peasant Omelet, mix the filling with the egg itself. Flavors can be added to scrambled eggs almost any time, but save fresh ingredients like herbs for the end. For stuffed eggs you can mix the cooked yolk with some finely chopped meat or fish, or set the eggs on a bed of cooked vegetables. Poached eggs, too, are good placed on a bed of vegetables and topped with a sauce. Shirred eggs are easiest of all—just put a spoonful or two of any flavoring in the ramekins before adding the eggs.

How to Cook Eggs

No matter how you cook them, there are two basic facts about eggs: they cook quickly at a relatively low temperature (about 140°F, 60°C) and fierce heat toughens them. Use low heat in cooking, except for omelets where the eggs are only partly cooked, and for soufflés where the eggs are protected by the dish. Respect cooking times, or the result can be overcooked egg whites which are tough, and dry yolks. Thirty seconds can make the difference between a perfect egg and one that is overdone. For the same reason, hot egg dishes should be served as soon as they are ready because they will continue to cook and overcook in the residual heat of the dish.

Judging the point at which an egg is perfectly cooked takes a little experience and a precise time cannot be given except for hard-cooked eggs. French cooks tell by appearance and sometimes by touch, especially for poached eggs. To French taste, eggs should be soft. Folded omelets should be slightly runny in the center, while scrambled eggs are soft and moist. In an ideal shirred or poached egg, as in a soft-cooked one, the white is just set and yolk still liquid.

How to Serve Eggs

The French do not serve eggs for breakfast, but prefer them as the first course of a meal. They can also be the main course of a light lunch or supper, usually as an omelet. The number of eggs to serve per person depends on the cooking method and on their role in the menu. A single poached, shirred or hard-cooked egg is enough for a first course, especially if accompanied by a substantial garnish, but two are needed for a main course. For omelets or scrambled eggs, two eggs per person are a minimum, even as an appetizer.

At dinner, eggs should be dressed up. Poached or hard-cooked eggs need a sauce to cover their pale appearance. Serve scrambled or poached eggs on toast or fried bread, or even in tartlet shells, so the crispness contrasts with the soft egg. The most dramatic, if risky, presentation is a soufflé. But because it is quick to make, a soufflé is well worth the effort. Even if it starts to fall, it still tastes good!

1/Bring water with vinegar to a rolling boil. Carefully crack eggs into the briskly boiling water. Transfer poached eggs to a bowl of cold water.

2/A properly poached egg will yield slightly when pressed with your finger. Trim eggs into neat ovals and drain on paper towels.

How to Poach Eggs

How to Poach Eggs

Eggs for poaching must be very fresh or the white will detach from the yolk in strings. Fill a wide, shallow non-aluminum saucepan two-thirds full of water. Add about three tablespoons vinegar for each quart of water. Bring water to a rolling boil. Break an egg into a bubbling portion of the water—the bubbles spin the egg so the white sets around the yolk. Repeat with up to five eggs. Reduce heat and poach three to four minutes. Remove eggs with a slotted spoon; whites should be just firm and yolks still soft. Place poached eggs in a bowl of cold water. When eggs are cool, remove from water and trim ragged edges with a knife or kitchen scissors. Return eggs to water. Poached eggs can be kept one to two days in cold water in refrigerator. Reheat by letting eggs stand in warm water a few minutes.

How to Hard-Cook Eggs

To help prevent cracking, use eggs at room temperature. Put enough water to cover eggs generously in a large non-aluminum saucepan. Bring to a boil. Carefully lower eggs into boiling water with a spoon. Return to a boil; reduce heat and simmer 10 to 12 minutes. Count cooking time from when water returns to a boil. Be careful not to simmer eggs more than 12 minutes as overcooked eggs will have a black line around the yolk. Drain eggs. Cover with cold water and let stand until cool. To peel, gently tap eggs all over to crack shell; remove shell with skin. If peeling is difficult, peel under cold running water. Peeled eggs can be kept at room temperature in a bowl of cold water up to 24 hours but they are best peeled when needed. Hard-cooked eggs that have been refrigerated or frozen are tough.

Scrambled Eggs with Fresh Herbs
Oeufs Brouillés aux Fines Herbes

Even if it's only parsley, a fresh herb makes all the difference in this simple dish.

4 slices bread
2 tablespoons vegetable oil
8 tablespoons butter
8 eggs

Salt and pepper to taste
2 tablespoons chopped mixed fresh herbs
    such as chervil, chives and tarragon

Cut 4 rounds from bread with a 3-inch cookie cutter. Heat oil and 2 tablespoons butter in a skillet. Fry bread rounds until golden brown on both sides. Drain on paper towels, arrange on a platter and keep warm. Whisk eggs with salt and pepper until slightly frothy. Quickly beat in herbs. Heat remaining 6 tablespoons butter in a medium, heavy skillet. Add eggs; stir constantly with a wooden spoon over low heat at least 3 minutes to start thickening. The slower the eggs cook, the smoother they will be. Cook to desired consistency—runny or fairly firm. Eggs will continue cooking in pan after it has been removed from heat. Spoon eggs onto fried bread rounds and serve immediately. Makes 4 servings.

Pipérade
Pipérade

This Basque recipe is really fancy scrambled eggs.

3 tablespoons olive oil
1 onion, thinly sliced
2 tomatoes, peeled, seeded, chopped,
    page 10
1 garlic clove, crushed

Salt and pepper to taste
1 red or green bell pepper, cored, seeded,
    cut in 1/4-inch dice
6 eggs, slightly beaten

Heat oil in a medium skillet. Add onion. Sauté until soft but not browned. Add tomatoes, garlic and salt and pepper. Cook over low heat 15 minutes or until thick and pulpy, stirring occasionally. Stir in bell pepper. Cook 5 minutes longer or until bell pepper is soft. Taste for seasoning. *Pipérade can be prepared to this point 4 hours ahead, covered and refrigerated. Just before serving, warm tomato mixture.* Beat eggs with a fork until frothy; stir into warm tomato mixture. Stir constantly over low heat until eggs have thickened but are still soft, at least 5 minutes, or eggs may be watery instead of smooth. Mixture will continue cooking in pan after it is removed from heat. Serve immediately. Makes 4 appetizer servings or 2 main-dish servings.

Cheese Omelet
Omelette au Fromage

The outside of an omelet should be golden brown and the inside runny or firm, but never hard.

4 to 5 eggs	**2 tablespoons butter**
Salt and freshly ground black pepper	**2 to 3 tablespoons grated or**
to taste	**finely diced Gruyère cheese**

Use a fork to beat eggs with salt and pepper in a small bowl until thoroughly mixed. Melt butter in a 9-inch omelet pan or skillet. When butter foams and just starts to brown, pour in eggs. Stir briskly over medium heat 8 to 10 seconds with the flat of a fork until eggs start to thicken. Quickly but carefully pull cooked egg mixture from sides of pan to center, then tip pan so uncooked egg mixture flows to sides of pan. Continue 30 seconds to 1 minute until egg is cooked as desired. Cook undisturbed 10 to 15 seconds to brown bottom. Sprinkle with cheese. To fold omelet, hold pan handle in your left hand. Tip pan towards you and give the handle a sharp tap with your right hand so edge of the omelet flips over, or use a fork to fold over edge of the omelet near handle. Half roll, half slide omelet onto platter so it lands folded in thirds, seam-side down. Straighten omelet with a fork and serve at once. Makes 2 servings.

Variations

Tomato Omelet (Omelette aux Tomates): Omit cheese. Peel, seed and coarsely chop 2 tomatoes, page 10. Melt 2 tablespoons butter in a small skillet. Stir in 1 finely chopped shallot, 1 crushed garlic clove, if desired, tomatoes and 1 teaspoon chopped mixed fresh herbs such as thyme, basil and parsley. Add salt and pepper to taste. Sauté, stirring, until thick and liquid has evaporated. Keep mixture hot and spoon into omelet just before folding.

Mushroom Omelet (Omelette aux Champignons): Omit cheese. Melt 2 tablespoons butter in a small saucepan. Sauté 4 ounces sliced mushrooms in butter until tender. Stir in 2 teaspoons flour and 3 to 4 tablespoons White Veal Stock, page 31, Chicken Stock, page 32, or milk. Cook 2 to 3 minutes, stirring constantly. Stir in 2 to 3 tablespoons whipping cream, a squeeze of lemon juice, and salt and pepper to taste. Keep mixture hot and spoon into omelet just before folding.

Chicken Liver Omelet (Omelette aux Foies de Volaille): Omit cheese. Melt 2 tablespoons butter in a small skillet. Sauté 2 large or 3 small chicken livers with 1 finely chopped shallot, if desired, in butter until livers are browned but still pink in center. Remove livers from pan and slice. Stir 1 teaspoon flour into skillet. Add 3 to 4 tablespoons White Veal Stock, page 31, or Chicken Stock, page 32. Cook 2 to 3 minutes, stirring constantly. Add sliced livers and salt and pepper to taste. Keep mixture hot and spoon into omelet just before folding.

1/Stir egg mixture with the flat of a fork until thickened, shaking pan to prevent sticking.

2/Fold a third of the omelet over the filling. Roll out onto plate so smooth underside of omelet faces up.

How to Make a Folded Omelet

Peasant Omelet
Omelette Paysanne

This hearty flat omelet can be made several hours ahead and served at room temperature.

1/4 lb. lean bacon, diced
1 medium potato, diced
1 small onion, diced
2 tablespoons finely chopped parsley

4 eggs
Salt and pepper to taste
2 tablespoons butter

Fry bacon in a medium skillet until fat is partially rendered. Stir in potato and onion. Stir constantly over medium heat until vegetables are browned and tender. Add parsley; keep warm. Use a fork to beat eggs and a dash of pepper in a medium bowl until thoroughly mixed; salt may not be needed as bacon is already salty. Heat butter in a 9-inch omelet pan or skillet. When butter foams, pour in egg mixture. Stir briskly 8 to 10 seconds with the flat of a fork until eggs start to thicken. Quickly but carefully pull cooked egg mixture from sides of pan to center, then tip pan so uncooked egg mixture flows to sides of pan. Continue 30 seconds to 1 minute until eggs are almost set. Stir in bacon mixture and continue stirring a few seconds. Cook undisturbed 15 to 20 seconds to brown bottom. Omelet will be almost firm on top. Remove from heat. Place a platter over top of omelet pan and invert pan and platter. Slide omelet back into pan and brown other side. Cut in wedges to serve hot or cold. Makes 2 servings.

Shirred Eggs
Oeufs en Cocotte

Serve toast fingers for dipping in these soft creamy eggs.

1/4 cup butter	**Salt and pepper to taste**
1/2 cup whipping cream	**8 eggs**

Preheat oven to 375°F (190°C). Spoon 1/2 tablespoon butter, 1 tablespoon cream, salt and pepper into 8 ramekins or custard cups. If ramekins are large enough for 2 eggs, double the amount of butter and cream in each ramekin and use only 4 ramekins. Place ramekins in a water bath, page 9. Heat ramekins in water bath on top of stove until butter has melted. Break 1 or 2 eggs into each ramekin. Bring water bath to a boil, then bake eggs in water bath in oven 7 to 10 minutes until whites are almost set; eggs will continue cooking in hot ramekins after removed from oven. Whites should be just set and yolks still soft when ready to serve. Serve immediately. Makes 4 servings.

Variations

Flavorings can be added to ramekins before adding cream. To each ramekin, add 2 tablespoons crumbled cooked bacon, browned sausage, chopped cooked chicken livers, diced ham or cheese, or sliced or diced cooked vegetables.

Eggs Mimosa
Oeufs Mimosa

The fluffy garnish of sieved egg yolks resembles mimosa blossoms.

6 hard-cooked eggs, page 52	**Warm water, if needed**
1-1/2 cups Mayonnaise, page 50	**1 small bunch watercress**

Dry peeled eggs thoroughly on paper towels. Halve eggs lengthwise and arrange 10 halves cut-side down in a circle on a platter. If Mayonnaise is too thick to coat the back of a spoon thickly, page 12, thin with a little warm water. If Mayonnaise is too thin, it will run off onto platter instead of clinging to eggs. Spoon Mayonnaise over eggs. Press yolks from remaining egg in a sieve over eggs so each egg is sprinkled with sieved yolk. Chop remaining egg white and sprinkle a little between each egg. Place a bouquet of watercress in center of platter. Eggs should be served within 2 hours or Mayonnaise will discolor. Makes 5 appetizer servings.

Variation

Eggs Mimosa with Shrimp (Oeufs Mimosa aux Crevettes): Mound 1 cup cooked, peeled shrimp in center of platter in place of watercress.

Poached Eggs Florentine
Oeufs Pochés Florentine

Florentine *refers to spinach, reputedly introduced to France by the princess Catherine de Medici.*

8 poached eggs, page 52, poached very soft
2-1/2 lbs. fresh spinach or
  2 (10-oz.) pkgs. frozen leaf spinach
Thin Basic White Sauce, page 40,
  made with 2 cups milk
2 tablespoons butter
Salt and pepper to taste

Pinch of nutmeg
2 egg yolks
3/4 cup grated Gruyère or
  5 tablespoons grated Parmesan cheese
1 teaspoon Dijon-style mustard
1/3 cup milk, if desired

Place cooked eggs in a bowl of cold water. If using fresh spinach, remove stems and wash leaves thoroughly. Fill a large saucepan three-fourths full of lightly salted water. Bring to a boil; plunge in spinach and bring back to a boil. Boil 5 minutes or until leaves are wilted, stirring occasionally. If using frozen spinach, cook according to package directions. Drain spinach; rinse with cold water. Squeeze to extract as much water as possible. Prepare Thin Basic White Sauce. *Poached Eggs Florentine can be prepared to this point 3 to 4 hours ahead.* Just before serving, transfer eggs to a bowl of warm water to heat them. Grease a shallow 1-1/2-quart baking dish. Preheat broiler. Melt butter in a medium saucepan. Add spinach. Toss with a fork until thoroughly heated. Season with salt, pepper and nutmeg. Spread spinach in prepared baking dish. Drain eggs on paper towels. Arrange eggs on top of spinach. Cover to keep warm. Bring white sauce to a boil, remove from heat and beat in egg yolks, 1/2 cup Gruyère cheese or 3 tablespoons Parmesan cheese, mustard, and salt and pepper to taste. Sauce should thickly coat the spoon, page 12; if too thick, stir in up to 1/3 cup more milk. Spoon sauce over eggs and spinach. Sprinkle with remaining cheese. Brown under broiler. *Poached Eggs Florentine can be kept hot 10 to 15 minutes in a water bath, page 9, but the eggs easily overcook.* Makes 8 appetizer or 4 main-dish servings.

Spoon thickened sauce over cooked spinach and poached eggs before browning under broiler.

How to Make
Poached Eggs Florentine

Cheese Soufflé
Soufflé au Fromage

A mixture of Parmesan and Gruyère is perfect for this soufflé. You can also use dry sharp Cheddar.

2 tablespoons dry breadcrumbs, if desired
3 tablespoons butter
2 tablespoons all-purpose flour
1 cup milk
Salt and pepper to taste

4 egg yolks
1/2 cup plus 1 tablespoon grated cheese
1 teaspoon prepared mustard or
   1/4 teaspoon dry mustard
6 egg whites

Preheat oven to 425°F (220°C). Generously butter a 5-cup soufflé mold. Sprinkle with bread-crumbs, if desired. Melt butter in a medium saucepan. Whisk in flour. Cook until mixture foams; do not brown. Whisk in milk. Bring to a boil, stirring constantly. Add salt and pepper. Reduce heat and simmer 2 minutes. Remove from heat. Beat egg yolks into hot sauce until thickened. Cool slightly. Beat in 1/2 cup cheese with mustard. Taste for seasoning. Mixture should be highly seasoned as egg whites will be added later. *Cheese Soufflé can be prepared to this point 3 to 4 hours ahead. Rub surface of cheese mixture with butter, page 13, to prevent a skin forming. If made ahead, cover and refrigerate. Thirty minutes before serving, preheat oven to 425°F (220°C).* Whip egg whites until stiff, page 7. If made ahead, heat cheese mixture over low heat, whisking constantly, until it is hot to the touch. Do not heat too long or cheese will become stringy. Thoroughly mix a fourth of the stiff egg whites into hot cheese mixture. Lightly fold cheese mixture into remaining egg whites, pages 10 and 11. Pour into prepared mold. Sprinkle with remaining 1 tablespoon cheese. Bake 12 to 15 minutes until soufflé is puffed and brown. Serve immediately. Makes 4 servings.

Eggs Benedict
Oeufs Bénédict

Like all dishes with Hollandaise Sauce, Eggs Benedict should be served warm, not hot.

6 poached eggs, page 52
1 cup Hollandaise Sauce, page 45
6 thick slices of cooked ham or
   Canadian bacon
3 English muffins or 6 slices bread

2 tablespoons sherry or Madeira
1 small can truffles, drained, or
   3 black olives
1 tablespoon butter

Keep cooked eggs warm in a bowl of warm water. Prepare Hollandaise Sauce and keep pan warm in a pan of warm water. Preheat oven to 250°F (120°C). Cut rounds from ham or bacon the same size as muffins; if using bread, cut 3-inch rounds. Place ham on a heatproof platter. Pour sherry or Madeira over ham. Tightly cover with foil and place in oven to warm. Cut 6 thick truffle slices or halve the olives, discarding pits. Split and toast muffins or toast bread and cut out 3-inch rounds. Spread muffins or toast with butter and place a slice of ham on top. Drain eggs. Dry thoroughly on paper towels and place on ham. Arrange on a warm platter. Spoon Hollandaise Sauce over eggs and top with a truffle slice or olive half. Serve immediately. Makes 6 appetizer servings or 3 main-dish servings.

Fish & Shellfish

Ask the top Paris chefs what foods they enjoy preparing most and all will put fish and shellfish high on their lists. What are their reasons? First, the delicate, lean flesh of seafood makes it the perfect companion for French cuisine's richest butter sauces. And second, the short cooking time makes seafood easy to prepare to order, so it can be served straight from the pan.

How to Choose Fish

For the freshest fish, buy as the French do—without a shopping list. What fish come to market depend on what has been caught by the fishermen and it is best to choose accordingly. Ask the fish man what he recommends—he'll welcome your interest. Better still, learn to recognize a fresh fish yourself. It's quite simple: a fresh whole fish looks good—it is moist and shiny, with bright eyes and little odor. Fresh fillets or steaks are slightly springy to the touch. Stale fish looks tired and its strong smell is unmistakable.

The French rarely use frozen fish, but whole fish and fish fillets that have been quickly frozen and properly stored are perfectly acceptable when the fresh equivalent is not available. Beware of frozen fish that has a strong smell when thawed.

Follow your natural inclination: Your senses will tell you if a fish is one you want to cook.

If you cannot choose your fish until you reach the market, how can you know whether you'll find the fish called for in the recipe you'd like to use? The great advantage of fish cookery is that fish are interchangeable. When you cannot find the sole fillets called for in a recipe, you can use halibut. Most fish fall into two categories: white fish like sole and cod, and richer fish like salmon and mackerel; see Types of Fish, opposite.

Shellfish are less easy to interchange than fish as there are so few kinds and each is very different. In case of need, crabmeat can often be used instead of lobster meat, and large shrimp or scampi double for rock lobster tails.

How to Prepare Fish for Cooking

At the market, fish are always sold cleaned and usually scaled. If any scales remain, scrape them off with a serrated knife, working from tail to head. The French usually leave on the heads of small fish such as trout for cooking, though you may remove them if you prefer. Trim tails to a "V" with scissors and cut off all fins. Check fillets to be sure no bones remain by running a finger across the flesh. Wash fish and fish fillets thoroughly in cold water, making sure the stomach cavity and gills of whole fish are clean. Dry well on paper towels or a cloth. Scallops should also be washed and dried.

How to Tell When Fish is Done

Fish is delicate—so are shellfish, despite their tough shells. To keep it juicy, no matter what the cooking method, there is one important rule to remember: seafood must never be overcooked. If overdone, fish becomes soft, dry and tasteless. Shellfish such as shrimp can go soft and others like scallops, lobster and mussels become unpleasantly tough and stringy.

How can you tell when seafood is done? As a fish cooks, three major transformations take place: its appearance changes from transparent to opaque, its temperature from cold to hot, and its texture from cohesive to flaky. To test small whole fish, fish fillets or scallops, poke the thickest part gently with a knife to see that no transparent center remains and the flesh flakes quite easily. If so, the fish is cooked. For very large fish, you can use a meat thermometer which will register 160° to 165°F (71° to 74°C) when the fish is done. Shellfish cooked in their shells must be judged by the time given in the recipe, because they cannot be tested.

Whatever the fish, remember that a few extra minutes mean the difference between being done and overcooked. Begin testing early and, if in doubt, undercook slightly.

How to Serve Fish

At the beginning of this century in France, fish was always followed by a meat course, but today the French serve fish as an appetizer or as a main course. Almost no accompaniment is needed with a fish appetizer. Lemon decorations, page 8, or parsley sprigs are possible, although neither is necessary if the fish is served in a sauce. When fish is the principal dish, you might want to serve a vegetable accompaniment. The French favorite is a boiled or steamed potato, though more and more chefs now add a green vegetable such as zucchini or green beans.

A sauce for fish may be based on the cooking liquid from the fish, or it may be made separately, like Hollandaise for poached fish. No matter! Half the pleasure of eating fish in France is the sauce that nearly always accompanies it!

Types of Fish

Most fish in each category can be substituted for another fish in the same category.

LARGE FISH
(usually sold as steaks or fillets)

White Fish	Rich Fish
California black sea bass (jewfish)	eel
carp	salmon
cod	swordfish
halibut	tuna
ocean perch	
red snapper	
spot bass (redfish)	
weakfish	

MEDIUM FISH
(sold whole, in steaks and fillets)

White Fish	Rich Fish
bluefish	eel
butterfish	mackerel
California whitefish	salmon
catfish	shad
flounder	tuna
fresh water bass	
haddock	
hake	
ling cod	
mullet	
pompano	
red snapper	
sea bass	

SMALL FISH
(used whole)

White Fish	Rich Fish
butterfish	fresh herring
California kingfish	
trout	

Norman Sole Fillets

Filets de Sole Normande

Norman fish dishes often contain generous amounts of butter and cream for which Normandy is famous.

1 qt. mussels
1/4 cup white wine
1/2 lb. cooked peeled shrimps
1-1/2 lbs. sole fillets
2 tablespoons butter
2 shallots, finely chopped

1/2 lb. mushrooms, thinly sliced
Fish Stock, page 32
Salt and white pepper to taste
Mushroom Velouté Sauce, see below
2 egg yolks
1/4 cup whipping cream

Mushroom Velouté Sauce:
Reserved fish cooking liquid
Reserved mushrooms
Strained mussel cooking liquid

3 tablespoons butter
3 tablespoons all-purpose flour

Wash mussels under running water, scraping with a small knife to remove any seaweed. Discard broken shells or open shells that do not close when tapped. Place mussels and white wine in a large non-aluminum saucepan. Cover and cook over high heat, tossing often, 3 to 4 minutes until opened. Remove mussels from opened shells, discarding unopened ones. Strain cooking liquid through cheesecloth; set aside. Halve shrimps lengthwise. Wash sole fillets; pat dry with paper towels. Spread the bottom of a medium skillet with 1 tablespoon butter. Cut a piece of waxed paper to cover skillet. Butter one side of waxed paper. Sprinkle shallots over butter in skillet. Place mushrooms on top. Fold fillets in half skin-side in and place narrow-side down on mushrooms. Pour Fish Stock over fillets. Add salt and white pepper. Simmer gently 7 to 10 minutes until fish can be flaked easily with a fork. Cool slightly. Lift out fillets and drain on paper towels. Reserve fish liquid and mushrooms. Butter a heatproof platter. Arrange fillets on platter and keep warm. Prepare Mushroom Velouté Sauce. Add mussels and shrimps to sauce and taste for seasoning. Whisk egg yolks and cream in a small bowl. Stir in a little hot sauce. Stir mixture into remaining sauce. Heat gently and stir until thickened slightly. Do not boil or sauce will curdle. Cut remaining 2 tablespoons butter in small pieces. Remove sauce from heat and stir in butter pieces. *Cooked fish can be covered and kept warm in 300°F (150°C) oven up to 15 minutes. Sauce can be kept hot in a water bath, page 9.* Just before serving, preheat broiler. Taste sauce for seasoning and spoon over fish. Brown under broiler. Makes 6 to 8 appetizer or 4 main-dish servings.

Mushroom Velouté Sauce:

Place fish liquid with mushrooms in a medium saucepan. Boil uncovered until reduced to about 2 cups. Add mussel liquid. Melt butter in a medium, heavy saucepan. Whisk in flour. Cook 1 to 2 minutes until foaming but not browned. Cool slightly. Whisk in fish liquid and mushrooms. Bring to a boil, whisking constantly. Simmer 2 minutes or until sauce is thick enough to coat a spoon, page 12. Makes 2 cups of sauce.

Variations

Sole Fillets with Shrimp & Mushrooms (Filets de Sole Joinville): Omit mussels. Add 1/4 cup white wine to fish stock before cooking fish.
Sole Fillets with Shrimp & Mussels (Filets de Sole Marguéry): Omit mushrooms.
Sole Fillets with Mussels & Mushrooms (Filets de Sole Dieppoise): Omit shrimps.

Trout in Parchment Paper
Truites en Papillote

Parchment paper is preferable to foil because it puffs and browns attractively in the oven.

4 (3/4- to 1-lb.) trout, cleaned,
  heads and tails on
Duxelles, see below

1/2 cup butter
Salt and pepper

Duxelles:
2 tablespoons butter
1 shallot, finely chopped
1/2 lb. mushrooms, finely chopped

2 tablespoons chopped parsley
Salt and pepper to taste

Preheat oven to 350°F (175°C). Rinse and dry fish. Prepare Duxelles. Cut 4 large heart shapes of parchment paper or foil large enough to enclose each fish, leaving a 2-inch border. Spread center of each paper with about 1/2 tablespoon butter. Place fish on butter. Sprinkle fish inside and out with salt and pepper. Spread Duxelles on top. Fold paper over fish, turn over paper edges and pleat to seal. *Fish can be prepared 3 to 4 hours ahead and refrigerated, but Duxelles must be cold before being spread on fish.* Place packets on a baking sheet. Bake 15 to 18 minutes until packets are puffed. Warm remaining butter in a water bath, page 9, or over very low heat, stirring constantly; butter should just soften but not melt and become oily. Rush fish packets on plates to the table before they cool and deflate. Cut before serving or let guests open their own. Serve softened butter separately. Makes 4 servings.

Duxelles:
Melt butter in a medium skillet. Add shallot. Cook over low heat 2 to 3 minutes until soft. Add mushrooms. Stir constantly over high heat until all moisture has evaporated. Remove from heat. Stir in parsley. Season with salt and pepper.

How to Make Trout in Parchment Paper

1/Pleat edges of parchment paper or foil to seal well.

2/Cut paper with a sharp dinner knife before serving or at the table.

Fish Croquettes
Croquettes de Poisson

The outside of a croquette, literally a crunchy morsel, *should be crisp and the center creamy.*

1-1/2 cups cooked fish, flaked,
  skin and bones discarded
Pinch of red (cayenne) pepper
Thick Basic White Sauce, page 40,
  made with 1 cup milk
Salt and pepper, if desired
2 eggs
1 tablespoon vegetable oil
1 tablespoon water

1 cup dry white breadcrumbs
1/2 teaspoon salt
1/4 teaspoon pepper
1/2 cup all-purpose flour
Béarnaise Sauce, pages 46-47, or
  Tomato Sauce, page 48
Oil for deep-frying
1 medium bunch parsley, washed, dried

Stir fish and red pepper into Thick Basic White Sauce. Taste for seasoning. Add salt and pepper, if desired. Spread mixture in a buttered ice-cube tray. Rub surface of mixture with butter, page 13, and refrigerate 2 to 3 hours until very firm. Beat eggs with 1 tablespoon oil and water. Put breadcrumbs in a shallow dish. Add 1/2 teaspoon salt and 1/4 teaspoon pepper to flour and sprinkle it on work surface. Turn out croquette mixture and cut in 1-inch squares. Roll squares on flour into cylinders about 3 inches long and 1 inch in diameter. Brush each cylinder with egg mixture and roll in breadcrumbs, making sure cylinders are completely coated. Refrigerate uncovered on a plate or baking sheet at least 30 minutes. *Fish Croquettes can be prepared to this point 6 hours ahead and refrigerated.* Prepare Béarnaise Sauce or Tomato Sauce. Keep sauce warm in a water bath, page 9. Heat oil for deep-frying to 360°F (180°C). Fry croquettes a few at a time 2 to 3 minutes until golden brown. Do not overcook or they will burst. Keep hot in a 300°F (150°C) oven with door ajar while frying remaining croquettes. Cool fat slightly. Dry parsley thoroughly and tie stems in a bunch with string. Wet parsley can cause hot fat to bubble and boil over. Lower parsley into fat in a basket or on a slotted spoon, **standing back as it will spatter.** Lift out after 10 seconds or when spattering stops. Drain briefly on paper towels. Cut or break off parsley stems and discard. Sprinkle leafy sprigs over croquettes. Serve immediately; serve sauce separately. Makes 10 to 12 servings.

Baked Sea Bass Niçoise
Loup au Four à la Niçoise

Olives, garlic, olive oil and tomatoes make the cuisine of Nice (say NEES) vigorous and colorful.

5 tablespoons olive oil	1 cup white wine or tomato juice
2 garlic cloves, crushed	1 (5- to 6-lb.) whole sea bass, scaled,
2 teaspoons paprika	cleaned, head on
1/4 cup tomato paste	1/2 cup pitted black olives
1 teaspoon dried thyme	1 lemon, thinly sliced
Salt and pepper to taste	

Preheat oven to 350°F (175°C). Heat oil in a small saucepan. Add garlic; cook 1 minute. Remove from heat and stir in paprika, tomato paste, thyme, salt and pepper and wine or tomato juice. Simmer 2 to 3 minutes; cool completely. Oil a large baking dish or roasting pan. Rinse and dry fish. Cut off fins; discard. Trim tail to a "V". Place fish in prepared baking dish or roasting pan. Score top of fish with deep diagonal slashes 2 inches apart. Spoon sauce over fish. *Bass can be prepared to this point 2 to 3 hours ahead and refrigerated.* Bake fish about 25 minutes, basting often. Stir olives into sauce. Bake 10 to 15 minutes longer until fish can just be flaked easily with a fork. Transfer fish to a platter or serve from baking dish. Garnish fish with overlapping lemon slices. Makes 4 servings.

Variations

Red Snapper or Mullet Niçoise (Rouget au Four à la Niçoise): Substitute red snapper or mullet for sea bass.
Cold Fish Niçoise (Poisson Froid à la Niçoise): Bake fish, cool to lukewarm; refrigerate at least 2 and not more than 8 hours. To serve, transfer to platter and decorate with lemon slices.

Fish Fillets Meunière
Filets de Poisson Meunière

The name refers to the flour coating which seals in the juices.

1-1/2 lbs. fish fillets	1 tablespoon chopped parsley
1/4 cup all-purpose flour	2 teaspoons chopped fresh herbs such as
1/4 teaspoon salt	chives, chervil or tarragon
Pinch of white pepper	Pinch each of salt and white pepper
Juice of 1 lemon	7 tablespoons butter

Wash fillets; pat dry with paper towels. Mix flour with 1/4 teaspoon salt and a pinch of white pepper. Coat fillets with flour mixture; pat off excess. Combine lemon juice, parsley, other herbs and a pinch of salt and white pepper. In a large skillet, heat 3 tablespoons butter until foaming; add fillets. If all fillets will not fit in 1 layer, cook in 2 batches, adding more butter if needed. Cook over medium-high heat 1 to 3 minutes until golden brown. Do not overcook or fish will fall apart. Turn fillets over and brown other side. Remove from skillet; keep warm on a hot platter. Wipe skillet with paper towels. Add remaining butter; heat until nut brown. Immediately add lemon juice mixture, swirling pan quickly to blend with butter. Pour foaming mixture over fish. Serve immediately. Makes 6 to 8 appetizer servings or 4 main-dish servings.

Baked Sea Bass Niçoise is pictured on the following pages.

Quenelles with Shrimp
Quenelles aux Crevettes

An equally delicious relative of the famous Quenelles of Nantua, which require crayfish in the sauce.

Cream Puff Pastry, page 160, made with
   1/2 cup flour
1-1/2 lbs. raw pike, shad, haddock,
   whiting or other firm fish fillets
3 egg whites, lightly beaten

1 cup whipping cream
Salt and pepper to taste
Pinch of grated nutmeg
Shrimp Sauce, see below

Shrimp Sauce:
1/4 cup butter
1/2 small onion, finely chopped
1 garlic clove, finely chopped
5 tablespoons all-purpose flour
3 cups milk
1 cup White Veal Stock, page 31, or
   Chicken Stock, page 32

3/4 lb. medium raw shrimp
Salt and pepper to taste
4 teaspoons brandy
2 tablespoons Tomato Sauce, page 48, or
   1 teaspoon tomato paste
1/3 cup whipping cream

Prepare Cream Puff Pastry, using less egg than called for to get a stiff mixture. Rub surface with butter while still warm to prevent skin from forming, page 13. Cool. Remove any pieces of skin or bone from fish. Grind fish in food processor or put through food grinder twice using the fine blade. For a finer texture, work ground fish through a fine sieve into a bowl. Refrigerate 1 hour or until chilled. Place bowl of ground fish in a pan of ice water. Gradually work in egg whites, beating vigorously with a wooden spoon. Gradually beat in Cream Puff Pastry. Beat in the cream gradually, followed by salt, pepper and nutmeg. Salt will slightly stiffen the mixture. Use immediately or refrigerate. Prepare Shrimp Sauce. Pour water 3 inches deep into a large shallow roasting pan or sauté pan. Add a large pinch of salt. Bring to a boil. Reduce heat and gently simmer. Shape one oval quenelle, using 2 tablespoons dipped in the pan of hot water. Drop quenelle into simmering water. If it breaks, add another egg white to remaining mixture and beat 5 minutes over ice. Shape remaining mixture into oval quenelles and drop them one by one into simmering water. Poach 10 to 15 minutes, depending on size. Remove with a slotted spoon; drain on paper towels. Preheat oven to 375°F (190°C). Arrange quenelles in buttered individual heatproof dishes or in 1 large buttered baking dish. Sprinkle with reserved shrimp or use shrimp to garnish after coating with sauce. Coat quenelles generously with sauce. Bake 10 to 15 minutes until sauce is browned and quenelles are slightly puffed. Makes 6 to 8 appetizer or 4 main-dish servings.

Shrimp Sauce:
Melt 2 tablespoons butter in a large skillet. Add onion and garlic. Stir constantly over low heat 5 minutes or until soft but not browned. Stir in flour. Cook, stirring constantly, until foaming but not browned. Add milk, stock, shrimp, salt and pepper. Bring to a boil; reduce heat and simmer 5 minutes. Remove shrimp and shell them, reserving meat. Crush shells. Add crushed shells and brandy to sauce. Simmer 10 minutes. Strain sauce. Stir in Tomato Sauce or tomato paste and cream. Bring to a boil. Taste for seasoning. Just before serving, remove sauce from heat and stir in remaining 2 tablespoons butter.

1/Holding a tablespoon in each hand, press mixture into egg shapes.

2/Arrange poached quenelles in a baking dish and coat with sauce. Garnish with reserved shrimp.

How to Make Quenelles with Shrimp

Sautéed Fish Steaks
Darnes de Poisson Sautées

Middle cut fish steaks are the best because they are a complete oval with no gap.

1 fish steak such as salmon, cod or bass, cut 3/4 inch thick
1/4 cup Béarnaise Sauce, pages 46-47, or 1/4 cup Hollandaise Sauce, page 45

1-1/2 tablespoons butter
Salt and pepper
1 slice lemon
1 teaspoon chopped parsley

Rinse fish steak; pat dry with paper towels. Prepare Béarnaise Sauce or Hollandaise Sauce. Keep sauce warm in a water bath, page 9. Heat butter in a medium, heavy skillet over medium heat until foaming. Add fish steak. Sauté 2 to 3 minutes until browned. Turn steak; sprinkle with salt and pepper. Sauté until second side is browned and flesh just flakes easily with a fork. Do not overcook. Put lemon slice on top. Sprinkle lemon with parsley. Serve immediately; serve sauce separately. Makes 1 serving.

Salmon Mousse
Mousse de Saumon

The rich flavor of salmon is best for this dish, but you can also use cod or smoked haddock.

1 (1-lb.) piece salmon	2 to 3 tablespoons Madeira
2 cups Fish Stock, page 32	Pinch of nutmeg
Salt and pepper	Salt and pepper to taste
2 envelopes gelatin	3/4 cup whipping cream
1/4 cup water	1 small cucumber
2 teaspoons tomato paste	8 slices hot toast

Rinse and dry salmon. Place in a medium saucepan. Pour stock over fish. Sprinkle with salt and pepper. Bring to a boil and poach over low heat 12 to 15 minutes until flesh just flakes easily with a fork. Cool in cooking liquid. Drain, reserving liquid in a saucepan. Discard skin and bone. Flake fish. Soak gelatin in 1/4 cup cold water to soften, page 9. Bring cooking liquid to a boil; remove from heat, add softened gelatin and stir until completely dissolved. Cool completely. In blender or food processor, blend salmon with gelatin mixture. Turn mixture into a large bowl. Stir in tomato paste, Madeira, nutmeg, salt and pepper. Place bowl in a larger bowl of ice water. Rinse a 1-1/4-quart charlotte mold or other metal mold with water. Stir salmon mixture until cold and on the point of setting. Whip cream until it holds a soft peak. Fold whipped cream into salmon mixture. Taste for seasoning and spoon into mold. Cover and refrigerate at least 2 hours or until firmly set. *Salmon Mousse can be made 2 days ahead and refrigerated, but serve it at room temperature.* Unmold mousse not more than 4 hours before serving. To unmold, carefully run a knife around edges and dip bottom of mold in a pan of lukewarm water for a few seconds. Unmold onto a serving plate. Use a vegetable peeler to remove alternate strips of peel from cucumber. Cut cucumber in thin slices. Press slices on sides and top of mousse. Serve with hot toast. Makes 8 to 10 appetizer servings.

Mussels in White Wine
Moules Marinière

Mussels are best cooked just before serving so they are plump and juicy.

3 qts. mussels	1 bouquet garni, page 7
1 cup white wine	Pepper to taste
3 shallots or 1 onion, very finely chopped	2 tablespoons coarsely chopped parsley

Scrape mussels clean. Wash thoroughly under cold running water and remove any weed. Discard broken shells or open ones that do not close when tapped. Put wine, shallots or onion, bouquet garni and pepper in a large non-aluminum saucepan. Do not add salt because mussels are salty. Bring to a boil, reduce heat and simmer 2 minutes. Add mussels. Cover and cook over high heat 3 to 4 minutes until mussels open, shaking occasionally. Use a slotted spoon to transfer mussels to individual bowls or a soup tureen, discarding any that are not open. Sprinkle with parsley. Taste cooking liquid for seasoning. Strain through cheesecloth or a fine strainer over mussels. Makes 4 servings.

Scallops Parisienne
Coquilles St. Jacques Parisienne

For economy, replace some of the scallops with white fish fillets poached 7 minutes and cubed.

1 lb. bay or sea scallops	**Duchess Potatoes, page 124**
2 cups Fish Stock, page 32	**3 tablespoons butter**
Pinch of salt	**1 onion, finely chopped**
Water	**3 tablespoons all-purpose flour**
6 oz. mushrooms, quartered	**1/2 cup whipping cream**
Juice of 1/2 lemon	**1/4 cup dry breadcrumbs**
Salt and pepper to taste	**2 to 3 tablespoons melted butter**

Rinse and drain scallops. Put stock in a large shallow saucepan. Add scallops and a pinch of salt. Cover and poach bay scallops 1 to 2 minutes or sea scallops 2 to 3 minutes until no longer transparent in center. Do not overcook or they will become tough. Cool slightly and drain, reserving cooking liquid. Discard small membrane on side of each scallop. Cut sea scallops in 2 or 3 slices. In a medium saucepan, combine 1/4 inch of water, mushrooms, lemon juice, salt and pepper. Cover tightly. Cook over high heat 3 to 5 minutes until liquid boils to top of pan and mushrooms are tender. Drain, reserving liquid. Preheat oven to 400°F (205°C). Prepare Duchess Potatoes. Butter 4 to 6 deep scallop shells or individual heatproof dishes. Using a pastry bag with medium star tube, pages 13 and 14, pipe a border of Duchess Potatoes around edges of dishes. Melt 3 tablespoons butter in a medium saucepan. Add onion. Cook until soft but not brown. Whisk in flour. Cook until foaming. Cool slightly and whisk in reserved cooking liquid from scallops and mushrooms. Bring sauce to a boil, whisking, and simmer 2 minutes. Add cream. If necessary, boil a few minutes until sauce is thick enough to coat a spoon, page 12. Taste for seasoning. Stir in mushrooms and scallops. Taste again and spoon into prepared shells or dishes. Sprinkle with breadcrumbs and melted butter. *Scallops Parisienne can be made 24 hours ahead, covered and refrigerated or frozen.* To keep them level, put scallop shells on cookie cutters on a baking sheet. Bake 10 to 15 minutes or until bubbling and browned. Makes 6 appetizer servings or 4 main-dish servings.

Snails with Garlic Butter
Escargots à la Bourguignonne

Serve snail shells in special plates or stand them upright on beds of rock salt.

1 shallot, finely chopped	**1 cup butter, softened**
1 to 2 garlic cloves, finely chopped	**36 snail shells**
3 tablespoons chopped parsley	**36 canned snails, drained thoroughly**
Salt and pepper to taste	

Preheat oven to 350°F (175°C). Beat shallots, garlic, parsley, salt and pepper into butter. Or combine shallots, garlic, parsley and butter in food processor, then add salt and pepper. Spoon 1/2 teaspoon butter mixture into each snail shell. Place snail on top; cover equally with remaining butter mixture. Arrange snail shells in 6 individual snail plates or on rock salt in shallow baking dishes. Bake 10 minutes or until butter bubbles. Serve immediately. Makes 6 servings.

Provençal Frogs' Legs
Cuisses de Grenouilles Provençale

Garlic can be adjusted to taste but in any Provençal dish it should always be noticeable.

1-1/2 lbs. fresh or frozen frogs' legs
  (10 to 15 pairs)
6 tablespoons butter
4 tomatoes, peeled, seeded, chopped,
  page 10, or 2 cups canned tomatoes,
  drained thoroughly, seeded, chopped
Salt and pepper to taste
1/4 cup all-purpose flour

1/2 teaspoon salt
1/4 teaspoon pepper
2 tablespoons vegetable oil
1 to 2 garlic cloves, finely chopped
2 shallots, chopped
1/2 cup white wine
2 tablespoons chopped parsley

Trim frogs' legs if necessary. Soak fresh ones in cold water 1 to 2 hours; drain on paper towels. Melt 1 tablespoon butter in a medium skillet. Add tomatoes, salt and pepper. Cook over medium heat, stirring occasionally, 10 minutes or until most moisture has evaporated. Mix flour with 1/2 teaspoon salt and 1/4 teaspoon pepper. Toss frogs' legs in flour mixture to coat. In another skillet, heat oil and 2 tablespoons butter until foaming. Add frogs' legs. Sauté over high heat about 2 minutes on each side. If necessary, cook in 2 batches to avoid crowding. Cook all frogs' legs together over medium heat 6 to 7 minutes longer until tender when pierced with a skewer. Transfer to a platter and keep warm. Add garlic and shallots to skillet. Cook 1 minute over medium heat. Stir in wine. Bring to a boil and simmer 1 minute. Stir in cooked tomatoes and parsley. Heat until bubbling; remove from heat. Stir in remaining 3 tablespoons butter. Taste for seasoning and pour over frogs' legs. Serve at once. Makes 6 to 8 appetizer servings or 4 main-dish servings.

Crab Gratin
Gratin de Crabe

Also delicious when cooked lobster or shrimp are substituted for the crab.

4 large cooked Dungeness crabs or
  1-1/2 lbs. crab meat
2 tablespoons butter
4 to 5 shallots, finely chopped
1 cup white wine
Thick Basic White Sauce, page 40,
  made with 1 qt. milk

2 teaspoons powdered mustard
3 tablespoons Dijon-style mustard
1 teaspoon brandy
2/3 cup whipping cream
Salt and pepper, if desired
1/2 cup grated Gruyère cheese

If using whole crabs, remove meat from claws and body, being careful to discard all pieces of membrane. Reserve any coral. There should be 1-1/2 lbs. or 4 cups crab meat. Preheat oven to 400°F (205°C). Melt butter in a medium saucepan. Add shallots. Stir over low heat 2 to 3 minutes. Add wine. Boil until reduced to about 1/3 cup. Stir into Thick Basic White Sauce with powdered mustard and Dijon-style mustard. Return sauce to low heat. Stir in brandy and cream. Remove from heat. Stir in crab meat and coral; taste for seasoning. Add salt and pepper, if desired. Spoon into crab shells or a buttered shallow baking dish. Rub with butter to prevent skin from forming, page 13. Sprinkle with grated cheese. *Crab Gratin can be prepared to this point 8 hours ahead, covered and refrigerated.* Bake 10 to 15 minutes until bubbling and browned. Makes 10 to 12 appetizer servings or 6 main-dish servings.

Lobster Américaine
Homard à l'Américaine

Rice Pilaf, page 127, is perfect to serve with this rich dish.

2 (1-1/2- to 1-3/4-lb.) live lobsters
4 tablespoons olive oil
1 onion, chopped
1 garlic clove, crushed
1/3 cup brandy
1-1/2 cups white wine
1 cup Fish Stock, page 32, or White
   Veal Stock, page 31, or water
4 tomatoes, coarsely chopped

1 bouquet garni, page 7
Pinch of red (cayenne) pepper
Salt and pepper to taste
4 tablespoons water
2 tablespoons tomato paste
1/3 cup butter
2 tablespoons all-purpose flour
2 tablespoons whipping cream
2 tablespoons chopped parsley

Place each lobster face-down flat on a board. Cover tail with a cloth. Hold lobster firmly behind head, away from claws. With point of a sharp heavy knife, pierce down to the board through the crossmark on center of head. Lobster is killed at once. Turn lobster around and continue splitting body as far as tail. Remove tail and cut it with its shell in thick slices, discarding intestinal tract. Discard head sacs. Crack claws. In a large skillet or shallow saucepan, heat oil. Add half the lobster pieces, cut-side down. Sauté 1 minute over high heat. Turn pieces over and continue cooking until shells turn red; remove from skillet. Repeat with remaining pieces. Add onion and garlic. Cook over low heat until soft but not browned. Return lobster pieces to skillet. Add brandy and flame, page 11. Stir in wine, stock, tomatoes, bouquet garni, red pepper, salt and pepper. Cover and simmer 20 minutes. Remove lobster tails and claws; extract meat, discarding shells. Cut meat in large cubes. Put remaining shells in a metal bowl and crush with a wooden pestle. Return shells to sauce. Mix 4 tablespoons water with tomato paste; add to sauce. Simmer 10 minutes. Strain through a fine strainer or cheesecloth, pressing on shells to extract all juices. Soften 2 tablespoons butter in a small bowl. Add flour and mash with a fork until smooth. Bring sauce to a boil. Whisk in flour mixture a little at a time. Reduce heat and simmer gently 1 to 2 minutes. Stir in lobster meat and cream. *Lobster Américaine can be prepared 24 hours ahead, covered and refrigerated or frozen. If freezing, add cream to sauce when reheating lobster.* Simmer lobster over low heat 2 to 3 minutes until lobster pieces are hot. Remove from heat and taste for seasoning. Stir in remaining butter in pieces. Sprinkle with parsley. Makes 4 servings.

Variation

If live lobsters are not available, use 6 raw frozen rock lobster tails in the shells; omit both crushing the shells and simmering them in the sauce.

If preparing ahead, cook or bake food for the minimum cooking time, so it won't overcook when you reheat it.

Oysters in Champagne
Huîtres au Champagne

Champagne is best for this luxury dish but any good dry white wine will do.

24 oysters	**Hollandaise Sauce, page 45**
1-1/2 cups champagne	**Few drops of lemon juice**
5 shallots, very finely chopped	**Salt and pepper, if desired**

Holding each oyster in a dish towel, pry open with a sturdy knife or bottle opener. Discard top shell. Carefully use knife to release each oyster from shell. Place oysters in a shallow saucepan. Wipe shells clean and arrange in a shallow baking dish or heatproof platter on a layer of rock salt to keep them level. Boil champagne and shallots in a small saucepan until about 2 tablespoons remain. Prepare Hollandaise Sauce; be careful not to add too much salt because oysters are naturally salty. Keep sauce warm in a water bath, page 9. Heat undrained oysters just until slightly above body temperature; remove from heat. Do not boil or overcook or oysters will be tough. Drain, adding oyster liquid to shallot mixture and boil again until about 2 tablespoons remain. Preheat broiler. Whisk shallot mixture into Hollandaise Sauce. Add lemon juice; taste for seasoning. Add salt and pepper, if desired. Spoon about 1 tablespoon sauce into bottom of each shell. Place 1 oyster in each shell and spoon remaining sauce over each oyster. Brown under broiler. Serve immediately. Makes 8 appetizer servings or 4 main-dish servings.

Scampi Newburg
Langoustines à la Newburg

Heat scampi and sauce in a chafing dish at the table.

Rice Pilaf, page 127	**Salt and pepper**
1/2 cup butter	**2 cups whipping cream**
1-1/2 lbs. cooked, peeled scampi or	**6 egg yolks**
large shrimp	**1/3 cup brandy**
1/2 teaspoon paprika	

Prepare Rice Pilaf. Grease a 1-quart ring mold and fill with rice, pressing lightly. Keep warm. Turn out onto a round platter just before preparing scampi mixture. Spread 3 tablespoons butter in a shallow saucepan or chafing dish. Add scampi or shrimp. Sprinkle with paprika, salt and pepper. Cover and heat over low heat 2 to 3 minutes. Whisk cream and egg yolks until blended. Add brandy to scampi mixture and flame, page 11. Remove from heat and stir in cream mixture. Heat gently, stirring constantly, until sauce thickens. Do not overheat or mixture will curdle. Cut remaining 5 tablespoons butter in small pieces. Remove from heat and add pieces of butter, shaking pan until butter mixes into sauce. Taste for seasoning. Spoon scampi into rice ring with a little sauce. Serve at once with remaining sauce served separately. Makes 4 servings.

Variation

Lobster Newburg (Homard à la Newburg): Substitute 3 cups (1-1/2 lbs.) cooked lobster meat for the scampi.

Poultry

From simple family meals built around a poached chicken to festive dinners featuring Roast Duck with Orange Sauce, poultry can play the main part in almost any menu. Poultry of one kind or another goes with virtually every sauce, vegetable and even fruit.

Birds are generally divided into two categories: those with white flesh and little natural fat and those with dark, rich meat and fatty skin. Chicken and turkey are most common in the first group, and duck is outstanding in the second.

Of all birds, chicken is the most versatile. It can be broiled, roasted, poached, braised—indeed, cooked almost any way. And chicken is as much at home with the delicate wine and cream sauces of the Loire Valley as with the robust garnish of bacon, potatoes, olives, tomatoes and mushrooms from Corsica.

For this reason you can change ingredients in chicken dishes almost at will, substituting red wine for white and zucchini strips for green beans. You can add or omit mushrooms, onions, garlic, bacon, tomatoes, herbs, or cream as it suits you. Each change in ingredients means a new name for the dish. If you substitute spring vegetables for the hearty garnish in Roast Chicken Fermière, you have Chicken with Spring Vegetables, omit the herb in Chicken with Tarragon and you get Chicken à la Crème.

Duck is a different matter. It is usually roasted to dissolve its fat and give a crisp skin. Because of its meaty flesh, duck is good with brown sauces, with fortified wines such as Madeira and sherry, and with fruit or sharp flavors like olives which complement its richness.

Turkey is the natural choice for serving large numbers. It is also a favorite for stuffing, which not only provides additional portions but extra flavor as well. Actually any bird can be stuffed. Mixtures are usually based on meat as in Turkey with Chestnuts or on cereals as in Stuffed Squabs Véronique. They can be varied by such additions as tiny sausages, nuts, apples or dried fruits such as raisins or prunes.

How to Choose & Cook Poultry

When buying poultry, try to choose plump chickens; a thin, bony chicken, no matter how well cooked, looks sad on the platter. Try to find ducks that are not too fat; French ducks are relatively lean. Small turkeys are usually more moist than large ones.

The goal in cooking poultry is to keep it moist. If cooked too long, a bird dries out, but if undercooked, it will be tough. One way to help retain juices is to cook a bird whole. Roast chicken is as much of a favorite in France as it is in the rest of the world. All except the largest birds are roasted at relatively high heat to ensure a crisp skin. Constant basting, especially during roasting of white-fleshed birds, is needed to keep poultry moist. A related French method which saves time and effort, is pot roasting *en cocotte*. The bird is browned all over in melted butter and then cooked in the oven in a covered casserole, often together with the garnish. This retains moisture so little or no liquid is needed.

Like fish and meat, chicken can be cooked in liquid, which both gives and receives flavor. Poaching, preferably in stock made beforehand with some chicken bones, is an efficient way to keep birds particularly moist. For this reason, it is the preferred method to cook a chicken which will be served cold, as in Chicken in Curry Mayonnaise. When poultry is cut in pieces, it is usually browned in fat first, then simmered in liquid from which is made a richly flavored sauce like the red wine sauce of Chicken in Wine.

How to Prepare Poultry Ahead

Poultry cooked in sauce reheats very well, so it can be refrigerated a day or two, or frozen. However, roasted or pot-roasted birds lose their fresh taste and crisp skin when reheated. They are much better cold: Serve cold white-fleshed birds with mayonnaise and duck with pickles, citrus or spicy poached fruit, or green salad. You can reheat sliced roasted chicken by adding it to a hot brown or white sauce if you are careful not to let it boil; sprinkle it with chopped parsley and surround it by butter-fried Croûtes, page 8.

How to Truss Poultry

Trussing encloses any stuffing and keeps the bird in a compact shape so it cooks evenly and does not dry during cooking.

Thread a trussing needle with string and make

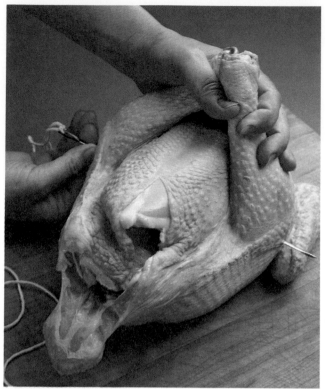

1/Insert trussing needle through leg at the joint. Push needle through the chicken and out other side.

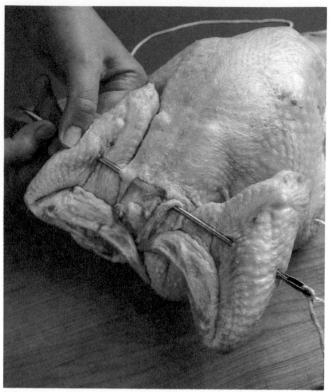

2/Insert needle into wing, making a long stitch from leg to wing. Push needle through neck skin, under backbone and through other wing. Cut and tie string.

a knot at the eye. For large birds, including ducks, remove the wishbone to make carving easier: Pull up the neck skin and use a small sharp knife to outline the wishbone and cut it free from the breastbone. Replace the skin in position.

Set the bird on its back on a board. Push the legs back and down toward the board. Insert the needle through the leg at the joint. Pass the needle through the body then through the other leg pulling the string to the other side of the bird.

Turn the bird on its breast. Fold the neck skin tightly over the backbone, enclosing any stuffing. Tuck wing tip bones under bird to hold neck skin. Insert the needle into a wing bone on the same side of the bird, leaving a stitch of string leading from the leg to the wing. Next, catch the neck skin and insert the needle under the backbone, then through the other side, catching the other wing. Pull the string through the bird and cut the string to free the trussing needle. Tie the ends of string from the leg and wing tightly together at the side. For unstuffed chickens, this is enough to hold the bird in shape. For stuffed chickens and all large birds: Thread the needle again. Run it through the tail, then through the end of both drumsticks. Tie the ends of string tightly together, thus closing the bird and preventing the stuffing from escaping.

How to Truss a Chicken

3/If chicken is stuffed or large, push threaded needle through the tail, then through drumsticks. Tie tightly.

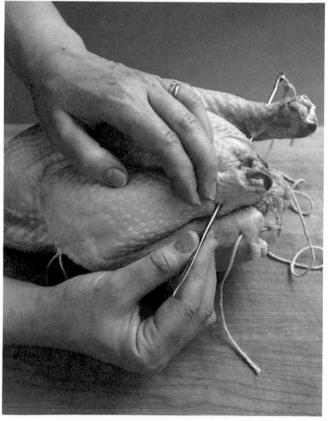

1/Pull leg away from chicken and cut off thigh through the joint.

2/Use a sharp knife to remove breast meat in slices.

How to Carve a Chicken

How to Check if Poultry is Done

For whole birds: Pierce the body with a two-prong fork and, if bird is small, lift it and tip the juices from inside. Note the color of the juices that escape. A white-fleshed bird is done when the juice is no longer pink, but clear. A duck is done French-style when the juice is no longer red, but light pink. However, many people prefer their duck well done, when the juice is clear.

For cut birds, stuffed birds and those too heavy to lift: Gently prick the thickest part of the leg with a two-prong fork and note the color of the juices. However, do not test too often or the bird will lose a good deal of juice.

How to Carve a Chicken

Set the bird on its back on a carving board, discard the trussing strings and leave the bird in a warm place 10 to 15 minutes.

Holding the chicken firmly with a two-prong fork, use a sharp knife to cut through the skin where the leg joins the body. When the leg is loosened, pull it out sharply to break the joint that attaches the thigh to the body. If necessary, use a knife to cut through this joint as you pull. Repeat with the other leg. For large birds, cut the legs in half, using the white line of fat on the underside as a guide to the position of the joint. Trim drumstick knuckles with poultry shears.

Use a sharp knife to remove the backbone, which is not served. With the knife, cut the breast piece in half along the breastbone and through the wishbone.

For large chickens, cut each piece of breast meat off the bird in thin slices.

How to Serve Poultry

A whole roast bird is impressive, but dexterity is needed to carve it neatly at the table. The French carve the bird in the kitchen where it can be reheated quickly if carving took too long. Then the pieces are arranged on a platter, coated with sauce—a poultry recipe without sauce is rare!—and decorated with any vegetables called for in the recipe. A sprinkling of chopped parsley or a bunch of watercress adds color.

Often the poultry dish you have chosen will already contain a generous amount of vegetables so there's no need to add an accompaniment. However, if the recipe has plenty of sauce, you may like to add rice, potatoes or noodles. The French would simply soak up the liquid with chunks of bread.

Corsican Pot-Roast Chicken
Poulet en Cocotte à la Corsoise

Olives and tomatoes give Mediterranean color to this chicken.

3 tablespoons vegetable oil
2 tablespoons butter
1/4 lb. bacon, cut in large dice
1 (3-1/2- to 4-lb.) roasting chicken,
   trussed, pages 75-76
Salt and pepper
2 medium potatoes
1 cup black olives, drained, pitted

1/4 lb. small mushrooms
4 medium tomatoes, peeled, halved,
   seeded, page 10
1 garlic clove, chopped
2 tablespoons brandy
1 tablespoon finely chopped parsley,
   if desired

Preheat oven to 400°F (205°C). Heat 2 tablespoons oil and 1 tablespoon butter in a large heavy casserole. Add bacon. Cook until browned. Remove and reserve. Add chicken to casserole and brown on all sides. Sprinkle lightly with salt and pepper. Cover and cook in oven 20 minutes. Cut potatoes in quarters and trim to uniform oval shapes with a small knife. Put in a small saucepan. Cover potatoes with cold water. Bring just to a boil; drain well. In a medium skillet, heat remaining 1 tablespoon oil and 1 tablespoon butter. Add potatoes. Sprinkle lightly with salt and pepper and brown quickly on all sides; do not cook further as potatoes will continue to cook in oven with chicken. Remove from heat. Add potatoes, olives, mushrooms, tomatoes, garlic and brandy to chicken. Cover and cook 30 to 40 minutes until chicken is tender. Taste liquid for seasoning. Discard trussing strings. Carve chicken and arrange in a deep serving dish. Spoon vegetable garnish and cooking liquid over chicken. Sprinkle with parsley. Makes 4 servings.

Roast Chicken Fermière   Photo on cover.
Poulet Rôti Fermière

Almost any young spring vegetables can be added to this dish.

1 (3-1/2- to 4-lb.) roasting chicken,
   trussed, pages 75-76
1 tablespoon butter
2 tablespoons vegetable oil
Salt and pepper

1 lb. potatoes
1/4 lb. bacon, diced
20 baby onions, peeled
1/2 lb. small mushrooms

Preheat oven to 400°F (205°C). Rub chicken with butter. Pour oil into a roasting pan. Place chicken on one thigh in pan. Sprinkle with salt and pepper. Roast chicken on one side 15 minutes, basting often. Cut potatoes in quarters and trim to uniform oval shapes with a small knife. Arrange around chicken and sprinkle with salt and pepper. Turn chicken to other side. Roast 15 minutes, basting chicken and potatoes often. While chicken roasts, cook bacon in a heavy skillet until browned. Remove and reserve. Brown onions on all sides in same skillet, shaking skillet to turn onions over. Remove and reserve. Quickly brown mushrooms in skillet. Add bacon, onions and mushrooms to roasting pan after chicken has roasted a total of 30 minutes. Place chicken on its back and roast 10 to 20 minutes longer; skin should be crisp and browned and the juice clear, page 77. Transfer chicken to a carving board. Taste vegetables for seasoning. Discard trussing strings and place chicken on a platter. Spoon vegetables and bacon around chicken. Makes 4 servings.

Chicken with Tarragon
Poulet à l'Estragon

If fresh tarragon is not available, use fresh rosemary, oregano, dill or Italian parsley.

Salt and pepper
1 (4- to 5-lb.) roasting chicken
  and giblets
1 (1-1/2-oz.) bunch fresh tarragon
6 tablespoons butter
1 onion, coarsely chopped

1 carrot, diced
1 to 2 qts. Chicken Stock, page 32
1 bouquet garni, page 7
Rice Pilaf, page 127
3 tablespoons all-purpose flour
1/3 cup whipping cream

Sprinkle salt and pepper in the chicken cavity. Place half the tarragon stems inside the cavity; reserve tarragon leaves. Truss chicken, pages 75 and 76. Melt half the butter in a large heavy casserole. Brown chicken on all sides in butter over medium heat. Stir in onion, carrot and reserved chicken giblets except for liver. Cook until lightly browned. Add enough stock to cover three-fourths of the chicken. Reserve and chill 1/4 cup stock. Add bouquet garni, remaining tarragon stems and a little salt and pepper to casserole. Cover and bring to a boil. Reduce heat and simmer 45 to 50 minutes or until juice runs clear, page 77. Transfer chicken to a platter. Cover with foil to keep warm. Skim excess fat from cooking liquid. Boil cooking liquid until reduced to about 2-1/2 cups. Taste for seasoning, then strain. *Chicken with Tarragon can be prepared to this point 2 days ahead, covered and refrigerated in its liquid or frozen. Reheat over medium heat.* Before serving, prepare Rice Pilaf. Fill a small saucepan two-thirds full of water. Bring to a boil. Add tarragon leaves and blanch by boiling 1 minute. Drain and rinse with cold water. Lift chicken from broth and keep warm. Mix flour and reserved cold stock in a cup to make a smooth paste. Gradually whisk paste into boiling broth and continue whisking until it thickens enough to coat a spoon lightly, page 12. Stir in cream and bring just to a boil. Add half the blanched tarragon leaves. Taste for seasoning. If carving the chicken at the table, spoon a little sauce over the whole chicken and sprinkle with remaining blanched tarragon leaves. Spoon Rice Pilaf around the chicken. Alternatively, carve the chicken into 8 pieces, page 77. Arrange the pieces on one side of the platter, coat them with sauce and decorate with remaining blanched tarragon leaves. Spoon Rice Pilaf onto other side of platter. Serve remaining sauce separately. Makes 4 to 6 servings.

For any roast or en cocotte *recipe—choose a dish in which chicken and garnish fit comfortably. If it is too large, the sauce may burn; if too small, the bird won't brown properly.*

Stuffed Squabs Véronique

Pigeons Farcis Véronique

Baby chickens are also used for this dish. Véronique *always refers to a garnish of green grapes.*

Stuffing, see below
4 squabs
1/4 cup butter
3/4 cup white wine
Salt and pepper
3/4 cup Chicken Stock, page 32

2 teaspoons potato starch or arrowroot
1 tablespoon water
3 tablespoons whipping cream
1 cup green seedless grapes (1/2 lb.)
1/2 teaspoon sugar, if desired

Stuffing:

3/4 cup coarse cracked wheat or
   whole buckwheat groats (kasha)
1 egg, slightly beaten

1-1/2 cups water or Chicken Stock, page 32
Salt and pepper
1/2 cup whole blanched almonds

Prepare Stuffing. Fill squabs with cooled Stuffing; truss, pages 75 and 76. Preheat oven to 375°F (190°C). Melt butter in a medium shallow casserole. Brown squabs in butter on all sides over medium heat. Remove from casserole. Stir in wine; boil until reduced by half. Return squabs to casserole. Sprinkle with salt and pepper. Cover and bake 25 to 30 minutes until juice runs clear, page 77. Place squabs on a platter. Discard trussing strings. Cover squabs with foil to keep warm. Discard fat from casserole. Pour in stock and bring to a boil, stirring to dissolve any brown juices on bottom of casserole. Strain into a saucepan and bring to a boil. Mix potato starch or arrowroot and water in a cup to make a smooth paste. Gradually whisk paste into boiling sauce and continue whisking until sauce thickens enough to coat a spoon, page 12. Stir in cream and bring just to a boil. Stir in grapes. Simmer 1 to 2 minutes. Taste sauce for seasoning, adding sugar if grapes are tart. Spoon sauce over squabs. Makes 4 servings.

Stuffing:

Preheat oven to 350°F (175°C). Mix cracked wheat or buckwheat groats and egg in a small heavy casserole over high heat. Stir constantly 5 to 6 minutes until grains are dry and separated. Stir in water or Chicken Stock, salt and pepper. Cover and bring to a boil. Bake cracked wheat 25 to 30 minutes or buckwheat groats 10 to 15 minutes. Place almonds on an ungreased baking sheet. Toast in oven 10 to 12 minutes until lightly browned. When grains of cracked wheat or buckwheat groats are tender and water is absorbed, remove from oven and cool slightly. Coarsely chop toasted almonds and stir into cracked wheat or buckwheat groats. Taste for seasoning. Cool and taste again before using.

Variation

Use Cornish hens instead of squabs, baking 30 to 40 minutes instead of 25 to 30 minutes.

The French rarely rinse their poultry before cooking it, so the skin will be crisp. If you'd like to wash it, or if you buy frozen poultry, be sure to pat it dry with paper towels before cooking it.

Anjou Chicken Sauté

Sauté de Poulet à l'Angevine

A rich chicken dish, traditionally made with white wine from Anjou in the Loire valley.

1 tablespoon vegetable oil
2 tablespoons butter
1 (3-1/2- to 4-lb.) roasting chicken,
    cut in 8 pieces, see below
18 to 20 baby onions, peeled
2 shallots, chopped
1/2 cup white wine

Salt and pepper
1/2 lb. mushrooms, cut in quarters
1/2 cup whipping cream
1 teaspoon potato starch or arrowroot
1 tablespoon water
1 tablespoon chopped parsley

Heat oil and butter in a large heavy skillet. Add chicken legs and thighs skin-side down. When they begin to brown, add wings and then breasts. Brown pieces on both sides. Remove from skillet. Stir onions into skillet and sauté, shaking skillet so onions brown evenly. Remove lightly browned onions from skillet. Stir in shallots. Sauté until soft but not browned. Remove from skillet. Return chicken pieces to skillet. Add 1/4 cup wine, salt and pepper. Cover tightly and cook over low heat 35 to 45 minutes until white meat is tender when pierced with a fork. Remove wing and breast pieces. Add mushrooms, sautéed onions and shallots. Cook remaining chicken 10 minutes longer or until very tender. *Anjou Chicken Sauté can be prepared to this point 2 days ahead, covered and refrigerated or frozen. Reheat slowly over medium heat.* Arrange chicken on a platter. Add onions and mushrooms. Cover with foil to keep warm. Stir remaining 1/4 cup wine into sauce. Bring to a boil. Continue to boil 2 to 3 minutes. Stir in cream and return just to a boil. Mix potato starch or arrowroot and water in a cup to make a paste. Gradually whisk paste into boiling sauce and cook, whisking until sauce thickens enough to coat a spoon, page 12. Taste for seasoning. Spoon sauce over chicken and sprinkle with chopped parsley. Makes 4 servings.

How to Cut up a Raw Chicken or Duck

So it cooks evenly and presents well, chicken or duck should be cut up into neat pieces, discarding the backbone. It can be divided into six or eight pieces, depending on its size and the recipe. With the point of a sharp knife, locate the *oysters* under the bird and cut around each one in a half circle. Cut down between the leg and body, following the outline of the thigh, until the leg joint is visible. Twist the leg sharply out to break the joint. Pull the leg away from the body, using the knife to cut the meat under the body away from the bone, including the *oyster*. Repeat with other leg.

Hold the knife at the end of the breastbone, where the breastbone and wishbone meet, and cut down to the wing joint, parallel to one side of the wishbone. Cut through the wing joint; in this way a portion of the breast is cut off with the wing. Repeat on the other side.

Using poultry shears or scissors, cut away the backbone and ribs, leaving the breast in a diamond-shaped piece. Cut away the meat from one side of the breastbone with a knife. Cut the breast in half along the breastbone with shears.

Depending on the recipe, cut the legs in half, using the white line of fat on the underside as a guide to the position of the joint.

After cooking, trim drumstick knuckles with poultry shears and, if you like, discard wing tips.

Chicken in Wine
Coq au Vin

Coq au Vin was designed to tenderize a tough old fowl and is now made throughout France.

1 (4- to 4-1/2-lb.) roasting chicken,
  cut in 8 pieces, page 81
Marinade, see below
1 tablespoon vegetable oil
1 tablespoon butter
1/4 lb. bacon, cut in large dice
18 to 20 baby onions, peeled
1/2 lb. mushrooms, cut in quarters

2 tablespoons all-purpose flour
1-1/2 cups Chicken Stock, page 32
1 garlic clove, finely chopped
2 shallots, finely chopped
1 bouquet garni, page 7
Salt and pepper
1 tablespoon chopped parsley

Marinade:
1-1/2 cups red wine
1 onion, thinly sliced
1 carrot, thinly sliced
1 celery stalk, thinly sliced

1 bouquet garni, page 7
1 garlic clove, sliced
6 peppercorns
2 tablespoons olive oil

Place chicken pieces in a deep bowl. Add marinade ingredients to chicken, adding olive oil last. Let stand 6 hours at room temperature or 10 to 12 hours in refrigerator; turn chicken pieces occasionally. If using oven, preheat to 350°F (175°C). Drain chicken, reserving marinade. Pat chicken dry with paper towels. Strain marinade; discard vegetables and seasonings. In a medium skillet, heat oil and butter. Fry bacon in fat until browned; remove from skillet. Sauté onions until lightly browned; remove from skillet. Sauté mushrooms until tender; remove from skillet. Place chicken pieces in skillet skin-side down. Brown both sides thoroughly over medium heat, 5 to 10 minutes. Remove from skillet. Discard all but 2 tablespoons fat from pan. Stir in flour; cook until foaming. Stir in reserved liquid from marinade, stock, garlic, shallots, bouquet garni and a little salt and pepper. Return chicken to skillet. Cover and bring to a boil. Reduce heat and simmer over medium heat or in oven 25 to 30 minutes until chicken is almost tender. Stir occasionally to prevent flour from sticking to skillet. Stir in onions and simmer 10 minutes longer. Place chicken on a platter. Cover with foil to keep warm. Discard bouquet garni. Stir mushrooms and bacon into sauce. If needed, boil sauce until thick enough to coat a spoon, page 12. Taste for seasoning. Spoon sauce over chicken. *Chicken in Wine can be prepared 3 days ahead, covered and refrigerated in its sauce or frozen. Reheat slowly over medium heat. Transfer to a platter.* Sprinkle with parsley. Makes 4 servings.

White meat cooks more quickly than dark, so when using chicken pieces, remove breast and wings from the pan first, leaving legs and thighs to simmer longer.

Chicken Bouchées
Bouchées à la Reine

Bouchées means mouthfuls *and they are indeed fit for a queen as the French title suggests.*

Bouchées, see below
1 (3-1/2- to 4-lb.) roasting chicken,
    trussed, pages 75-76
1 onion, halved
1 carrot, halved
1 bouquet garni, page 7
6 peppercorns
5 to 6 cups White Veal Stock, page 31,
    or Chicken Stock, page 32, or water

Water
1/2 lb. mushrooms, cut in quarters
Juice of 1/2 lemon
Salt and pepper
4 tablespoons butter
4 tablespoons all-purpose flour
3 egg yolks
1/2 cup whipping cream

Bouchées:
Puff Pastry, pages 154-155, made with
    1-1/4 cups butter

Egg Glaze, page 7

Prepare Bouchées. Place chicken in a medium, heavy casserole with onion, carrot, bouquet garni, peppercorns and enough stock or water to barely cover. Cover and slowly bring to a boil. Reduce heat and simmer 1 to 1-1/4 hours until juice runs clear, page 77. Turn chicken at least once during cooking. Cool to lukewarm in liquid. Drain cooled chicken, reserving liquid. Simmer liquid until reduced to about 3 cups. Remove chicken meat from bones. Cut meat in 1/2-inch dice, discarding skin. In a small saucepan, combine 1/4 inch of water, mushrooms, lemon juice, salt and pepper. Cover and cook over high heat 4 to 5 minutes, until liquid boils to top of pan and mushrooms are tender; drain, reserving liquid. Melt butter in a medium saucepan. Whisk in flour. Cook over medium heat 1 to 2 minutes until foaming but not browned. Cool slightly, then whisk in reduced stock and mushroom cooking liquid. Bring to a boil, whisking constantly. Cook and whisk 2 minutes or until mixture thickly coats a spoon, page 12. Stir in diced chicken and mushrooms. Taste for seasoning. *Filling can be prepared to this point 2 days ahead, covered and refrigerated or frozen.* To serve, reheat bouchées a few minutes in a 250°F (120°C) oven. Reheat chicken filling over medium heat. Beat egg yolks and cream in a small bowl. Stir in a few tablespoons of hot filling. Add yolk mixture to remaining filling. Mix thoroughly. Stir over low heat until mixture thickens slightly. Sauce should be fairly thick so it doesn't soak bouchées. Do not boil or it will curdle. Taste for seasoning. Fill each bouchée generously with filling and top with a reserved pastry "hat." Serve immediately. Makes 8 appetizer servings or 4 main-dish servings.

Bouchées:
Prepare Puff Pastry, completing all 6 turns. Refrigerate at least 1 hour. Preheat oven to 425°F (220°C). Sprinkle water on a baking sheet. Roll out dough about 1/4 inch thick. Cut out sixteen 3-1/2-inch rounds with a fluted cookie cutter. Place half the rounds on prepared baking sheet. Brush with Egg Glaze. Use a plain cookie cutter to cut a 2-1/2-inch circle from center of each remaining round to form rings. Place rings on top of glazed rounds and press gently to seal. Refrigerate 15 minutes. Brush with Egg Glaze. Bake 15 to 20 minutes until puffed and browned well. Transfer to a rack to cool. While bouchées are still warm, remove and reserve center "hat" that has formed. Scoop out any uncooked dough with a teaspoon. *Bouchées can be stored 3 to 4 days in an airtight container or they can be frozen, unbaked or baked.*

Chicken Kiev
Poulet à la Kiev

An herb-and-butter surprise is hidden in each deep-fried chicken breast.

1/3 cup butter
Grated peel and juice of 1 lemon
1 tablespoon finely chopped parsley
1 tablespoon finely chopped fresh tarragon
   or 1 teaspoon dried tarragon
1 teaspoon finely chopped chives
Salt and pepper

4 boneless chicken breasts
1/4 cup all-purpose flour
1 egg
1/2 tablespoon vegetable oil
1/2 tablespoon water
3/4 cup dry white breadcrumbs
Oil for deep-frying

Cream butter in a small bowl. Beat in lemon peel and juice, parsley, tarragon, chives and plenty of salt and pepper. Shape into a 3-inch square cake on a sheet of waxed paper. Cover and put in freezer or refrigerator until very firm. Remove skin from chicken breasts. Place breasts on a flat surface. With knife tip, cut a deep slit in thick edge of each breast to make a pocket; do not cut through opposite side of breast. Cut 4 sticks from chilled herb butter. Slip one stick into each pocket. Press pocket edges together with your fingertips. No butter should be visible. Mix flour with 1/4 teaspoon salt and a pinch of pepper on a plate. In a wide shallow bowl, beat egg, oil and water. Roll chicken breasts in seasoned flour, dip both sides in beaten egg mixture and coat thoroughly with breadcrumbs. Refrigerate uncovered without breasts touching each other 2 to 3 hours or overnight. Bread coating will dry and be crisp when fried. *Prepared breasts can also be wrapped and frozen. Thaw 6 to 7 hours uncovered in refrigerator before frying.* Heat oil for deep-frying to 360°F (180°C) on a deep-fat thermometer. Deep-fry 2 breasts at a time until golden brown, about 5 minutes. Drain on paper towels and serve immediately. Chicken Kiev can be kept hot 5 to 10 minutes in a 250°F (120°C) oven with oven door open. Makes 4 servings.

Chicken in Curry Mayonnaise
Poulet Elizabeth

Created by the Cordon Bleu cooking school in London for the coronation of Queen Elizabeth II.

1 (3-1/2- to 4-lb.) roasting chicken,
    trussed, pages 75-76
1 onion, quartered
1 carrot, quartered
2 celery stalks
1 bouquet garni, page 7

6 peppercorns
Salt
Curry Mayonnaise, see below
1/4 to 1/2 teaspoon paprika
Watercress, if desired

Curry Mayonnaise:
1-1/2 cups Mayonnaise, page 50
1 tablespoon vegetable oil
1 small onion, finely chopped
2 teaspoons curry powder

1/4 cup tomato juice
1/4 cup red wine
1 tablespoon apricot jam
1 tablespoon warm water, if needed

Place chicken in a medium, heavy casserole with onion, carrot, celery, bouquet garni, peppercorns, salt and enough water to barely cover. Cover casserole. Slowly bring to a boil; reduce heat. Simmer 1 to 1-1/4 hours until juice runs clear, page 77. Turn chicken at least once during cooking. Cool to lukewarm in liquid. Transfer to a platter to cool completely. Cover chicken and refrigerate. Reserve cooking liquid to use as light chicken stock for another recipe. *Chicken can be cooked to this point 24 hours ahead, covered and refrigerated.* Prepare Curry Mayonnaise. Not more than 1 hour before serving, remove trussing strings and cut chicken into 8 pieces, discarding skin. Arrange chicken pieces on a platter and coat with Curry Mayonnaise. Serve remaining mayonnaise separately. Sprinkle paprika over chicken to add color. Garnish platter with watercress, if desired. Makes 4 servings.

Curry Mayonnaise:
Prepare Mayonnaise. Heat oil in a medium saucepan. Sauté onion until soft but not browned. Stir in curry powder. Simmer 2 minutes to blend flavors. Stir in tomato juice and red wine. Boil to reduce liquid by half. Stir in apricot jam. Cool and strain, pressing to extract as much liquid as possible. Stir curry mixture into Mayonnaise, adding less or more to taste. If needed, add 1 tablespoon warm water to thin mayonnaise so it coats a spoon, page 12.

Roast Duck with Orange Sauce
Canard à l'Orange

Boiling the orange peel softens it and reduces its bitterness.

3 navel oranges
1 (4- to 5-lb.) duck, reserve neck and
   gizzard for Orange Sauce
Orange Sauce, see below
Salt and pepper

3 tablespoons brandy
1/2 cup White Veal Stock, page 31,
   or Chicken Stock, page 32
1 tablespoon Grand Marnier

Orange Sauce:
Reserved peel of 2 oranges
1/4 cup sugar
1/4 cup water
1/4 cup vinegar
Duck neck and gizzard
3 tablespoons vegetable oil

1 onion, diced
1 carrot, diced
2 tablespoons all-purpose flour
2-1/2 cups White Veal Stock, page 31,
   or Chicken Stock, page 32

Preheat oven to 400°F (205°C). Use a vegetable peeler to peel 2 oranges thinly. Place a few strips of peel inside duck, reserving remaining peel for sauce. Truss duck, pages 75 and 76. Prepare Orange Sauce. Place duck on one thigh in a roasting pan. Sprinkle with salt and pepper. Prick all over to release fat during cooking. Roast duck in oven 1-1/2 to 2 hours until skin is crisp and browned and juice runs pink or clear, page 77. Roast duck on one side 20 minutes. Turn on other side. Cook 20 minutes longer. Place on back for remaining cooking time. Spoon excess fat from roasting pan occasionally. Use a serrated knife to cut skin and pith from 2 peeled oranges. Separate sections, discarding membrane and reserving any juice. Put orange sections in a small pan with 2 tablespoons brandy. Flute remaining orange, page 8, cut in half and thinly slice for garnish. Place cooked duck on a platter. Remove trussing string. Cover duck with foil to keep warm. Discard fat from roasting pan. Pour in stock. Bring to boil, stirring to dissolve any brown juices on bottom of pan. Strain into Orange Sauce with juice from orange segments. Add remaining 1 tablespoon brandy and Grand Marnier. Heat over low heat without boiling. Taste for seasoning. Stir in orange segments. Spoon a little sauce over duck and arrange orange segments on platter. Garnish with fluted orange slices. Serve remaining sauce separately. Makes 3 to 4 servings.

Orange Sauce:
Cut reserved orange peel into very thin strips. Put them in a small saucepan two-thirds full of cold water; bring to a boil. Blanch peel by boiling 3 to 4 minutes. Drain, rinse in cold water and drain again; set aside. In a small heavy saucepan, heat sugar in 1/4 cup water until dissolved, then bring to a boil. Continue to boil until liquid turns a light brown caramel, page 11. Immediately remove from heat and pour in vinegar; **stand back as vinegar vapor can sting your eyes.** Heat gently until caramel is dissolved. Cut duck neck and gizzard into chunks. Heat oil in a medium, heavy saucepan. Sauté giblet chunks in oil until well browned. Remove from pan. Stir in diced onion and carrot. Cook over low heat until they just begin to brown. Stir in flour. Cook and stir until browned; do not let flour scorch. Pour in stock and bring to a boil, stirring often. Stir in browned giblets with caramel mixture. Simmer 40 to 50 minutes until sauce is thick enough to coat a spoon, page 12, and reduced to 1-1/2 to 2 cups. Skim sauce and stir occasionally. Strain sauce, pressing vegetables to extract as much liquid as possible. Taste for seasoning. Stir in strips of orange peel. *Orange Sauce can be prepared to this point 1 day ahead, covered and refrigerated.*

Duck Sauté with Madeira
Sauté de Canard au Madère

Use port instead of Madeira for an excellent variation of this recipe.

1 tablespoon vegetable oil
1 (4- to 5-lb.) duck, quartered
1 onion, chopped
1-1/2 tablespoons all-purpose flour
3/4 cup red wine
3/4 to 1 cup Brown Beef Stock, page 30,
   or Chicken Stock, page 32
1 bouquet garni, page 7

2 shallots, chopped
1 garlic clove, crushed
Salt and pepper
1/4 lb. mushrooms, thinly sliced
3 tablespoons Madeira
Croûtes, page 8
1 tablespoon chopped parsley, if desired

Heat oil in a large skillet. Sauté duck pieces cut-side down in oil 1 to 2 minutes to seal in juices. Turn over and cook skin-side down 15 to 20 minutes until browned well and all fat has been rendered so duck will not be greasy. Remove duck and discard all but 2 tablespoons fat. Stir in onion; sauté until lightly browned. Stir in flour. Cook and stir over medium heat until browned. Immediately add wine, stock, bouquet garni, shallots, garlic and salt and pepper. Return duck to skillet. Cover and simmer 20 to 25 minutes until tender when pierced with a skewer or done as desired, page 77. Add more stock if sauce becomes thick. Add mushrooms and Madeira. Simmer 2 to 3 minutes longer until mushrooms are tender. Sauce should be just thick enough to coat a spoon, page 12. To thin sauce, add more stock; to thicken sauce, simmer until reduced. Discard bouquet garni. Taste sauce for seasoning. *Duck Sauté with Madeira can be prepared to this point 2 days ahead, covered and refrigerated or frozen. Reheat in a large saucepan over medium heat.* Prepare Croûtes. Arrange duck pieces on platter. Spoon mushrooms and sauce onto duck and place Croûtes around platter edge. Sprinkle duck with parsley. Makes 4 servings.

Turkey with Chestnuts
Dinde aux Marrons

Traditional Christmas turkey in France is stuffed with chestnuts. Try the same stuffing with chicken.

1-1/2 lbs. fresh chestnuts or 1 (2-lb.)
   can whole unsweetened chestnuts
5 to 6 cups Chicken Stock
   or Turkey Stock, page 32
Salt and pepper
6 tablespoons butter
2 onions, chopped
3/4 lb. ground pork fat

3/4 lb. lean pork, ground
3 tablespoons brandy
1 teaspoon allspice
1/4 teaspoon nutmeg
1 (6- to 8-lb.) turkey
1 cup white wine
1 bunch watercress

To peel fresh chestnuts, pierce tops with a pointed knife and place in a medium saucepan. Cover with cold water. Bring to a boil and immediately remove from heat. Drain and peel a few at a time, leaving remaining chestnuts in hot water. If they cool and become difficult to peel, reheat quickly; don't cook chestnuts or they will be impossible to peel. Place peeled fresh chestnuts in a medium saucepan with 3 cups stock and salt and pepper. Cover and simmer 20 to 30 minutes until tender. Cool to lukewarm and drain. If using canned chestnuts, drain. Preheat oven to 350°F (175°C). In a medium skillet, melt 2 tablespoons butter. Stir in onions. Cook until soft but not browned. Add fat and lean pork and brown, stirring to break up meat. Stir in brandy, allspice, nutmeg and salt and pepper to taste. Cook over medium heat 2 minutes to blend flavors. Remove from heat and gently stir in chestnuts so they don't break. Taste for seasoning. Cool thoroughly. Stuff turkey and truss, pages 75 and 76. *Turkey can be stuffed with chilled stuffing 3 to 4 hours ahead and refrigerated.* Spread breast and legs of turkey with 4 tablespoons butter. Sprinkle with salt and pepper and place turkey on its side in a roasting pan. Pour 1 cup stock into pan. Loosely cover bird with foil and roast in oven 3 to 3-1/2 hours until juice runs clear, page 77. During cooking, turn turkey from one side to the other and then onto its back, basting often. If pan gets dry add more stock. Remove foil during last 1/2 hour of cooking so turkey browns well and skin becomes crisp. Transfer turkey to a platter. Cover with foil to keep warm. Stir wine and remaining 1 to 2 cups stock into roasting pan. Bring to a boil, stirring to dissolve any brown juices on bottom of pan. Reduce gravy until flavor is concentrated; taste for seasoning. Strain. Remove trussing strings from turkey. Spoon a little gravy over bird and serve the rest separately. Garnish platter with watercress. Makes 8 servings.

Meat

The word *meat* brings to mind the main course of the most important meal of the day. French cooks have devoted their greatest energy to producing hundreds of meat dishes from simple combinations like Calves' Liver with Onions to the lavish Tournedos Rossini with its Truffle Sauce and *foie gras*. The French attitude to meat cookery is wide-ranging. Although they love juicy done-to-a-turn roasts and steaks they have no less regard for braises and stews in rich well-flavored sauces. And they like to garnish their meat with vegetables that form an integral part of the main dish itself. A grand roast, feels a French cook, is neglected without a group of glazed carrots, onions and potatoes. Even a broiled chop deserves a sprig of watercress.

How to Choose & Store Meat

The best guide to meat quality is the grade. This varies in different countries. In the U.S., beef, veal and lamb are USDA-graded *prime*, *choice*, *good* and *standard* in descending order of quality. Pork is graded U.S. 1 to 4 in descending order. But you can also tell a lot by sight. The most obvious sign is color. Good beef should have a generous marbling of fat, and if you prefer the mature flavor of aged beef, look for bright red flesh tinged with purple. Lamb, pork and veal are best when clear and light-colored, a sign that the animal is young. Lamb should be deep pink, pork a pinkish-beige and veal a delicate rose. When tinged with red, veal is on its way to becoming beef; insipid and tough, it combines the worst of both meats. Dark red lamb is really mutton.

Good meat, no matter what the animal, is never flabby. In beef and pork the fat should be white or creamy, not yellow. This is less important in lamb because the fat color varies with age and breed. Veal, a young meat, has little fat but it should be moist and shiny.

Store meat loosely wrapped in the coldest part of the refrigerator and use it as soon as possible. If you buy frozen meat or are thinking of freezing raw meat yourself, you'll find that lamb and pork are best. The flavor and texture of beef are never quite the same after freezing. Veal deteriorates even more because of its high water content. All meat should be well trimmed. Some butchers are more thorough than others, so before you cook, make sure all obvious sinews and cartilage have been removed. Then cut away all but a thin outside layer of fat.

How to Cook Meat

Whatever the meat or method of cooking, keep two goals in mind: meat must be both moist and tender when served.

Luxury cuts of meat that are tender by nature are usually cooked by the dry-heat methods of roasting or pan-frying. Broiling also belongs to this category but the French prefer to pan-fry so they can take advantage of the concentrated meat-flavored pan juices to make a good sauce. In dry-heat cooking, the meat is seared briefly either in the oven for roasting, or on top of the stove for pan-frying. High heat is used so a crust is formed quickly, enclosing the meat juices. Thus minimum cooking at a high temperature keeps the meat moist while retaining its natural tenderness. It is important not to overcook or the juices will burst from the protective crust, leaving the meat dry and tasteless—classic attributes of an overcooked steak!

Cooking with moist heat—by stewing or poaching—is less exacting. These methods suit less tender cuts of meat, as they call for slow simmering in flavored liquid so tough fibers are softened. During cooking an exchange takes place: Juices escape from the meat to flavor the sauce, and at the same time flavors from the sauce penetrate the meat. The result is a new taste greater than just the sum of the ingredients. Here long slow cooking makes the meat tender while liquid keeps it moist.

1/Roasts: If you don't have a meat thermometer, insert a skewer into center of meat and leave it for 30 seconds. If skewer is quite hot, the roast is cooked.

2/Steaks: Press steaks with your finger: rare steak yields easily, medium steak gives a slight resistance.

How to Tell When Meat is Done

How to Tell When Meat is Done

The degree of doneness you prefer for roasted or broiled and pan-fried meats is very much an individual matter, so adjust the degree of cooking to your taste. To retain all their flavor, red meats like beef and lamb, and variety meats like liver and kidneys, are often cooked only to *rare*. White meats, which rely less on their natural juices for moistness, are cooked until light pink, for veal, or *well done*, for pork. All meats cooked by moist heat should be very well done. One traditional French test is to see if the meat can be cut easily with a spoon.

Calculating cooking time from the weight of a piece of meat can give you only a rough guide as cuts vary in thickness and tenderness. For small pieces of meat the French rely on touch, pressing steaks and crushing stew meat between their fingers. For large cuts, they test the internal temperature of the meat with a skewer, though a meat thermometer can be used also. See the table on page 92.

Pan-Fried & Broiled Meats

For *very rare*, cook meat just long enough to sear all surfaces; it will be soft when pressed with your finger.

For *rare*, turn meat over as soon as juices bubble to the surface. Turn to brown the other side, then cook until the meat offers little resistance when pressed.

For *medium*, turn the meat over when drops of juice are clearly visible on the surface. When pressed, the meat will be slightly firm.

When *well done*, meat is very firm to the touch, showing the heat has reached the center. Any escaping juices should be clear.

Braised, Stewed & Poached Meats

For large pieces of meat, insert a skewer into the thickest part of the piece of meat; you should be able to pull it out easily.

For small pieces, insert a skewer or two-prong fork into the meat cubes; the meat should fall easily from the skewer. You should also be able to crush the cubes of meat between your fingers.

Roasts

To determine degree of cooking, insert a meat thermometer into the center of the meat. If you don't have a meat thermometer, push a skewer into the center of the meat and leave it for 30 seconds. It should be warm to hot to the touch when withdrawn.

Is It Done?				
Stage	Color of Meat When Cut	Meat	Thermometer	Skewer
rare	deep pink	beef lamb liver kidneys	140°F (60°C)	warm
medium	light pink	beef lamb veal	160° to 165°F (70° to 72°C)	quite hot
well done	white	veal pork	170° to 175°F (75° to 77°C)	very hot

How to Prepare Meat Ahead

Meats cooked in liquid are even better when reheated because the sauce mellows on standing. They can be kept in the refrigerator up to 2 days and freeze well if covered with sauce.

Meats cooked by dry heat should not be cooked far ahead. Red meats, whether roasted, broiled or pan-fried, overcook easily if kept warm and should not stand more than a few minutes. Roasted white meats can be left for half an hour or so in a low oven without coming to harm. Left-over roast meats are best served cold, though white meat can be reheated gently in a sauce.

How to Serve Meat

French ideas on serving depend both on the type of meat and how it is cooked. Roasts require expensive cuts, so they are usually reserved for festive occasions and given a variety of accompaniments as in Roast Veal with Spring Vegetables. For an impressive platter in the French style, carve most of a roast or any large piece of meat, and arrange the slices overlapping on the dish with the vegetables in colorful mounds around the meat. Place the uncut end of the roast at the end of the platter, and moisten the meat with gravy. The smaller the piece of meat, the more limited the accompaniment; it may be only one or two vegetables, usually including potatoes.

Veal, the most delicate of meats, is usually paired with a light vegetable such as Spinach Puree, page 116, asparagus tips, or Glazed Carrots, page 121. Green beans and dried white beans are classic partners for lamb, while pork takes to robust garnishes like Braised Red Cabbage, page 119, or fruits which cut the richness of the meat. With beef, the choice is wide open, for the French serve it with practically all vegetables.

Beef Stew Bourguignonne

Boeuf à la Bourguignonne

One of the most popular of all French recipes, the best beef Bourguignonne needs well-aged stew beef.

Marinade, see below
1-1/2 lbs. beef chuck or heel of round,
  cut in 1-1/2-inch cubes
1 (1/2-lb.) piece lean bacon, diced
4 tablespoons vegetable oil
16 to 20 baby onions, peeled
1/2 lb. mushrooms

3 tablespoons all-purpose flour
1 cup Brown Veal or Beef Stock, pages 30-31
Salt and pepper to taste
Croûtes, page 8
1 tablespoon chopped parsley

Marinade:
1 bottle red wine (3 cups)
1 onion, sliced
1 carrot, sliced
1 bouquet garni, page 7
1 garlic clove, crushed

6 peppercorns
2 whole cloves
10 juniper berries, if desired
Pinch of salt
2 tablespoons vegetable oil

Prepare Marinade. Add beef, pushing it under liquid. Cover and refrigerate 24 to 48 hours, stirring occasionally. Put bacon in a saucepan. Cover generously with water. Boil 2 to 3 minutes. Drain and rinse with cold water. Drain beef, reserving Marinade with the carrot and onion separately. Dry beef thoroughly on paper towels. In a heavy casserole, heat 2 tablespoons oil. Brown beef a few pieces at a time on all sides over medium-high heat, removing pieces as browned. Fry bacon in oil until browned but not crisp; remove. Sauté onions until browned; remove. Sauté mushrooms until tender and lightly browned; remove. If using oven, preheat to 325°F (165°C). Discard excess fat from casserole and add 1/2 cup Marinade. Bring to a boil, stirring to dissolve brown juices on casserole bottom. Pour into a small bowl and reserve. In same casserole, heat remaining 2 tablespoons oil. Add reserved onion and carrot from Marinade. Cook over medium heat, stirring occasionally, until soft but not browned. Stir in flour. Cook, stirring constantly, until mixture is a rich brown. Do not burn. Stir in remaining Marinade, juices from casserole, stock and a little salt and pepper. Do not add much salt at this point as the bacon will add more. Return beef to casserole and bring stew to a boil. Cover tightly, reduce heat and simmer on top of stove or in oven, stirring occasionally, 2-1/2 to 3 hours until meat is very tender. Transfer beef pieces to another casserole or large saucepan and strain sauce over them. Add garnish of bacon, onions and mushrooms. Simmer 15 minutes or until onions are tender and flavors are blended. Taste for seasoning. *Beef Stew Bourguignonne can be prepared to this point 2 days ahead, covered and refrigerated or frozen. It tastes best when prepared at least 1 day ahead. Reheat over medium heat or in a 350°F (175°C) oven.* Prepare Croûtes. Serve stew from casserole or spoon into a shallow bowl. Sprinkle with parsley and arrange Croûtes around edge. Makes 4 servings.

Marinade:
Mix all ingredients in a deep non-aluminum bowl.

Tournedos Rossini
Tournedos Rossini

Foie gras, truffles and tournedos steak make one of the most luxurious of all dishes.

2 cups Basic Brown Sauce, pages 42-43
1 tablespoon tomato paste, if desired
4 thick slices canned truffles with liquid
4 tablespoons Madeira
Croûtes, see below
1 tablespoon vegetable oil

1 tablespoon butter
4 tournedos steaks, 1-1/2 to 2 inches thick
Salt and pepper to taste
1/2 cup Brown Veal Stock, pages 30-31
4 slices canned foie gras or foie gras
   pâté, cut 3/8 inch thick

Croûtes:
4 slices white bread
3 tablespoons vegetable oil

3 tablespoons butter

Prepare Basic Brown Sauce, whisking in tomato paste for more color if desired. Drain truffles, adding liquid to sauce with Madeira. Simmer 10 minutes or until glossy. Preheat oven to 250°F (120°C). Prepare Croûtes. *Sauce and Croûtes can be prepared 8 hours ahead; cover and refrigerate sauce.* Heat oil and butter in a large heavy skillet. Fry steaks over high heat 3 to 4 minutes on each side for rare. Sprinkle with salt and pepper after turning. Place steaks on a heatproof platter; keep warm in oven. Discard fat from skillet. Add stock, stirring over medium heat to dissolve brown juices. Boil until reduced slightly and flavor is concentrated. Strain liquid into sauce. Simmer 2 minutes. Taste for seasoning. Place each steak on a Croûte and top with a slice of foie gras. Heat 1 to 2 minutes in oven. Do not heat too long because foie gras melts easily. Spoon a little sauce over each steak. Top with a truffle slice. Serve remaining sauce separately. Makes 4 servings.

Croûtes:
Cut rounds from bread the same size as tournedos steaks. Heat oil and butter in a medium skillet. Fry bread rounds in hot fat until browned on both sides. Drain on paper towels.

Steak Tartare
Steak Tartare

Guests can compose their own Steak Tartare, adding onion, mustard, capers and parsley to their tastes.

1 to 1-1/4 lbs. very freshly ground
   sirloin or tenderloin
5 fresh egg yolks
Salt and pepper
4 spring onions, cut in thin rounds

1 large onion, very finely chopped
4 teaspoons Dijon-style mustard
2 tablespoons capers, drained
2 tablespoons chopped parsley

Just before serving, mix meat with 1 egg yolk and plenty of salt and pepper. Mixture should be highly seasoned. Shape mixture into 4 patties and place on serving plates. Use the back of a spoon to make a hollow in each patty. Slide 1 raw egg yolk into each hollow. Garnish with onion rounds, chopped onion, mustard, capers and parsley. Serve immediately. Makes 4 servings.

Beef Casserole with Olives & Vegetables
Boeuf en Daube

Tough cuts of meat cooked en daube *should become tender enough to cut with a spoon.*

Marinade, see below
1 (3-1/2- to 4-lb.) beef chuck or
   round roast, cut in 2-inch cubes
3/4 lb. lean salt pork, cut in small chunks
1 pig's foot, washed
1-1/2 lbs. tomatoes, peeled, seeded,
   chopped, page 10, or 3 cups
   (1-1/2 lbs.) canned tomatoes,
   drained, chopped

1 lb. carrots, sliced in thick rounds
Pepper to taste
1-1/2 cups White Veal Stock, page 31, or
   Brown Beef Stock, page 30
1 lb. mushrooms, sliced
1 lb. baby onions, peeled
3/4 cup green olives, pitted
3/4 cup black olives, pitted

Marinade:
2 tablespoons wine vinegar
2 cups red wine
1 onion, sliced
1 carrot, sliced
1 large bouquet garni, page 7
1 thinly pared strip orange peel

2 garlic cloves, crushed
6 peppercorns
1 whole clove
1/2 teaspoon coriander seeds
2 tablespoons olive oil

Prepare Marinade. Add beef, pushing it under marinade. Cover and refrigerate 24 to 48 hours, stirring occasionally. In a large saucepan, generously cover salt pork and pig's foot with cold water. Boil 10 minutes. Drain, rinse with cold water and drain again. Preheat oven to 300°F (150°C). Remove beef from Marinade, reserving Marinade with vegetables and seasonings. Tie marinade vegetables, herbs, orange peel and spices in a piece of cheesecloth. In a large heavy casserole, layer beef, salt pork and pig's foot with tomatoes and carrots. Pour in marinade. Add pepper, stock and cheesecloth bag of vegetables. Do not add salt as salt pork will add enough to season the beef. Gradually bring to a boil. Cover tightly and cook in oven 2-1/2 to 3 hours until beef is very tender. Remove pig's foot, pull meat from bone and shred with a fork. Return meat to casserole with mushrooms, baby onions and green and black olives. Cook 15 to 20 minutes longer until onions are done. Discard cheesecloth bag. Taste sauce for seasoning. Serve from casserole or spoon into a bowl. *Beef Casserole can be made 2 days ahead, covered and refrigerated or frozen. Reheat in a 350°F (175°C) oven or over medium heat on top of stove. Skim off fat and taste for seasoning.* Makes 6 to 8 servings.

Marinade:
Mix all ingredients in a deep non-aluminum bowl.

Beef Wellington
Boeuf en Croûte

Work quickly when wrapping beef so the buttery brioche dough won't melt.

Brioche dough, pages 166-167
1 (3- to 4-lb.) whole beef fillet
Salt and pepper
2 tablespoons vegetable oil
Duxelles, see below

Egg Glaze, page 7
1-1/2 cups Madeira Sauce or
   Truffle Sauce, page 44
1 bunch watercress, if desired

Prepare Brioche dough; let rise and refrigerate until firm enough to roll out, at least 3 hours or overnight. Trim fillet and tie into a compact bundle using trussing string. Sprinkle with salt and pepper. Heat oil in a large skillet. Brown beef on all sides over high heat, 8 to 10 minutes. Cool completely. Prepare Duxelles; refrigerate. Lightly grease a baking sheet. On a cloth towel, roll out Brioche dough to a rectangle 6 inches longer and wider than trussed beef. Spread dough with cooled Duxelles, leaving a 2-inch border of dough. Remove strings from fillet and place upside-down on Duxelles. Cut a 2-inch square from each corner of dough and brush edges of the rectangle with Egg Glaze. Lift one long edge of dough to top of fillet. Fold over the opposite edge to enclose fillet. Press gently to seal. Fold ends to make a neat package. With the help of the cloth towel, roll enclosed fillet over onto prepared baking sheet so seam is underneath. Brush with Egg Glaze. Cut leaves and other decorative shapes from leftover dough and attach to top of pastry with Egg Glaze. Brush decorations with Egg Glaze. Use a sharp knife to cut 3 equally spaced holes in top of dough. Insert a roll of foil or the smaller end of a plain pastry tube in each hole to let steam escape. Cover and refrigerate 2 to 3 hours until dough is firm. *Beef Wellington can be prepared to this point 8 hours ahead, covered and refrigerated.* Prepare Madeira Sauce or Truffle Sauce. Preheat oven to 425°F (220°C) 1 hour before serving. Bake Beef Wellington 30 minutes or until dough is browned and beef is cooked to rare, 140°F (60°C) on a meat thermometer. Check pastry after 15 minutes and if it is becoming too brown, reduce oven temperature to 400°F (205°C). Transfer to a large platter and keep warm 10 to 15 minutes. Juices will become more evenly distributed and meat will also be easier to cut. Garnish with watercress. Serve sauce separately. Makes 6 servings.

Variation

Use Puff Pastry, pages 154-155, made with 1-1/3 cups butter, instead of Brioche dough.

Duxelles
Duxelles

Mushrooms used as a flavoring or stuffing are sautéed with shallots and seasonings.

2 tablespoons butter
2 shallots, finely chopped
1 lb. mushrooms, finely chopped

1 tablespoon chopped parsley
Salt and pepper

Melt butter in a medium skillet. Add shallots. Stir over medium heat until soft but not browned. Add mushrooms. Cook over high heat, stirring often, until dry. Remove from heat and add parsley. Season with salt and pepper. Makes 2 cups of Duxelles.

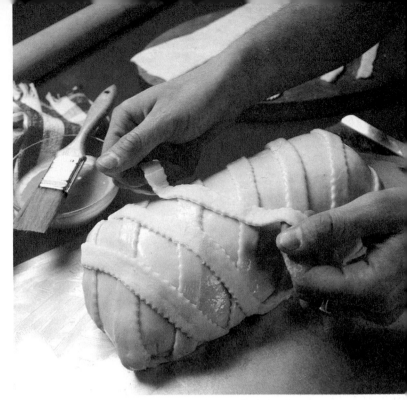

1/Place beef on Duxelles and enclose with pastry.

2/Use Egg Glaze to attach decorative dough shapes.

How to Make Beef Wellington

Steak in Red Wine Sauce
Entrecôte Marchand de Vin

A respectable wine is a must for this sauce. Try a good Bordeaux and drink the rest with your steak.

1 tablespoon vegetable oil
1 tablespoon butter
4 fillet, club or Porterhouse steaks or
  2 sirloin steaks, cut 1 inch thick
Salt and pepper to taste
3 shallots, finely chopped

1 garlic clove, finely chopped, if desired
1-1/2 cups red wine
2 tablespoons chopped parsley
1 tablespoon chopped fresh herbs such as
  chives, tarragon and basil
1 bunch watercress, if desired

Heat oil and butter in a large heavy skillet. Fry steaks over high heat 2 to 3 minutes on each side for rare. Sprinkle with salt and pepper after turning. Transfer steaks to a heatproof platter; keep warm in a 300°F (150°C) oven. Let skillet cool slightly, then add shallots and garlic. Cook over medium heat about 1 minute until shallots begin to soften. Add wine, stirring over medium heat to dissolve brown juices on bottom of skillet. Boil until liquid is reduced by at least half and flavor in concentrated. Remove from heat. Add parsley and other herbs. Taste for seasoning. Pour sauce over steaks, garnish with watercress and serve immediately. Makes 4 servings.

Pot au Feu
Pot au Feu

The broth is the soup followed by meat and vegetables served with pickles, horseradish and mustard.

Pot au Feu Stock, see below, or mixture of
   3 qts. Brown Beef Stock, page 30, or
   White Veal Stock, page 31, and
   3 qts. water
3 lbs. short ribs or chuck
3 lbs. bottom round, eye round, heel of
   round or rolled rump roast
2 lbs. beef marrow bones
6 onions (about 1 lb.), halved
6 carrots (about 1 lb.), halved,
   cut in 3-inch lengths

3 medium turnips (about 1 lb.),
   cut in quarters
6 leeks (about 1 lb.) halved,
   cut in 3-inch lengths
6 stalks celery, cut in 3-inch lengths
Salt and pepper to taste
1 cup uncooked vermicelli or very fine
   noodles or 1 small loaf French bread

Pot au Feu Stock:
2 lbs. veal bones, cracked in 2 or 3 pieces
1 onion, quartered
1 large carrot, quartered
1 large bouquet garni, page 7

1 whole clove
Salt to taste
10 peppercorns
6 qts. water

Prepare Pot au Feu Stock. Tie each cut of beef into a compact cylinder using trussing string. Add beef to hot stock. Simmer 2 to 3 hours until meat is nearly tender. Wrap marrow bones in cheesecloth so marrow does not fall out during cooking. Tie each type of vegetable in a piece of cheesecloth so it is easy to lift out after cooking. Add marrow bones, onions and carrots to stock. Simmer 20 minutes. Add turnips, leeks, celery, salt and pepper. Simmer 30 minutes or until meat is very tender. *Pot au Feu can be made 2 days ahead, covered and refrigerated, but undercook it slightly to allow for reheating. Reheat over medium heat.* If serving broth with vermicelli or noodles, spoon 1 to 2 quarts broth into a large saucepan 10 minutes before meat is cooked; bring broth to a boil, add vermicelli or noodles and simmer 5 minutes or until tender. If serving broth with bread, cut bread in 1/2-inch diagonal slices and toast in 350°F (175°C) oven 10 to 15 minutes until golden brown. Remove beef and vegetables from broth and discard trussing string. Carve round or rump roast in 3/8-inch slices and arrange overlapping down the center of a large platter. Cut short ribs or chuck in pieces and pile at each end. Arrange vegetables around meat. Cover platter with foil and keep warm in a 300°F (150°C) oven. Add cooked vermicelli or noodles and their broth to cooking liquid. Skim off as much fat as possible. Reheat and taste for seasoning. If serving with toasted bread, unwrap marrow bones and spread bread with marrow; place bread in soup bowls and pour broth over it. If not using marrow for bread, add bones to platter of meat and give guests spoons for scooping out marrow. After serving broth in soup bowls, serve meat and vegetables. Makes 8 servings.

Pot au Feu Stock:
If you don't have a heavy cleaver, ask a butcher to crack the bones. Place all ingredients in a large pot. Slowly bring to a boil, 20 to 30 minutes. Skim stock often. Reduce heat and simmer uncovered 2-1/2 to 3 hours, skimming occasionally. Strain.

Pepper Steak
Steak au Poivre

For stronger flavor, use more pepper. For mild flavor, scrape pepper off steak before cooking.

2 tablespoons peppercorns
4 steaks, 3/4 to 1 inch thick
2 tablespoons vegetable oil
2 tablespoons butter

Salt to taste
1/4 cup brandy
1 cup whipping cream

Roughly crush peppercorns in a mortar and pestle or with a rolling pin or bottom of a heavy saucepan. Firmly press into both sides of steaks. Cover and refrigerate 2 to 3 hours. Heat oil and butter in a large heavy skillet. Fry steaks over high heat 2 to 3 minutes on each side for rare. Sprinkle with salt after turning. Remove from skillet. Discard fat and return steaks to skillet. Flame with brandy, page 11. Remove steaks and keep warm. Add cream to skillet and simmer 2 to 3 minutes, stirring to dissolve brown juices. Transfer steaks to individual serving plates. Taste sauce for seasoning, pour over steaks and serve immediately. Makes 4 servings.

Parslied Leg of Lamb
Gigot d'Agneau Persillé

Parsley coating gives a crisp brown crust to roast leg of lamb.

1 small (5- to 6-lb.) leg of lamb
2 tablespoons vegetable oil
1 onion, quartered
1 carrot, quartered
Salt and pepper
1 to 1-1/2 cups Brown Veal Stock,
   pages 30-31, or water

1/2 cup chopped parsley
1 cup fresh white breadcrumbs
1 garlic clove, finely chopped
1/3 cup butter, melted
1/2 cup white wine
1 bunch watercress, if desired

Preheat oven to 450°F (230°C). Trim skin and all but a thin layer of fat from lamb. Pour oil into a large roasting pan. Add onion and carrot. Place lamb on top. Sprinkle lamb with salt and pepper. Roast in oven 10 to 15 minutes until browned. Reduce oven temperature to 400°F (205°C) and continue roasting. Including first 10 to 15 minutes, allow 9 to 11 minutes per pound for rare or 13 to 15 minutes for medium, basting frequently and adding stock if pan becomes dry. Mix parsley, breadcrumbs and garlic. Remove lamb from oven 10 minutes before it is completely cooked and spread evenly with breadcrumb mixture. Sprinkle with melted butter. Return to oven 10 more minutes or until coating is lightly browned. Transfer lamb to a platter and let stand in a warm place 10 to 15 minutes before carving. Juices will become more evenly distributed and meat will also be easier to cut. To make gravy, discard excess fat from roasting pan, reserving onion and carrot. Add wine and 1 cup stock. Boil, stirring to dissolve any brown juices. Simmer 5 to 10 minutes to concentrate flavor. Strain into a small saucepan. Skim off excess fat. Bring to a boil and taste for seasoning. Cover and keep warm over very low heat until ready to serve. Carve lamb in the kitchen and replace it on bone for serving or carve it at the table. Place lamb on a platter and decorate with watercress. Serve gravy separately. Makes 6 servings.

Lamb & Vegetable Stew
Navarin d'Agneau

Best in springtime, made with as many fresh vegetables as possible.

1-1/2 lbs. boned shoulder of lamb,
   cut in 1-1/2-inch chunks
Salt and pepper
2 tablespoons vegetable oil
12 to 16 baby onions, peeled
2 tablespoons all-purpose flour
1 tablespoon tomato paste
1 garlic clove, finely chopped
1 bouquet garni, page 7
3 to 4 cups White Veal Stock, page 31,
   Brown Beef Stock, page 30, or
   Chicken Stock, page 32

2 tomatoes, peeled, seeded, chopped,
   page 10
8 baby carrots, peeled, or
   2 large carrots, quartered
1 turnip, cut in eighths, trimmed to ovals
1-1/2 lbs. small new potatoes or 3 to 4
   large potatoes, quartered,
   trimmed to ovals
1 cup fresh peas, blanched, or
   1 pkg. frozen peas
2 tablespoons chopped parsley, if desired

Sprinkle lamb with salt and pepper. In a large heavy casserole, heat oil. Brown lamb a few pieces at a time on all sides over medium-high heat, removing pieces as browned. Sauté onions until browned; remove. Stir in flour. Stir over medium heat until foaming. Add tomato paste, garlic, bouquet garni and 3 cups stock. Return lamb to casserole. If needed, add more stock to cover lamb. Bring to a boil; cover tightly. Reduce heat and simmer 1 hour. Skim off fat. Add tomatoes and carrots with more stock to cover, if needed. Cover and simmer 30 minutes. Add turnip, potatoes and browned onions. Simmer 10 minutes longer. Add peas. Cook 20 minutes longer or until meat is tender. Frozen peas should be added after turnips and potatoes have simmered 20 minutes and should be cooked only 8 to 10 minutes. Discard bouquet garni. Taste for seasoning. Sauce should have body but will not be thick enough to coat a spoon. If necessary, remove meat and vegetables and boil sauce to thicken slightly. Return meat and vegetables to sauce. *Lamb & Vegetable Stew can be prepared 2 days ahead, covered and refrigerated or frozen. Vegetables should be slightly undercooked to allow for reheating. Reheat stew over medium heat.* Sprinkle with parsley and serve in the casserole. Makes 4 servings.

Lamb Chop & Potato Casserole
Côtes de Mouton Champvallon

A simple dish that needs no last-minute attention.

4 lamb chops
1 tablespoon vegetable oil
3 tablespoons butter
2 large onions, thinly sliced
6 potatoes, thinly sliced
Salt and pepper to taste

Pinch of chopped fresh thyme or
  dried thyme
4 tablespoons chopped parsley
1 garlic clove, halved
2 cups White Veal Stock, page 31

Preheat oven to 350°F (175°C). Trim excess fat and gristle from chops. In a large skillet, heat oil and 2 tablespoons butter. Brown chops on both sides over medium-high heat. Remove chops and discard all but 2 tablespoons fat. Sauté onions until just transparent and remove. Add potatoes, salt, pepper, thyme and 2 tablespoons parsley. Mix well. Generously grease a 2-quart shallow baking dish and rub with garlic. Spoon half the potato mixture into dish. Place chops on top. Cover with remaining potato mixture. Pour in enough stock to cover potatoes. Dot with remaining butter. Bake uncovered 45 to 60 minutes until potatoes and chops are tender when pierced with a fork. Top of potatoes should be golden brown and most of the liquid should have been absorbed. Sprinkle with remaining parsley. Serve in baking dish. Makes 4 servings.

Veal Chops Dijonnaise   Photo on pages 2 and 3.
Côtes de Veau à la Dijonnaise

Simmer this dish on top of the stove or in your oven. If you prefer, use pork chops instead of veal chops.

1 tablespoon vegetable oil
1 (1/3-lb.) piece lean bacon,
  cut in 1/4-inch cubes
16 to 20 baby onions, peeled
4 large veal chops
Salt and pepper to taste
1 tablespoon all-purpose flour

1/2 cup white wine
1/2 cup White Veal Stock, page 31, or
  Chicken Stock, page 32
1 bouquet garni, page 7
1/4 cup whipping cream
2 tablespoons Dijon-style mustard
1 tablespoon chopped parsley, if desired

If using oven, preheat to 350°F (175°C). Heat oil in a large skillet. Fry bacon in oil until browned; remove. Sauté onions until browned; remove. Sprinkle veal chops with salt and pepper. Brown chops on both sides over medium-high heat. Remove chops and discard all but 2 tablespoons fat. Stir in flour. Cook, stirring constantly until foaming. Stir in wine, stock, bouquet garni and pepper to taste. Do not add salt as the bacon may be salty enough to season the dish. Bring just to a boil, stirring occasionally. Return chops and bacon to skillet. Cover, reduce heat and simmer 25 to 30 minutes on top of stove or in oven. Add onions. Cook 15 minutes longer or until chops and onions are tender. *Veal Chops Dijonnaise can be cooked to this point 2 days ahead, covered and refrigerated or frozen. Reheat over medium heat.* Overlap chops on a platter. Cover with foil and keep warm. Taste sauce and, if necessary, reduce until it coats a spoon, page 12, and flavor is concentrated. Add cream. Return just to a boil; remove from heat and stir in mustard. Do not boil mustard or it will become bitter. Discard bouquet garni. Taste sauce for seasoning and spoon with onion and bacon garnish over chops. Sprinkle with parsley and serve. Makes 4 servings.

Roast Veal with Spring Vegetables
Rôti de Veau Printanière

The same spring vegetables are also good with roast pork or lamb.

1 (3- to 4-lb.) rolled veal roast
1/4 cup butter, softened
2 teaspoons mixed herbs such as thyme,
  oregano and rosemary

Salt and pepper
2 to 3 cups White Veal Stock, page 31
1 cup white wine
Spring Vegetables, see below

Spring Vegetables:
1 lb. baby or medium carrots
2 teaspoons sugar
Salt and pepper
5 to 6 tablespoons butter
3/4 to 1 lb. green beans,
  cut in 3-inch lengths

24 baby onions, peeled
1-1/2 lbs. baby new potatoes
2 tablespoons chopped parsley

Preheat oven to 350°F (175°C). Trim veal and tie into a compact cylinder with trussing string. Spread with butter. Sprinkle with herbs, salt and pepper. Place in a roasting pan with 1/2 cup stock and 1/2 cup white wine. For slightly pink meat (160°F, 70°C, on a meat thermometer), roast 30 minutes per pound, adding more stock if pan gets dry; baste often. Prepare vegetables; set aside until meat is done. Let roast rest on a platter in a warm place 15 to 20 minutes. Juices will become more evenly distributed and meat will also be easier to cut. To make gravy, add remaining stock and wine to roasting pan and bring to a boil, stirring. Strain into a small saucepan. Bring to a boil and taste; if necessary, boil until flavor is concentrated. Taste for seasoning. Discard trussing strings and carve veal in 3/8-inch slices. Overlap slices down the center of a large platter. Arrange vegetables around veal. Spoon a little gravy over meat and serve remaining gravy separately. Makes 6 to 8 servings.

Spring Vegetables:
Peel baby carrots or quarter medium carrots. Put in a medium saucepan with water to cover, 1 teaspoon sugar, a pinch of salt and 1 tablespoon butter. Boil uncovered 15 to 20 minutes until nearly all liquid has evaporated and carrots are tender. Cook green beans in a medium saucepan full of boiling salted water 10 to 12 minutes until just tender. Drain, rinse with cold water and drain thoroughly. Melt 2 tablespoons butter in a heavy skillet. Add baby onions, remaining 1 teaspoon sugar and a pinch of salt and pepper. Cook over low heat 15 to 20 minutes, shaking pan occasionally, until onions are tender and lightly browned. Cook potatoes in boiling salted water 15 to 20 minutes until just tender; drain. Just before serving, reheat each vegetable separately over low heat, adding 1 tablespoon butter and a pinch of salt and pepper to both beans and potatoes. When reheating vegetables in butter, shake pan instead of stirring to prevent vegetables from breaking up. Add 1 tablespoon chopped parsley to both carrots and potatoes.

Roast Veal Orloff
Rôti de Veau Orloff

Named for Prince Alexis Fedorovich Orlov, Russian ambassador to France in the 19th century.

1 (3-1/2- to 4-lb.) boneless veal roast
3 tablespoons butter
Salt and pepper to taste
1 cup white wine
1-1/2 cups White Veal Stock, page 31
Onion Puree, see below
Thick Basic White Sauce, page 40,
   made with 4 cups milk

Duxelles, page 96
2 egg yolks, if desired
1/2 teaspoon Dijon-style mustard,
   if desired
1/2 cup grated Gruyère cheese or
   1/4 cup grated Parmesan cheese
1 scant cup milk or light cream

Onion Puree:
5 medium onions, thinly sliced
3 tablespoons butter

Salt and pepper to taste

Preheat oven to 350°F (175°C). Trim veal and tie into a compact cylinder with trussing string. Spread with butter. Sprinkle with salt and pepper. Place in a roasting pan. Pour in 1/2 cup wine and 1/2 cup stock. For slightly pink meat (160°F, 70°C, on meat thermometer), roast 30 minutes per pound, adding more stock if pan gets dry; baste often. Prepare Onion Puree. Remove meat from pan and let stand in a warm place. Stir 2 tablespoons Basic White Sauce into Duxelles; taste for seasoning. Stir 1/2 cup Basic White Sauce into Onion Puree; taste for seasoning. *Meat, Basic White Sauce, Onion Puree and Duxelles mixtures can be prepared 24 hours ahead, covered and refrigerated.* Discard trussing strings and carve meat in 3/8-inch slices. Arrange slices on a heatproof platter, spreading alternate slices with Onion Puree and Duxelles mixtures and propping the first slice with veal ends so meat stands upright like a sliced loaf. Spread any leftover Duxelles and Onion Puree mixtures on top of meat. Bring remaining Basic White Sauce to a boil. Remove from heat and beat in egg yolks. Stir in mustard and 1/3 cup Gruyère cheese or 3 tablespoons Parmesan cheese. If necessary add a little milk but sauce should be quite thick. Taste for seasoning. Preheat broiler. Cover top of the meat with a third of the sauce. Thin remaining sauce with enough milk or light cream so it is just thick enough to coat a spoon, page 12. Taste for seasoning. Spoon thinned sauce over meat to coat both meat and platter. Sprinkle with remaining cheese. Wipe platter rim clean. *Roast Veal Orloff can be prepared to this point 24 hours ahead, covered and refrigerated or frozen. If reheating, omit egg yolks from sauce so it doesn't separate when it thaws. Reheat on the heatproof platter in a 350°F (175°C) oven 25 to 30 minutes until sauce is bubbling and browned.* If meat is not chilled, place platter under broiler and heat until sauce is bubbling and browned. Makes 6 to 8 servings.

Onion Puree:
In a large heavy saucepan, generously cover onions with cold water. Boil 5 minutes; drain. Melt butter in same pan. Add onions, salt and pepper. Cover with buttered foil and pan lid. Cook over low heat 10 to 15 minutes until onions are very soft. Do not brown. Press through a sieve or puree in food processor. Return to saucepan. Cook a few minutes until nearly all moisture has evaporated, stirring constantly.

1/Spread slices with onion and mushroom mixtures.   2/Spoon sauce over top of reshaped roast.

How to Make Roast Veal Orloff

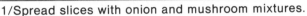

Alsatian Sauerkraut
Choucroûte Alsacienne

Sauerkraut is not the same without boiled potatoes and a stein of beer.

1 (1-lb.) piece of lean bacon
6 cups fresh or canned sauerkraut (3 lbs.)
6 tablespoons lard or vegetable oil
1-1/2 lb. fresh loin of pork, on the bone
2 whole cloves
1 garlic clove
10 juniper berries

1 large onion, peeled
2 cups white wine, water or
  a mixture of both
1 (3-1/2- to 4-1/2-lb.) cooked ham hock,
  or butt or shank of cooked ham
6 to 8 frankfurters
Salt and pepper

Put bacon in a large saucepan and generously cover with cold water. Cover saucepan and simmer 1 hour. Drain. Rinse fresh or canned sauerkraut in cold water. Squeeze sauerkraut with your hands to extract all water; pull into strands. Preheat oven to 350°F (175°C). Heat 3 tablespoons lard or oil in a large casserole. Layer half the sauerkraut over melted lard and place pork loin on top. Add remaining sauerkraut so it almost covers pork. Tie cloves, garlic and juniper berries in a piece of cheesecloth and bury in the sauerkraut with the onion. Dot with remaining 3 tablespoons lard or sprinkle with remaining oil. Add wine or water. Cover tightly and cook in oven 30 minutes. Add ham and bacon, burying them in the sauerkraut. Cook 1 hour longer or until pork is tender; if all liquid is not absorbed, boil a few minutes on top of stove. *Alsatian Sauerkraut can be prepared to this point 2 days ahead, covered and refrigerated. Reheat in a 350°F (175°C) oven.* In a medium saucepan, generously cover frankfurters with cold water and bring almost to a boil. Reduce heat and poach 10 to 12 minutes. Drain and slice ham hock, pork loin and piece of bacon, discarding skin, bones and bag of seasonings. Taste sauerkraut for seasoning. Pile sauerkraut on a large platter and overlap meats on top. Drain frankfurters and arrange around edge of platter. Serve very hot. Makes 8 to 10 servings.

Veal Stew with Cream
Blanquette de Veau

Veal breast gives richness and flavor while veal shoulder adds solid meat.

1 lb. boneless veal shoulder,
   cut in 2-inch pieces
2 lbs. veal breast, including bones,
   cut in chunks
2 onions, quartered
1 whole clove
2 carrots, quartered
1 bouquet garni, page 7
Green top of 1 leek, if desired
1-1/2 qts. White Veal Stock,
   page 31, or water

Salt and pepper to taste
Water
1/2 lb. mushroom caps, quartered if large
Juice of 1/2 lemon
5 tablespoons butter
24 to 30 baby onions, peeled
3 tablespoons all-purpose flour
1/2 cup whipping cream
Pinch of nutmeg
Cooked rice or Rice Pilaf, page 127

In a large saucepan, generously cover veal shoulder and breast with cold water. Bring to a boil. Reduce heat and simmer 5 minutes, skimming often. Drain; rinse veal with warm water. Place in a large casserole with quartered onions, clove, carrots, bouquet garni, leek and enough stock or water to just cover. Add salt and pepper. Cover and bring to a boil. Reduce heat and simmer, skimming occasionally, 1-1/4 to 1-1/2 hours until veal is very tender. In a medium saucepan, combine 1/4 inch of water, mushroom caps, salt, pepper and 1 teaspoon lemon juice. Cover and cook over high heat 5 minutes or until mushrooms are tender. Set mushrooms aside and add cooking liquid to simmering blanquette. Melt 2 tablespoons butter in a large shallow saucepan. Add baby onions with a little salt and pepper. Cover and cook over very low heat 15 to 20 minutes until onions are tender but not browned, shaking pan occasionally to turn onions. When veal is tender, remove from broth; reserve broth. Melt remaining 3 tablespoons butter in a medium saucepan. Stir in flour. Cook, stirring constantly, until foaming but not browned. Remove from heat and strain in reserved broth. Bring to a boil, stirring constantly; reduce heat and simmer 10 to 15 minutes until sauce is thick enough to coat a spoon, page 12. Stir in cream. Add meat, baby onions and mushrooms to sauce. Season to taste with a little more lemon juice, nutmeg, salt and pepper. Warm over low heat 5 to 10 minutes to blend flavors; do not boil. *Veal Stew with Cream can be made 2 days ahead and refrigerated, but slightly undercook onions to allow for reheating. Reheat over medium heat.* Keep hot in a water bath, page 9, until ready to serve. Serve in a shallow serving dish. Serve with plain rice or Rice Pilaf. Makes 6 servings.

Cassoulet
Cassoulet

A traditional hearty meat and bean stew which originated in the Languedoc region of southern France.

Cooked Beans, see below
1 (1/2-lb.) piece lean salt pork,
  rind scored deeply
1 small (3-1/2- to 4-lb.) duck,
  cut in 6 pieces, page 81
Salt and pepper
2 tablespoons lard or vegetable oil
1 lb. shoulder or breast of lamb,
  cut in 1-1/2-inch pieces
1 lb. boneless pork loin or shoulder,
  cut in 1-1/2-inch cubes

2 onions, chopped
4 garlic cloves, chopped
1/4 cup white wine
4 medium tomatoes, peeled, seeded,
  chopped, page 10, or 2 cups canned
  tomatoes, drained, chopped (about 1 lb.)
1 bouquet garni, page 7
3/4 lb. Toulouse or fresh garlic sausage

Cooked Beans:
2 lbs. dried white beans
1 carrot, quartered
1 onion, halved

4 whole cloves
1 bouquet garni, page 7
Salt and pepper

Prepare Cooked Beans. In a large saucepan, generously cover salt pork with cold water. Boil 10 minutes. Drain; rinse with cold water. Preheat oven to 300°F (150°C). Sprinkle duck with salt and pepper. In a large casserole or skillet, heat lard or oil and brown duck pieces on all sides over medium-high heat. Lower heat and cook 10 to 15 minutes longer to dissolve all fat. Remove duck and pour off all but 2 tablespoons fat. Sprinkle lamb pieces with salt and pepper. Brown a few at a time in fat. Remove lamb from skillet as browned. Sprinkle pork cubes with salt and pepper. Brown a few at a time in remaining fat. Remove pork from skillet as browned. Stir in onions. Sauté until lightly browned. Add garlic. Sauté a few seconds. Add wine, stirring to dissolve any brown juices. In a very large deep casserole, layer beans, browned duck, lamb, pork and tomatoes, ending with beans. Add bouquet garni. Place salt pork on top. Add garlic mixture and just enough reserved bean liquid to cover beans. Do not add salt as salt pork is quite salty. Cover and bake 2 to 3 hours until meat is nearly tender. If mixture becomes dry during cooking, add more liquid. If it is too soupy, remove lid. Add sausage and cook 1 hour longer. Cassoulet should be moist but not soupy. Remove salt pork and sausage; slice and return to casserole. Taste for seasoning. *Cassoulet can be prepared to this point 2 days ahead and refrigerated or frozen. To reheat, preheat oven to 375°F (190°C) and bake about 1 hour until very hot and browned.* If Cassoulet is already warm, increase oven temperature to 375°F (190°C). Bake 45 minutes longer to brown. Discard bouquet garni. Serve in the casserole. Makes 8 to 10 servings.

Cooked Beans:
Place beans in a large bowl or saucepan. Cover generously with cold water and soak overnight. Drain. In a large saucepan, place beans, carrot, onion studded with cloves, and bouquet garni. Cover with water. Cover and simmer 1 to 1-1/4 hours until beans are almost tender, seasoning with salt and pepper halfway through cooking. Drain beans, discarding onion, carrot and bouquet garni and reserving liquid to add to meat.

Loin of Pork with Caramelized Apples
Filet de Porc Normande

To use pork tenderloin, cook the meat on top of the stove 40 to 50 minutes until very tender.

1 tablespoon vegetable oil
1 tablespoon butter
1 (2-lb.) boned pork loin, rolled, tied
2 medium onions, sliced
2 tart apples, peeled, cored, sliced
3 tablespoons Calvados or
  other apple brandy

1 tablespoon all-purpose flour
1-1/2 cups White Veal Stock, page 31, or
  Chicken Stock, page 32
Salt and pepper
Caramelized Apple Slices, see below
1/3 cup whipping cream

Caramelized Apple Slices:
2 tablespoons butter
2 firm apples, unpeeled, cut in
  3/8-inch slices

2 tablespoons sugar

Preheat oven to 350°F (175°C). Heat oil and butter in a large ovenproof skillet. Brown pork on all sides over medium-high heat. Remove from skillet. Add onions. Cook until soft but not browned, stirring occasionally. Add peeled apple slices and continue cooking over medium-high heat until apples and onions are golden brown. Return pork to skillet. Flame with Calvados, page 11. Stir flour into cooking liquid in skillet. Add stock, salt and pepper and bring to a boil; cover. Reduce heat and cook in oven, stirring occasionally, 1-1/2 to 2 hours until meat is tender. *Pork can be prepared 2 days ahead, covered and refrigerated or frozen. Reheat chilled pork in a 350°F (175°C) oven.* Prepare Caramelized Apple Slices. Remove pork from skillet, cover with foil and keep warm. Strain the sauce into a medium saucepan, pressing to puree the apples. Boil until thick enough to coat a spoon, page 12. Add cream, bring just to a boil and taste for seasoning. Carve pork in 3/8-inch slices and arrange on a platter. Spoon sauce over pork and garnish with Caramelized Apple Slices. Makes 4 servings.

Caramelized Apple Slices:
Heat butter in a skillet. Dip one side of each apple slice in sugar. Cook sugar-side down in hot butter over high heat 4 to 5 minutes until sugar is caramelized. Sprinkle remaining sugar over apples. Turn over and cook 4 to 5 minutes longer. Do not overcook or apples will be mushy.

Loin of Pork with Caramelized Apples and Braised Red Cabbage, page 119.

Stuffed Pork Tenderloin Chasseur
Filet Mignon de Porc Farci Chasseur

A chasseur *garnish contains mushrooms, which supposedly were gathered by hunters, or* chasseurs.

Stuffing, see below
3 pork tenderloins (about 2 lbs.)
2 tablespoons butter
2 tablespoons all-purpose flour
3/4 cup white wine
1-1/2 cups White Veal Stock, or
   Brown Veal Stock, pages 30-31

3 teaspoons tomato paste
2 shallots, finely chopped
Salt and pepper
1/2 lb. mushrooms, thinly sliced

Stuffing:
2 tablespoons butter
1 onion, finely chopped
1/4 lb. lean pork, ground
1/4 lb. ground pork fat
1 tablespoon chopped parsley
1 teaspoon mixed fresh herbs such as
   sage, thyme and marjoram or
   1/3 teaspoon mixed dried herbs

1 cup fresh white breadcrumbs
Salt and pepper
1 egg, slightly beaten

Prepare Stuffing. Preheat oven to 350°F (175°C). Use a sharp knife to split tenderloins lengthwise two-thirds of the way through. Open them flat. Place between 2 sheets of waxed paper and pound each with a mallet or rolling pin to flatten. Sandwich 3 tenderloins with 2 layers of stuffing. Tie meat into a neat loaf shape with trussing string. Heat butter in a medium casserole. Add pork. Brown on all sides over medium-high heat. Remove pork from casserole. Stir in flour. Cook until lightly browned. Add wine, stock, tomato paste, shallots, salt and pepper. Return pork to casserole. Cover and bring just to a boil. Cook in oven 1-1/2 to 2 hours until very tender. Add mushrooms 10 minutes before end of cooking time. *Stuffed Pork Tenderloin can be prepared to this point 2 days ahead, covered and refrigerated or frozen. Reheat in a 350°F (175°C) oven.* Transfer pork to a carving board, cover with foil and keep warm. Strain cooking liquid into a medium saucepan and boil until thick enough to coat a spoon, page 12. Discard trussing string from meat. Carve meat in 1/2-inch slices. Arrange slices overlapping on a platter. Spoon mushrooms over slices. Top with a little sauce and serve the rest separately. Makes 4 servings.

Stuffing:
Melt butter in a medium saucepan. Add onion. Cook over medium heat until soft but not browned. Remove from heat and stir in lean and fat pork, parsley, mixed herbs, breadcrumbs and plenty of salt and pepper. Stir in egg. Cook 1 teaspoon stuffing in a skillet and taste for seasoning; stuffing should be highly seasoned.

Braised Ham Piémontaise
Jambon Braisé Piémontaise

This recipe dates from the 18th century when grand presentations were common.

1 (12- to 16-lb.) processed or
   regular ham, or uncooked country ham
4 carrots, quartered
4 onions, quartered
2 whole cloves
1 large bouquet garni, page 7
10 peppercorns
3 tablespoons butter
3 carrots, diced
3 onions, diced
3 celery stalks, diced

2 cups dry white wine
1/4 cup brandy
4 to 5 cups Brown Veal Stock, pages 30-31
2 to 3 teaspoons arrowroot or
   potato starch
2 to 3 tablespoons Madeira
Salt and pepper, if desired
Rice Piémontaise, page 128
1 bunch watercress, if desired
1-1/2 cups grated Parmesan cheese

If using uncooked country ham, scrub with cold water and trim off some of the fat. If ham is salty, soak in cold water 12 to 24 hours, changing water 2 or 3 times. Drain ham and put in a large pot with quartered carrots and onions, cloves, bouquet garni and peppercorns. Cover with cold water. Bring to a boil, skimming occasionally. Cover, reduce heat and simmer 12 minutes per pound plus 12 additional minutes. Cool ham in cooking liquid to lukewarm. Discard cooking liquid. Regular or processed hams do not need boiling. Use a knife to peel skin from ham. Trim off all but a thin layer of fat. Preheat oven to 350°F (175°C). Melt butter in a large casserole or roasting pan; add diced carrots, onions and celery. Cook over medium heat 5 to 7 minutes until soft but not brown, stirring often. Add wine. Simmer 5 minutes. Add brandy and 3 cups stock. Place ham in stock mixture. Cover tightly and cook in oven 1 hour. *Ham can be cooked 2 days ahead, covered and refrigerated. Reheat in casserole in a 350°F (175°C) oven 45 minutes or until a skewer inserted in center for 30 seconds is hot to the touch when withdrawn.* Transfer ham to a roasting pan. Raise oven temperature to 450°F (230°C). Strain cooking liquid into a medium saucepan, pressing vegetables to extract all juices; skim off fat. Spoon a little liquid over ham. Roast ham, basting often, 10 to 15 minutes until ham is glazed. Add remaining stock to strained cooking liquid. Boil until flavor is concentrated. Mix arrowroot or potato starch and enough Madeira to make a smooth paste. Add to boiling sauce to thicken it slightly, whisking constantly. Taste for seasoning. Spread Rice Piémontaise on a large platter with watercress. Place ham on top of rice. Serve sauce and bowl of Parmesan cheese separately. Makes 12 to 16 servings.

Sautéed Sweetbreads

Ris de Veau Panés

This luxurious garnish is a perfect match for delicate sweetbreads.

2 to 3 pairs calves' sweetbreads
   (1-1/2 lbs.)
1 slice lemon
Salt
1/2 cup all-purpose flour
1/2 teaspoon salt
1/4 teaspoon pepper
6 to 8 tablespoons butter
1 (1/4-inch) slice prosciutto or
   uncooked smoked ham, finely diced
   (about 1/4 lb.)

2 medium potatoes, boiled, cut in
   1/2-inch cubes
1/4 lb. mushrooms, thinly sliced
2 tomatoes, peeled, seeded, chopped,
   page 10, or 1 cup canned tomatoes,
   drained, chopped (about 1/2 lb.)
1 tablespoon chopped parsley, if desired

Soak sweetbreads 2 to 3 hours in a bowl of cold water, changing water once or twice. Drain, rinse with cold water and drain again. Place sweetbreads in a large saucepan. Generously cover with cold water. Add lemon and a pinch of salt. Bring slowly to a boil, skimming occasionally. Reduce heat and simmer 5 minutes. Drain sweetbreads and rinse with cold water. Peel, removing ducts. Press between 2 plates with a 2-pound weight on top. Refrigerate 1 hour. Mix flour with 1/2 teaspoon salt and pepper. Cut sweetbreads in diagonal 1/2-inch slices. Lightly coat both sides with flour mixture. Heat 4 tablespoons butter in a large skillet. Fry sweetbreads over medium heat 8 to 10 minutes until tender and golden brown on both sides. Fry in 2 batches, if necessary. Remove from skillet. Add ham and potatoes. Cook over medium heat, stirring occasionally, until golden brown. Add more butter if skillet is dry. Remove ham and potatoes, cover with foil and keep warm. Add 2 more tablespoons butter to skillet. Cook mushrooms and tomatoes over high heat, stirring constantly, 5 minutes or until mushrooms are tender and tomatoes pulpy. Taste for seasoning. Return sweetbreads to skillet, turning to coat with mixture. Reduce heat and cook 2 to 3 minutes longer to blend flavors. Gently stir in potatoes and ham. *Sautéed Sweetbreads can be prepared 2 days ahead, covered and refrigerated or frozen. Fry potatoes separately in butter and add to sweetbreads during reheating so they do not lose their crispness. Reheat chilled sweetbreads over medium heat.* Transfer to a platter and sprinkle with parsley. Makes 4 servings.

Sautéed Kidneys with Mustard
Rognons Sautés à la Moutarde

Cook this recipe in a chafing dish at the table.

3 to 4 veal kidneys or 6 to 8
   lamb kidneys (1-1/2 lbs.)
2 tablespoons vegetable oil
2 tablespoons butter
3 tablespoons brandy

1 cup whipping cream
Salt and pepper to taste
2 to 3 teaspoons Dijon-style mustard
1 tablespoon chopped parsley, if desired

Skin kidneys, if necessary, and cut out the core with scissors or a sharp knife. Cut veal kidneys in 1/2-inch slices and lamb kidneys in half to form crescents. In a chafing dish or medium skillet, heat oil and butter until very hot. Add half the kidneys; if using lamb kidneys, place them cut-side down. Sauté 1 to 2 minutes until browned on outside but rare in the center. Remove from skillet. Add more butter and oil, if needed, and quickly sauté remaining kidneys. Remove kidneys and drain in a strainer. Return kidneys to skillet; heat quickly until very hot and flame with brandy, page 11. Stir in cream, salt and pepper. Bring just to a boil. Remove from heat. Stir in mustard and taste for seasoning. Warm over low heat 1 to 2 minutes to blend flavors. Do not boil mustard or it will become bitter. Sprinkle with parsley and serve immediately. Makes 4 servings.

Calves' Liver with Onions
Foie de Veau à la Lyonnaise

A la Lyonnaise refers to a garnish of onions cooked in butter.

1/2 cup butter
8 onions, thinly sliced
Salt and pepper to taste

2 tablespoons vegetable oil
8 slices calves' liver (about 1-1/2 lbs.)

Melt 2 tablespoons butter in a large heavy shallow saucepan. Add onions and salt and pepper. Cover with a piece of buttered foil, then a pan lid. Cook over low heat, stirring occasionally, 20 to 30 minutes until onions are very soft. Remove lid and foil. Continue cooking onions until light golden. Do not burn. Taste for seasoning. *Onions can be cooked 2 to 3 hours ahead and kept at room temperature.* Heat oil and 2 tablespoons butter in a large skillet. For medium-rare liver, sauté 2 to 3 minutes on each side until lightly browned. Arrange liver on a platter. Reheat onions and spoon on top of liver. Heat remaining 1/4 cup butter in a small skillet and cook until it turns nut brown. Immediately pour brown butter over onions and serve. Makes 4 to 6 servings.

Vegetables

A French dinner without vegetables is hard to imagine. As appetizers, they are a lively and versatile complement to almost any main course. As accompaniments, vegetables contribute lightness and color, while potatoes and rice, with their more neutral flavors, are the perfect background for rich meats and sauces. And it is vegetables that make possible the huge variety of dishes in the French repertoire by flavoring its stocks and sauces. Their role may be unseen because the vegetables used for flavor are often strained from a dish before serving, but it is nonetheless vital.

How to Choose & Store Vegetables

Fresh vegetables are easy to recognize because they look good: bright-colored, firm, and with no brown spots or wilted leaves. Because freshness is the key to flavor, try to cook them as soon as possible. If they must be stored, keep greens and softer vegetables like tomatoes and zucchini loosely covered in the bottom of the refrigerator. Do not leave them sealed in plastic or they will rot. Roots, particularly onions, are best kept at room temperature, even if the kitchen is warm. Potatoes should never be kept in the refrigerator as they blacken.

How to Cook Vegetables

So you can substitute one vegetable for another in a recipe, it is important to recognize the three main categories: green vegetables from above the ground, roots from below the ground, and squash-type vegetables. All need different treatment in cooking.

Green vegetables such as spinach, peas, leeks, green beans, asparagus, cabbage, broccoli and cauliflower overcook very easily, losing taste and color. They should be cooked as fast as possible over high heat in large quantities of boiling salted water. Leave the pan uncovered so the vegetables do not stew. To keep their color, at the end of cooking, drain and rinse them at once with plenty of cold water to cool them immediately. Drain thoroughly so they do not "weep" when served; spinach retains so much water that it must be squeezed by handfuls to get rid of the excess. The French often dry their green vegetables still further by reheating them in butter over low heat.

Cooking of root vegetables such as carrots, potatoes, turnips or onions should start in cold salted water to extract over-strong flavor. Cook in a covered pan, simmering rather than boiling, so they are cooked completely without breaking up the outside. Root vegetables are not usually rinsed because their color is less fragile than that of greens, but they must be well drained.

Squash-type vegetables include tomatoes, mushrooms, bell peppers and eggplant, as well as members of the squash family. Many of them are hot-climate plants and recipes are typical of the Mediterranean, involving long slow cooking to develop flavor. Rarely cooked in water, they are most often sautéed or baked.

For all vegetables, only a rough guide can be given to cooking times because they vary enormously with the age and size of the vegetables—and how tender you want them to be. There are two ways to test cooking, the first being to taste a small piece. For most recipes, the vegetable should have lost its toughness but still be firm and, for a green vegetable, slightly crisp. If you don't want to cut into the vegetable, poke it with a two-prong fork to check that it has lost its toughness. The fork should penetrate the vegetable quite easily but there should be a degree of resistance indicating that it is still slightly crisp.

How to Prepare Vegetables Ahead

Few vegetables should be kept waiting because whether cooked or raw, their taste depends on freshness. However, cooked root vegetables can be stored covered in the refrigerator and reheated in butter the following day. Greens can have the same treatment, though their flavor will not be quite so lively. Potatoes taste stale if refrigerated after cooking—unless they are in a casserole such as Gratin of Potatoes in Cream. Squash-type vegetables are more accommodating, and most recipes using them are even improved if made a day or two ahead so the flavors blend. If you have cooked vegetables left over, they are good made into a salad with Vinaigrette, page 131, or Mayonnaise, page 50. For a hot dish, convert them to a gratin by coating the vegetable—or a mixture of vegetables—with a white sauce in a shallow baking dish. Sprinkle the top generously with grated cheese or breadcrumbs, moisten with butter and bake until browned. Delicious!

How to Serve Vegetables

The French like to serve fresh baby green or root vegetables as simply as possible. They boil them in salt water, drain and reheat in butter. Traditionally, steaming has never been very popular in France. More mature vegetables may be pureed and blenders and food processors have taken over the work of sieving. Vegetable purees are always laced with butter and cream to bring out their flavor. Many squash-type vegetables and a few greens like cabbage and endive take kindly to braising with stock, or to baking in the oven. Zucchini, eggplant and potatoes are among the few vegetables that are good deep-fried. One excellent treatment for root vegetables is to glaze them: They are cooked gently with butter, a little sugar and sometimes with water, until tender and very shiny. Sugar develops their flavor and for a winter dinner, the combination of roast veal or beef with a garnish of glazed carrots, onions and little turnips is hard to beat.

Green Peas with Lettuce & Onions
Petits Pois à la Française

The bigger the peas, the longer they need to cook, so cooking time can vary from 20 to 45 minutes.

1 head romaine lettuce	1 bouquet garni, page 7
3 to 4 cups fresh peas, shelled	1/2 cup water
6 to 8 green onions, cut in 2-inch lengths	Salt and pepper to taste
2 teaspoons sugar	1 tablespoon all-purpose flour, if desired
2 to 4 tablespoons butter	

Coarsely shred lettuce. Put in a medium, heavy saucepan with peas, green onions, sugar, 2 tablespoons butter, bouquet garni, water, salt and pepper. Cover and simmer over low heat 20 to 45 minutes until peas and green onions are tender, shaking pan occasionally to prevent sticking. Discard bouquet garni. *Green Peas with Lettuce & Onions can be cooked to this point 24 hours ahead, but should be slightly underdone to allow for reheating. If made ahead, cover and refrigerate. Just before serving, reheat peas over medium heat.* If peas are a little dry, add remaining 2 tablespoons butter in pieces, shaking pan occasionally until butter is melted and absorbed. If there is too much liquid in the peas, use a fork to mix flour with remaining butter. Add mixture to peas in small pieces, shaking pan over heat until liquid thickens slightly. Taste for seasoning. Spoon into a serving dish. Makes 4 servings.

Variation

Use 2 (10-ounce) packages frozen baby peas and reduce cooking time to 15 to 20 minutes.

Spinach Puree
Purée d'Epinards

Serve beside Carrot Puree or Mashed Potatoes for an attractive color contrast.

1-1/2 lbs. fresh spinach or 1 (10-oz.) pkg. frozen leaf spinach	1 cup light cream or milk
1 tablespoon butter	Salt and pepper to taste
1 tablespoon all-purpose flour	Pinch of nutmeg

Remove stems from fresh spinach and wash leaves thoroughly. Fill a large saucepan three-fourths full of water. Bring water to a boil and add a large pinch of salt. Boil fresh spinach 5 minutes or until tender, stirring occasionally. Cook frozen spinach according to package directions. Drain cooked spinach, rinse with cold water and drain again. Squeeze by handfuls to extract as much water as possible; set aside. Melt butter in a small saucepan. Whisk in flour. Cook over low heat, whisking constantly, until mixture foams but doesn't brown. Remove from heat and whisk in cream or milk. Bring to a boil, whisking constantly. Add salt, pepper and nutmeg. Reduce heat and simmer 3 to 5 minutes. Puree spinach with cream sauce in 3 portions in food processor or blender. Pour into a medium, heavy saucepan and heat 2 to 3 minutes over medium heat. Puree should be soft enough to fall from the spoon without being soupy. Taste for seasoning. *Spinach Puree can be prepared 2 days ahead, covered and refrigerated or frozen. Reheat chilled puree over low heat.* Makes 4 servings.

Variation

Light Spinach Puree (Purée Légère d'Epinards): Omit cream sauce. Puree cooked spinach with 1 cup whipping cream in 3 portions in food processor or blender. Melt 1 tablespoon butter in a medium saucepan, add spinach puree and heat as directed above.

Leek Gratin   Photo on pages 2 and 3.
Poireaux au Gratin

Most vegetables can be made into a gratin—good as an appetizer or with a main course.

6 to 8 medium leeks (about 1 lb.)	1/2 cup grated Gruyère cheese or
Medium Basic White Sauce, page 40, made with 2 cups milk	1/4 cup grated Parmesan cheese

Trim leeks, discarding green tops. Quarter lengthwise, cutting almost to the root. Wash very thoroughly. Preheat oven to 425°F (220°C). Put leeks in a medium saucepan with enough boiling salted water to cover. Boil 12 to 15 minutes until tender; cooking time depends on size. Drain, rinse with cold water and drain again. Grease a 1-quart shallow baking dish. Spoon a thin coat of Medium Basic White Sauce over bottom of prepared baking dish. Cut leeks in 2-1/2-inch lengths. Arrange over white sauce and coat with remaining sauce. Sprinkle with cheese. *Leek Gratin can be prepared 24 hours ahead, covered and refrigerated or frozen. Bake chilled gratin in a 400°F (205°C) oven 15 to 20 minutes until bubbling and browned.* Bake gratin 10 to 15 minutes until bubbling and browned. Makes 4 servings.

Spinach Soufflé
Soufflé aux Epinards

"A soufflé," say the French, "is a bit of theatre"—the perfect opening for a grand dinner.

3 tablespoons dry breadcrumbs
3/4 lb. fresh spinach or 1 (10-oz.)
  pkg. frozen spinach
1/4 cup butter
2 tablespoons all-purpose flour
3/4 cup milk
1/2 cup whipping cream

Salt and pepper to taste
Pinch of nutmeg
4 egg yolks
6 egg whites
1/4 cup grated Gruyère cheese or
    3 tablespoons grated Parmesan cheese

Preheat oven to 425°F (220°C). Thickly butter a 1-quart soufflé dish, being sure edge is greased well so mixture won't stick. Sprinkle buttered dish with 2 tablespoons breadcrumbs. Remove stems from fresh spinach and wash leaves thoroughly. Fill a large saucepan three-fourths full of water. Bring to a boil and add a large pinch of salt. Boil fresh spinach 5 minutes or until tender, stirring occasionally. Cook frozen spinach according to package directions. Drain cooked spinach, rinse with cold water and drain again. Squeeze by handfuls to extract as much water as possible. Finely chop spinach with a knife or in food processor; do not puree. Melt 2 tablespoons butter in a medium saucepan. Add spinach. Stir over medium heat until dry. Melt remaining 2 tablespoons butter in a small saucepan. Whisk in flour. Cook over low heat, whisking constantly, until mixture foams but doesn't brown. Remove from heat and whisk in milk and cream. Add salt, pepper and nutmeg. Bring to a boil, whisking constantly. Reduce heat and simmer 3 to 5 minutes. Stir in spinach and heat thoroughly. Remove from heat; beat egg yolks into hot mixture to thicken. Taste for seasoning. Mixture should be highly seasoned. *Spinach Soufflé can be prepared to this point 3 to 4 hours ahead. Rub surface of spinach mixture with butter, page 13, to prevent a skin forming. If made ahead, cover and refrigerate. Thirty minutes before serving, preheat oven to 425°F (220°C).* Whip egg whites until stiff, page 7. Heat spinach mixture over low heat, whisking constantly, until it is hot to the touch. Remove from heat and thoroughly mix in one-fourth of the stiff egg whites. Add this mixture with 3 tablespoons Gruyère cheese or 2 tablespoons Parmesan cheese to remaining stiff egg whites; fold together lightly, pages 10 and 11. Spoon into prepared soufflé dish and sprinkle with a mixture of remaining breadcrumbs and cheese. Bake 12 to 15 minutes until soufflé is puffed and brown. Serve immediately. Makes 4 servings.

Braised Endive
Endives Braisées

Unlike many green vegetables, endive are best when they are cooked until very soft.

4 to 6 heads Belgian endive
   (about 1-1/2 lbs.)
3 tablespoons butter
Salt and pepper to taste

1 teaspoon sugar
Squeeze of lemon juice
2 tablespoons water
1 tablespoon chopped parsley

Preheat oven to 350°F (175°C). Discard any wilted leaves from endive and trim stems. Do not wash them. With a knife point, hollow stems slightly so endive cook more evenly. Thickly coat bottom and sides of a 1-quart shallow baking dish with butter. Place endive in prepared baking dish and sprinkle with salt, pepper, sugar, lemon juice and water. Press a piece of buttered foil over endive and cover with a lid. Cook in oven 50 to 60 minutes until endive cores are very tender. If dish gets dry during cooking, add more water. Endive should brown lightly without burning. *Braised Endive can be prepared 24 hours ahead, tightly covered and refrigerated. Reheat chilled endive in the baking dish in a 350°F (175°C) oven.* Arrange endive on a platter or leave in baking dish. Sprinkle with parsley. Serve hot. Makes 4 servings.

Braised Cabbage
Choux Braisés

Good with beef and pork.

1 medium head firm green cabbage,
   halved, cored
1/4 lb. bacon, diced
1 onion, sliced

Salt and pepper to taste
1/4 cup Brown Beef Stock, page 30, or
   White Veal Stock, page 31

Preheat oven to 350°F (175°C). Shred cabbage. Brown bacon in a 2-quart casserole. Stir in onion. Sauté until onion is golden brown. Add shredded cabbage, salt and pepper; mix thoroughly. Pour in stock. Cover and bake 30 to 40 minutes until cabbage is very tender, stirring once or twice. Remove lid toward end of cooking time if cabbage mixture is very moist. Taste for seasoning. Serve hot. Makes 4 servings.

Braised Red Cabbage   Photo on page 109.
Choux Rouges Braisés

A favorite in the cooking of the Ardennes region in northern France.

1 medium head red cabbage, halved, cored
2 tablespoons butter
1 onion, sliced
1 tablespoon sugar

1 tablespoon vinegar
1/2 cup red wine
Salt and pepper to taste

Preheat oven to 350°F (175°C). Shred cabbage. Heat butter in a 2-quart casserole. Stir in onion. Sauté until soft but not browned. Add sugar. Cook, stirring constantly, until sugar caramelizes. Add shredded cabbage and vinegar; stir thoroughly. Add red wine, salt and pepper. Cover and bake 45 to 55 minutes until cabbage is very tender, stirring once or twice. Remove lid toward end of cooking time if cabbage is very moist. Taste for seasoning, adding a little more sugar or vinegar if necessary. *Braised Red Cabbage can be prepared 1 to 2 days ahead and refrigerated. Reheat over medium heat.* Serve hot. Makes 4 servings.

Cauliflower with Egg & Breadcrumbs
Choufleur à la Polonaise

Be careful not to overcook cauliflower—it should remain slightly crisp.

1 medium cauliflower
3 tablespoons butter
1/4 cup fresh breadcrumbs

Salt and pepper to taste
1 hard-cooked egg, page 52, finely chopped
1 tablespoon chopped parsley

Divide cauliflower into flowerets, discarding stem. Put cauliflower in a medium saucepan of boiling salted water so pieces are covered. Boil 8 to 10 minutes until just tender. Drain. Rinse with cold water and drain again. Grease a medium, deep round casserole or heatproof bowl. Arrange cauliflower so tops of flowerets press against bowl sides and stalks point toward center, filling bowl. Press lightly with a saucepan lid or plate and let stand 5 minutes. *Cauliflower can be prepared to this point 6 hours ahead, covered and refrigerated. Before serving, cover bowl with foil and reheat in a 250°F (120°C) oven 15 to 20 minutes.* Unmold cauliflower onto a platter; it will resemble a whole cauliflower. Cover with foil and keep warm. Melt butter in a small skillet. Fry breadcrumbs in butter until golden brown, stirring constantly. Add salt and pepper. Immediately sprinkle breadcrumbs over cauliflower. Top with hard-cooked egg and parsley. Serve hot. Makes 4 servings.

Asparagus with Butter Sauce
Asperges au Beurre

Asparagus is also delicious with Hollandaise Sauce, page 45.

2 lbs. fresh asparagus
Melted Butter Sauce, see below

Melted Butter Sauce:
1 cup butter
2 tablespoons water

Juice of 1/2 lemon
Salt and pepper to taste

Choose asparagus spears of the same thickness so they cook evenly. Snap stems to remove fibrous ends. Peel lower part of stem with a vegetable peeler. Tie asparagus spears with string in serving-size bundles. *Bundles can be prepared 6 to 8 hours ahead. Refrigerate with stem ends standing in a bowl of cold water.* To cook, place bundles flat in a large shallow saucepan of boiling salted water. Water should cover asparagus and bundles should not overlap. Cover and boil 8 to 10 minutes until stems are almost tender when pierced with a knife. Prepare Melted Butter Sauce. Drain asparagus. Transfer to a platter and remove strings. Pour a little Melted Butter Sauce over asparagus and serve remaining sauce separately. Serve hot. Makes 4 servings.

Melted Butter Sauce:
Cut butter into small cubes. Combine water, lemon juice, salt and pepper in a small non-aluminum saucepan over low heat. Whisk in butter piece by piece, removing from heat occasionally and whisking constantly so butter softens and thickens sauce without melting; base of pan should never be more than warm. Taste for seasoning, adding more lemon juice if needed. Serve immediately. Melted Butter Sauce can be kept warm for a few minutes by placing pan in a container of lukewarm water, but the butter tends to melt and make the sauce oily. If sauce does separate, it cannot be reemulsified. Makes about 1 cup of sauce.

Sautéed Cucumbers
Concombres Sautées

Light and refreshing with lamb or fish—especially salmon.

4 cucumbers
3 tablespoons butter
Salt and pepper to taste

1 tablespoon chopped fresh mint,
dill or parsley

Peel cucumbers, cut in half lengthwise and scoop out seeds with a teaspoon. Slice each half once again lengthwise, then crosswise into 2-inch sticks. Put in a medium saucepan of boiling salted water. Boil 4 to 5 minutes until almost tender; drain. *Cucumbers can be boiled 6 hours ahead, covered and refrigerated.* Melt butter in a large skillet. Add cucumbers. Sauté 3 to 4 minutes until just tender. Do not overcook or they will be bitter. Remove from heat. Add salt, pepper and mint, dill or parsley. Toss and transfer to a serving dish. Makes 4 servings.

1/Snap off fibrous ends of asparagus spears.

2/Arrange asparagus in bundles and tie with string.

How to Make Asparagus with Butter Sauce

Glazed Carrots
Carottes Vichy

Named for the town of Vichy, which is also famous for its mineral water.

1 lb. baby carrots, trimmed, or	**2 tablespoons butter**
large carrots, quartered or sliced	**1/2 teaspoon salt**
2 teaspoons sugar	**1 tablespoon chopped fresh mint or parsley**

Put carrots in a medium shallow saucepan with sugar, butter, salt and water to cover. Bring to a boil. Reduce heat and simmer uncovered 8 to 12 minutes for baby carrots or 15 to 20 minutes for large carrots until almost tender. Boil rapidly until all the liquid has evaporated to form a shiny glaze. Toward the end of cooking time, watch carefully so sugar does not caramelize. Taste for seasoning. *Glazed Carrots can be cooked 24 hours ahead, but leave a little liquid for reheating. If made ahead, cover and refrigerate.* Just before serving, reheat over medium heat. Remove from heat. Add chopped mint or parsley; toss. Spoon into a serving dish. Makes 4 servings.

Carrot Puree
Purée de Carottes

Golden Carrot Puree is a pretty addition to any main course.

1-1/2 lbs. carrots, sliced
1/4 cup whipping cream
1 tablespoon butter

1/2 to 1 teaspoon sugar, if desired
Salt and pepper to taste

Put carrots in a large saucepan and cover with water. Add pinch of salt. Boil 8 to 12 minutes until carrots are very tender; drain. Puree with cream in blender or food processor. Melt butter in a medium saucepan. Add Carrot Puree and heat over low heat. Add sugar, salt and pepper. If puree is soupy, cook and stir until it thickens. It should fall easily from a spoon. Taste for seasoning. *Carrot Puree can be made 2 to 3 days ahead, covered and refrigerated. Just before serving, reheat over low heat.* Spoon into a serving dish and serve very hot. Makes 4 servings.

How to Make Carrot Puree

1/Add pureed cooked carrots to melted butter. Mixture should fall thickly from a spoon.

2/Use a rubber spatula to make decorative ripples on the surface of the finished puree.

Ratatouille
Ratatouille

This vegetable stew originated in Provence and is served as an appetizer or an accompaniment.

1 medium eggplant (about 1/2 lb.),
    halved, cut in 3/8-inch slices
1/2 lb. small zucchini, cut in
    1/2-inch slices
1/4 cup olive oil
2 medium onions, thinly sliced
4 large tomatoes (about 1 lb.), peeled,
    seeded, chopped, page 10, or 2 cups
    canned tomatoes, drained, chopped

2 red or green peppers, cored,
    seeded, sliced
2 garlic cloves, crushed
1 teaspoon dried basil
1/2 teaspoon dried thyme
1/2 teaspoon ground coriander
Pinch of crushed aniseed
Salt and pepper to taste
1 tablespoon chopped parsley

Sprinkle eggplant and zucchini slices with salt and let stand 30 minutes. Drain, rinse with cold water and dry on paper towels. Heat 2 tablespoons olive oil in a large casserole. Add onions. Sauté until soft but not browned. Layer onions, eggplant, zucchini, tomatoes and peppers in casserole. Mix garlic, basil, thyme, coriander, aniseed, salt and pepper. Sprinkle on casserole, then mix vegetables thoroughly. Spoon remaining 2 tablespoons olive oil over vegetables. Cover casserole and simmer over medium heat 30 to 40 minutes until vegetables are tender. Do not overcook or vegetables will become soft and watery. If mixture is soupy, remove lid for last 10 minutes of cooking time. Taste for seasoning. *Ratatouille can be prepared 3 days ahead, but it should be slightly underdone to allow for reheating. If preparing ahead, cover and refrigerate. Reheat chilled Ratatouille over medium heat.* Serve hot or at room temperature. Stir in chopped parsley just before serving. Makes 4 servings.

Mashed Potatoes
Purée de Pommes de Terre

Good mashed potatoes are fluffy from beating with milk and butter over heat.

3 to 4 medium potatoes (1-1/2 lbs.),
    peeled
1/2 to 3/4 cup milk

3 tablespoons butter
Salt and white pepper to taste
Pinch of nutmeg

Cut each potato in 2 or 3 equal pieces. Put in a medium saucepan and cover with cold salted water. Cover and bring to a boil. Simmer 15 to 20 minutes until tender; potatoes should be quite soft. In a small saucepan, scald milk by bringing it just to a boil. Drain potatoes and press through a sieve or ricer, or mash in the pan with a potato masher. Beat in butter, 1/2 cup hot milk, salt, white pepper and nutmeg. Continue beating over low heat until puree is light and fluffy. Heat causes grains of starch in the potatoes to expand. If needed, add more milk to make a soft puree that just falls from the spoon. Taste for seasoning. *To keep Mashed Potatoes warm 30 minutes, leave in the pan, smooth the top and pour a little hot milk over top to prevent drying. Just before serving, beat until smooth.* Spoon into a serving dish. Makes 4 servings.

Potatoes Anna
Pommes Anna

A golden brown cake of thinly sliced potatoes.

3 to 4 medium potatoes (1-1/2 lbs.), peeled   **5 to 6 tablespoons butter**
2 tablespoons vegetable oil   **Salt and pepper**

Preheat oven to 400°F (205°C). Slice potatoes 1/8 inch thick. Do not soak in water as this removes the starch needed to hold slices together. Heat vegetable oil and 2 tablespoons butter in a 7- to 8-inch skillet with an ovenproof handle, tipping skillet to coat sides with fat; do not let butter brown. Remove from heat. Arrange a layer of potato slices overlapping in a spiral in bottom of skillet. When potatoes are unmolded, the spiral design will show on the top. Add another layer of potatoes—these don't need to be arranged in a pattern. Sprinkle lightly with salt and pepper and dot with butter. Continue adding layers of potatoes with seasoning and butter until all potatoes are used and skillet is full. Cook over medium heat 10 to 15 minutes until potatoes are browned on the bottom. To test, slide a metal spatula down side of the potato cake and lift slightly—you should be able to smell the browned butter. For a crisp bottom crust, leave uncovered; for a softer potato cake, cover with foil. Place skillet in center of oven. Cook 25 to 30 minutes, pressing potatoes occasionally with a spatula, until tender when tested with a skewer. *Potatoes Anna can be prepared 6 to 8 hours ahead, covered and kept at room temperature. Reheat over low heat.* To serve, loosen edge of potato cake with a spatula. Place a platter over skillet and invert so potato cake falls onto platter; it should be golden brown. Makes 4 servings.

Duchess Potatoes
Pommes Duchesse

These potatoes contain egg yolks, making them thick enough for piping rosettes or a decorative border.

3 or 4 medium potatoes (1-1/2 lbs.), peeled   **Pinch of nutmeg**
3 tablespoons butter   **3 egg yolks**
Salt and white pepper to taste

Cut each potato in 2 or 3 equal pieces. Put in a medium saucepan and cover with cold salted water. Cover pan and bring to a boil. Simmer 15 to 20 minutes until tender; potatoes should be quite soft. Drain. Return potatoes to pan and heat very gently, shaking occasionally until dry. Press hot potatoes through a sieve or ricer. Return to pan. Beat in butter, salt, white pepper and nutmeg. Continue beating over low heat until potatoes are light and fluffy. Heat causes grains of starch in the potatoes to expand. Remove from heat and beat in egg yolks. Taste for seasoning. Puree should hold its shape and stick to a spoon. *Potatoes can be prepared a few hours ahead, covered and kept at room temperature. Puree will stiffen as it cools so a little milk must be added before piping.* Grease a baking sheet or, if piping a potato border, the edge of a heatproof dish. Spoon puree into a pastry bag fitted with a medium star tube, pages 13 and 14, and pipe large rosettes, figure eights or small mounds of potato on the baking sheet or a border around the serving dish. *Duchess Potatoes can be piped several hours ahead, covered and kept at room temperature.* Just before serving, heat broiler or oven to 450°F (230°C). Broil or bake 5 to 10 minutes until browned. Makes 4 servings.

Gratin of Potatoes in Cream
Gratin Dauphinois

A rich version of scalloped potatoes. Curdling is prevented by parboiling the potatoes in milk.

1 garlic clove, halved	**Salt and pepper to taste**
3 or 4 potatoes (1-1/2 lbs.), peeled	**Pinch of nutmeg**
1-1/2 cups milk	**1/3 cup grated Gruyère cheese**
1-1/2 cups whipping cream	**1 tablespoon butter**

Rub a 1-1/2-quart shallow baking dish with garlic, then generously butter dish. Slice potatoes about 1/4 inch thick. Do not soak in water as this removes the starch needed to hold slices together. Bring milk to a boil in a large saucepan. Add potato slices. Boil 15 minutes or until partly tender. Drain; discard milk or use for soup. Return potatoes to saucepan. Add cream, salt, pepper and nutmeg. Bring to a boil. Reduce heat and simmer 10 to 15 minutes until potatoes are tender but not falling apart. Preheat broiler. Mixture should be very moist. Taste for seasoning. Spoon into prepared baking dish. Sprinkle with cheese and dot with butter. *Gratin of Potatoes in Cream can be prepared 1 to 2 days ahead, covered and refrigerated. Reheat in a 350°F (175°C) oven until bubbling.* Broil warm potatoes until golden brown. Serve in baking dish. Makes 4 to 6 servings.

French Fried Potatoes
Pommes Frites

Use mature potatoes rather than waxy new ones; mature potatoes hold less water and fry more crisply.

8 medium potatoes, peeled	**Salt**
Oil for deep-frying	

Cut potatoes in sticks 3/8 inch wide and 2-1/2 to 3 inches long. *Potatoes can be cut and soaked in cold water 1 to 2 hours ahead. Thoroughly drain on paper towels; wet potatoes can spatter dangerously when put in hot oil.* Heat oil to 350°F (175°C) or until a small cube of bread dropped in oil browns in 1 minute. Put part of the potatoes in a wire basket; do not fill basket too full or potatoes will stick together. Carefully lower basket into hot oil. If oil bubbles furiously, remove basket and reduce temperature of oil. Fry potatoes 8 to 12 minutes until soft and just beginning to brown. Remove basket and transfer potatoes to paper towels. Let drain until ready to finish frying. Continue frying remaining potatoes. *French Fried Potatoes can be prepared to this point 2 hours ahead.* Reheat oil to 375°F (190°C) or until a small cube of bread dropped in oil browns in 20 seconds. Fry partially cooked potatoes 1 to 2 minutes until golden brown, shaking basket occasionally to prevent sticking together. This second frying makes the potatoes very crisp. Drain thoroughly but quickly on paper towels. Sprinkle with salt and serve immediately. Makes 4 servings.

Rice Pilaf
Riz Pilaf

If you use stock instead of water, the pilaf will have a richer flavor.

2 tablespoons butter
1 onion, finely chopped
1-1/2 cups long-grain rice

3 cups Chicken Stock, page 32, or water
1 bouquet garni, page 7
Salt and pepper to taste

Preheat oven to 350°F (175°C). Melt butter in a medium, heavy saucepan with an ovenproof handle. Add onion. Sauté until soft but not browned. Add rice. Sauté 2 minutes, stirring constantly, until butter is absorbed and rice grains are transparent. Add Chicken Stock or water, bouquet garni, salt and pepper. Press a piece of buttered foil over rice and cover with a lid. Bring to a boil. Place in oven and cook 18 minutes. If liquid has evaporated but rice is not cooked, add more liquid and cook a few more minutes until tender. Remove from oven and let stand covered 10 minutes. Remove lid and discard bouquet garni. Stir rice with a fork to fluff. Taste for seasoning. *Rice Pilaf can be prepared 2 to 3 days ahead, covered and refrigerated or frozen. Reheat chilled rice in a 350°F (175°C) oven. Use a dish with a wide surface area for reheating so rice will heat quickly and evenly.* Makes 5 to 6 servings.

Rice Pilaf with Mushrooms
Pilaf aux Champignons

Serve this rice dish steaming hot as a first course or with a meat or poultry main course.

1/4 cup butter
1 onion, chopped
1/4 lb. lean bacon, diced
1-1/2 cups long-grain rice

1/4 lb. fresh mushrooms, sliced
1 qt. White Veal Stock, page 31, or
    Brown Beef Stock, page 30
Salt and pepper to taste

Preheat oven to 350°F (175°C). Melt 2 tablespoons butter in a medium, heavy saucepan with an ovenproof handle. Add onion and bacon. Sauté until transparent but not browned. Add rice. Sauté 3 to 4 minutes, stirring constantly, until rice is transparent. Melt remaining 2 tablespoons butter in a medium saucepan. Add mushrooms. Sauté 2 to 3 minutes until tender. Stir stock into rice with mushrooms, salt and pepper. Press a piece of buttered foil over rice and cover with a lid. Bring to a boil. Place in oven and cook 18 minutes. If liquid has evaporated but rice is not cooked, add more liquid and cook a few more minutes until tender. Remove from oven and let stand covered 10 minutes. Remove lid. Stir rice with a fork to fluff. Taste for seasoning. *Rice Pilaf with Mushrooms can be prepared 2 to 3 days ahead, covered and refrigerated or frozen. Reheat chilled rice in a 350°F (175°C) oven.* Makes 5 to 6 servings.

Rice Piémontaise
Riz Piémontaise

This dish is an integral part of Braised Ham Piémontaise, page 111, but is also delicious on its own.

1-1/2 cups butter	**Salt and pepper**
4 cups long-grain rice	**1-1/3 cups grated Parmesan cheese**
7 cups White Veal Stock, page 31	

In a large heavy saucepan, melt 1 cup butter. Add rice, stock, salt and pepper. Cover and bring to a boil. Reduce heat and simmer 18 to 20 minutes. *Rice can be cooked 2 to 3 days ahead, covered and refrigerated. Slowly reheat chilled rice over low heat.* Let hot rice stand covered in a warm place 10 minutes. Remove lid; dot rice with remaining 1/2 cup butter and sprinkle with grated cheese. Let stand 1 to 2 minutes, then stir with a fork to fluff. Taste for seasoning. Makes 12 to 16 servings.

Fresh Noodles
Nouilles Fraîches

Basic pasta can be cut in a variety of widths and topped with any number of sauces.

2 cups all-purpose flour	**2 tablespoons warm water**
3 small eggs, slightly beaten	**3 to 4 tablespoons butter**
1 teaspoon salt	**Salt and pepper to taste**
1 tablespoon olive oil	

Sift flour onto a flat surface. Make a well in the center. Put eggs, 1 teaspoon salt, olive oil and water in the well. Work flour into the mixture with your fingertips. Add more water if needed; dough should be smooth and soft but not sticky. Lightly flour work surface and work dough by pushing it away with the heel of your hand and gathering it up with a metal spatula until dough forms a rough ball. Cover with an inverted bowl and let stand 1 hour so dough will lose some of its elasticity. If making noodles by hand, divide dough in half. On a floured board, roll out each half as thin as possible. Let dough rest 30 minutes to 1 hour until fairly stiff and dry. Roll loosely into a jelly-roll shape and cut into 3/8-, 1/2- or 3/4-inch slices to make noodles. Spread noodles on a floured cloth towel or hang over a chair back to dry 1 to 2 hours. If making noodles with a pasta machine, divide dough into 3 or 4 balls. Put each ball through the machine 3 or 4 times on the first setting until very smooth. Put through once on each of the thinner settings or until dough is very thin. Cut dough into noodles as described above and dry 2 to 3 hours. *If making noodles a week ahead, coil them loosely and let stand uncovered 12 to 24 hours to dry thoroughly. Wrap in a plastic bag and refrigerate or freeze.* To cook noodles, bring a very large pan of salted water to a boil; noodles must have room to cook without touching. Add noodles and return to a boil. Reduce heat and simmer uncovered 2 to 3 minutes until tender. Noodles should be slightly chewy. Fresh noodles cook more quickly than packaged noodles. Drain and rinse noodles with hot water to reduce starch. Immediately melt butter and add noodles. Heat, tossing constantly and season lightly with salt and pepper. Serve immediately. Makes 4 to 6 servings.

Salads

Salads in France are very different from those popularized in the U.S. There is much less variety in France and the green salad reigns supreme. It is made with one kind of lettuce and tossed with a simple dressing of oil and vinegar with none of the additions of chopped onion, garlic and herbs often served in the North American version. The Frenchman has no urge to vary these ingredients, except to use seasonal greens. This is because green salad plays a different role in France, traditionally being served after the main course to refresh the palate before the cheese.

Many French first course salads are scarcely more complicated. They are based on one raw or cooked vegetable, mixed or sprinkled with a simple dressing. For instance, in summer the ripest tomatoes are sliced and marinated in Vinaigrette with a little chopped shallot and fresh herbs. Sliced cucumber is mixed with yogurt and topped with chives. School children are brought up on grated carrot seasoned with Vinaigrette. Crudités, a mixture of three or four fresh vegetables, each of different color and texture, is the standard restaurant appetizer.

However, times are changing and more elaborate salads are becoming popular as the opening to a meal. They vary from classics like Niçoise Salad, made with green beans, tuna, black olives, cucumbers and tomatoes, to imaginative combinations that mix fish with meat and a few nuts for texture. The French dislike of fruit in salads is changing too, so now you may find a few segments of grapefruit or mandarin orange on your salad plate.

How to Prepare Salads

There is nothing to camouflage salad ingredients, so they must be the best. In mixed salads, look for color contrast like that in Rice Salad, with peppers, carrots, tomatoes and peas against a white background of rice. Texture is important too, the aim being a balance of soft and crisp. With this in mind, it's best to shred raw vegetables such as carrots or cabbage in fine pieces, or cut them in thin julienne sticks, so you don't have to bite into hard lumps. Briefly cook strong ingredients such as peppers so they won't dominate a salad, but be sure to leave them slightly crisp. If overdone they'll lack texture and flavor. Always drain and dry fresh and cooked vegetables thoroughly so they don't dilute the dressing.

How to Dress Salads

Dressing for a salad is at least as important as the ingredients. Again, the French like to keep it simple. Vinaigrette, the most common dressing, is based on only four ingredients: oil, vinegar, salt and pepper. Its character is changed to a startling extent not only by the oil, which can vary from neutral vegetable oil to fruity olive or walnut oil, but also by the vinegar. Most popular is a mild red or white wine vinegar, but you could try a herb vinegar. Or, use lemon juice for a truly Mediterranean touch. Mustard, finely chopped herbs, shallots, garlic, pickles or capers are also possible additions, but the French like to use them mainly with strongly flavored ingredients like cooked meats and root vegetables.

Mayonnaise, page 50, is popular but less versatile than Vinaigrette as a dressing. It can overwhelm delicate flavors and it would mask the vivid color in a salad using red cabbage for instance. So mayonnaise is usually reserved for dry foods like cooked poultry or fish and for root vegetables. It is never used in a green salad.

Within these guidelines, the choice of dressing is very much up to you. Try mayonnaise if you like a rich dish, but use Vinaigrette if you want delicate vegetables to stand out clearly. And always remember that a dressing should accentuate the flavors of the ingredients without overwhelming them.

How to Serve Salads

Salad ingredients should be mixed gently but thoroughly with dressing. Robust ingredients such as root vegetables and rice benefit from marinating in the dressing for at least an hour, so the flavors blend. On the other hand, green vegetables should remain crisp and must be mixed with dressing just before serving. If they sit for even half an hour with dressing, the leaves will become soggy. Exceptions are escarole, curly endive and dandelion greens which will lose some of their toughness if dressed up to an hour ahead of time. Add only enough dressing to flavor and moisten salad vegetables. Always taste a salad after mixing, as some ingredients absorb more seasoning than you might expect.

Lastly comes the decoration. A salad should be carefully arranged in a dish of appropriate size. Many salads have enough color to need no further garnish. But, for some, a sprinkling of parsley or a topping of thinly sliced lemon makes all the difference.

How to Prepare Salad Greens

Give salad greens special attention, choosing those that are bright and green. Divide heads into leaves, discarding stems and any wilted leaves.

Be sure to wash greens thoroughly. Soak the leaves briefly in a sink of cold water to loosen any soil, then lift them out one by one so the dirt stays at the bottom of the sink. If necessary, wash again in cold water, or run each leaf under cold running water.

Dry the leaves well so the dressing clings and the salad does not taste watery. Either pat the leaves dry with paper towels, or whirl them in a salad basket or a salad spinner. Do not shred the leaves with a knife; leave them whole, or tear them in two or three pieces depending on their size and texture.

Greens can be washed up to a day ahead and refrigerated, lightly wrapped in a dish towel.

How to Dry Salad Greens

After thoroughly washing salad greens, gently pat dry with a towel or whirl in a salad basket or salad spinner.

Vinaigrette
Vinaigrette

An excellent salad dressing to bring out delicate vegetable flavors.

1 tablespoon vinegar or	**1/2 teaspoon Dijon-style mustard,**
2 teaspoons lemon juice	**if desired**
Salt and pepper to taste	**3 tablespoons vegetable oil**

Whisk vinegar or lemon juice with salt, pepper and mustard, if desired. Gradually whisk in oil until Vinaigrette is blended and slightly thickened. Taste for seasoning. *Vinaigrette can be made up to 1 month ahead and kept tightly covered at room temperature. Whisk vigorously to blend before using.* Makes 1/4 cup of Vinaigrette.

Variations

Add one or more of the following ingredients just before using: 1/2 garlic clove, crushed; 1 shallot, finely chopped; 1 teaspoon chopped mixed fresh herbs such as parsley, tarragon, chives, basil or oregano.

Green Salad
Salade Verte

To give just a hint of flavor, rub a cut clove of garlic around the salad bowl before adding the greens.

1 lb. lettuce or other greens such as	**Vinaigrette, see above**
watercress, chicory, spinach or	**Salt and pepper, if desired**
dandelion leaves	

Carefully wash salad greens. Tear, do not cut, into pieces and dry thoroughly, opposite. Just before serving, add Vinaigrette to salad greens. Toss well. Taste for seasoning. Add salt and pepper, if desired. Serve immediately because most greens will soften rapidly and become soggy. Makes 4 to 6 servings.

Raw Vegetable Salad
Crudités

Mix and match the colors and textures for this fresh appetizer according to the seasons.

Celery Root with Mayonnaise, page 134   **Tomato Salad, see below**
Cucumber Salad, page 135

Prepare Celery Root with Mayonnaise, Cucumber Salad and Tomato Salad. Arrange salads in separate mounds on a long or circular platter. Makes about 12 servings.

Variations

One or more of the following salads can be added to the platter or substituted for any of the above salads.

Beet Salad (Salade de Betteraves): Mix 1/4 cup Vinaigrette, page 131, with 2 cups diced, peeled cooked beets. Makes 2 to 3 servings.
Cabbage Salad (Salade de Choux): Finely shred 1/2 head red or white cabbage. If using red cabbage, immediately toss with 2 tablespoons vinegar from 1/2 cup Vinaigrette, page 131, to prevent cabbage from discoloring. Add remaining Vinaigrette ingredients and 1 teaspoon chopped fresh dill or 1/2 teaspoon dill seed. Toss well. If using white cabbage, toss with Vinaigrette and dill. Makes 4 servings.
Carrot Salad (Salade de Carottes): Grate 3 large carrots, discarding yellow core. Toss grated carrots, 1/4 cup Vinaigrette, page 131, and a pinch of sugar. Makes 4 servings.
Fennel Root Salad (Salade de Fenouil): Trim and thinly slice 2 medium fennel bulbs. Add to lightly salted boiling water; boil 2 minutes. Drain; rinse with cold water and drain thoroughly. Toss fennel with 1/4 cup Vinaigrette, page 131, made with lemon juice. Makes 4 servings.
Pepper Salad (Salade de Poivrons): Core and remove seeds from 2 red, green or yellow bell peppers. Slice into strips. Add to boiling water; boil 1 to 2 minutes until crisp-tender. Drain. Toss with 1/4 cup Vinaigrette, page 131, made with olive oil and garlic. Makes 2 to 3 servings.

Tomato Salad
Salade de Tomates

Vine-ripe tomatoes make all the difference in this salad.

1 lb. fresh ripe tomatoes, cored, sliced   **Salt and pepper, if desired**
1 teaspoon sugar
1/4 cup Vinaigrette, page 131, made with
  garlic, shallot and 1 tablespoon
  parsley or 1 teaspoon fresh
  oregano or basil

Arrange tomato slices overlapping in a medium serving dish. Whisk sugar into Vinaigrette and taste for seasoning. Add salt and pepper, if desired. Spoon over tomatoes. Cover and let stand 1 to 2 hours at room temperature to blend flavors. Serve at room temperature. Makes 4 servings.

Celery Root with Mayonnaise
Céleri Rémoulade

If you can't find celery root, use stalk celery and do not blanch it.

1 medium celery root
Juice of 1 lemon
1 cup Mayonnaise, page 50

2 teaspoons Dijon-style mustard
Salt and pepper to taste

Peel celery root. Rub white portion with lemon juice to prevent discoloration. Cut in very thin strips. If celery root is pleasantly crunchy, leave raw. If tough and fibrous, cover strips with cold water in a medium saucepan. Bring to a boil and blanch by boiling 1 minute or until cooked but still crunchy. If celery root is very fibrous, blanch 3 to 5 minutes. Drain. Combine Mayonnaise with mustard. Stir in celery root. Add salt and pepper. Add more mustard, if needed. Cover and let stand 1 to 2 hours at room temperature to blend flavors. Serve at room temperature. Makes 4 to 6 servings.

How to Make Celery Root with Mayonnaise

1/Peel celery root with a sharp knife. Rub white portion with lemon juice to prevent discoloration.

2/Guide the knife with your knuckles to cut thin slices before cutting into thin strips.

Dandelion Salad
Salade de Pissenlits

Use any tough-leaf winter greens such as escarole and curly endive.

3/4 lb. dandelion greens
5 to 6 slices bacon, diced
1 garlic clove, crushed
3 tablespoons wine vinegar

2 hard-cooked eggs, page 52, chopped
Pinch of pepper
Salt, if desired

Pull dandelion heads apart. Trim stalks, wash heads thoroughly and dry on paper towels. Place in a medium salad bowl. Fry bacon in a medium skillet until browned and crisp. Add garlic. Sauté 20 seconds longer. Pour hot bacon and fat over salad greens and immediately toss until they wilt slightly. Pour vinegar into skillet. Bring to a boil, stirring to dissolve any browned bits of bacon. Pour over greens. Add eggs and pepper; toss. Taste for seasoning. Salad should be quite peppery. If bacon was salty, more salt may not be necessary. Makes 4 servings.

Cucumber Salad
Salade de Concombres

A cool combination!

1 large cucumber, peeled, thinly sliced
Salt
3/4 cup plain yogurt

1-1/2 tablespoons chopped fresh chives
Salt and pepper, if desired

Sprinkle cucumber with salt and let stand 30 minutes to draw out bitter juices. Rinse with cold water. Drain thoroughly and dry on paper towels. In a medium bowl, mix cucumber with yogurt and 1 tablespoon chives. Taste for seasoning. Add salt and pepper, if desired. Place in a serving dish and sprinkle with remaining 1/2 tablespoon chives. Cover and refrigerate 2 to 4 hours. Makes 4 servings.

Potatoes Vinaigrette
Pommes de Terre Vinaigrette

A bistro standard, French potato salad is delicious with hot sausage.

1-1/2 lbs. medium potatoes, unpeeled
3/4 cup Vinaigrette, page 131,
  made with mustard

Salt and pepper, if desired
1 tablespoon finely chopped fresh chives

Place potatoes in a large saucepan with enough salted water to cover. Cover and bring to a boil. Simmer 15 to 20 minutes until just tender. Drain potatoes and cool slightly. Peel and cut into pieces. Place in a medium serving dish. Pour Vinaigrette over warm potatoes. Mix gently and taste for seasoning. Add salt and pepper, if desired. Cover and let stand up to 2 hours at room temperature. Gently stir in chives just before serving. Makes 4 servings.

Niçoise Salad
Salade Niçoise

A Mediterranean salad from Nice—a city on the Riviera.

10 to 12 anchovy fillets
1/2 cup milk
3/4 lb. green beans
1 (7-oz.) can tuna in oil, drained, flaked
1/2 cup Vinaigrette, page 131, made with
   lemon juice, olive oil and garlic

1 small or 1/2 large cucumber, peeled,
   sliced very thin
1/4 cup black Italian or Greek-style
   olives, halved, pitted
3 medium tomatoes, peeled, cut in quarters

Soak anchovy fillets in milk 30 minutes. Drain and rinse with cold water; drain thoroughly. In a large saucepan, boil enough salted water to cover green beans generously. Add green beans; boil 8 to 10 minutes until just tender. Split anchovy fillets lengthwise with a knife. Spread tuna on bottom of a salad bowl. Cover with green beans. Moisten with a little Vinaigrette and cover completely with cucumber, overlapping slices to make a flat layer. Spoon most of remaining Vinaigrette over cucumber layer. Arrange anchovy fillets in a lattice pattern on top. Place an olive half cut-side down in center of each lattice. Arrange tomato quarters around edge of salad and brush with remaining Vinaigrette. Serve at room temperature. *Niçoise Salad can be made up to 8 hours ahead, covered and refrigerated.* Makes 4 servings.

Cooked Vegetable Salad
Macédoine de Légumes

Warm vegetables will absorb the dressing more easily than cold ones.

2 medium carrots, diced
1/2 celery root or 1/2 lb.
   medium turnip, diced
1 cup shelled peas

1 cup green beans, cut in 1/2-inch lengths
1/4 cup Vinaigrette, page 131
1/3 to 1/2 cup Mayonnaise, page 50
Salt and pepper, if desired

In a medium saucepan, cover carrots and celery root or turnip generously with cold salted water. Cover and boil 10 to 12 minutes until just tender. Drain thoroughly. In a medium saucepan, boil enough salted water to cover both peas and green beans. Add peas and green beans; boil 5 to 8 minutes until crisp-tender; drain. Rinse with cold water and drain thoroughly. Mix Vinaigrette with warm vegetables. When cool, mix vegetables with enough Mayonnaise to bind lightly, being careful not to add too much Mayonnaise or salad will be heavy. Taste for seasoning. Add salt and pepper, if desired. Cover and let stand 1 to 2 hours at room temperature to blend flavors. Serve at room temperature. Makes 4 servings.

Rice Salad
Salade de Riz

Be careful not to overcook the rice—it should be firm, not sticky.

1-1/4 cups long-grain rice
1 slice lemon
1 carrot, diced
1/2 green bell pepper, cored, seeded, diced
1/2 red bell pepper, cored, seeded, diced
1/2 cup green peas

1 medium tomato, peeled, seeded,
   cut in strips, page 10
1 celery stalk, thinly sliced
1/2 cup Vinaigrette, page 131
Salt and pepper, if desired

In a large saucepan, boil 3 to 4 quarts salted water. Add rice and lemon. Boil 10 to 12 minutes until rice is just tender. Lemon will keep rice white. Drain; discard lemon. In a strainer, rinse rice with hot water to wash away starch. Poke a few drainage holes in rice with the handle of a spoon and leave rice in strainer 10 to 15 minutes to dry. Generously cover carrot with salted water in a medium saucepan. Boil 8 to 10 minutes until tender. Drain. Boil enough salted water to cover peppers generously and boil 1 minute. Drain. Rinse with cold water and drain thoroughly. Repeat this process with peas, boiling 5 to 8 minutes until just tender. Drain peas. Rinse with cold water and drain thoroughly again. *Rice and vegetables can be prepared up to 12 hours ahead, covered and refrigerated.* Not more than 2 hours before serving, carefully mix cooked vegetables, tomato, celery and rice. Add Vinaigrette to vegetable mixture. Mix well and taste for seasoning. Add salt and pepper, if desired. Pile salad in a bowl. Serve at room temperature. Makes 4 servings.

Beet Salad with Nuts
Salade de Betteraves aux Noix

The texture contrasts are refreshing.

2 plump heads Belgian endive (1/2 lb.)
A few bunches (1/4 lb.) lambs' lettuce or
   1 small head very green lettuce
   (1/4 lb.)

2 large cooked beets
1/2 cup Vinaigrette, page 131
Salt and pepper, if desired
1/2 cup walnuts, coarsely chopped

Wipe endive. Discard any wilted leaves; trim stems. Cut into 1-inch diagonal slices. Thoroughly wash lettuce to remove all sand; dry well. Mix endive and lettuce in a salad bowl. *Greens can be prepared several hours ahead, covered and refrigerated.* Just before serving, cut beets in medium dice. Add to greens. Toss salad with Vinaigrette. Taste for seasoning. Add salt and pepper, if desired, and sprinkle with walnuts. Serve at room temperature. Makes 6 servings.

Cakes & Pastries

French pastry chefs often say their entire repertoire is built on a few basic recipes: all the rest are variations. With knowledge of preparations such as Génoise Cake, Cream Puff Pastry, Puff Pastry, Pastry Cream and Chantilly Cream, there is almost no end to the cakes and pastries you can make. Génoise and Butter Cream, for example, are combined in both Christmas Log and Strawberry Cake. Cream Puffs and Chantilly Swans use Cream Puff Pastry and Chantilly Cream. Napoleons, Apple Turnovers and Palm Leaves are based on Puff Pastry.

Very often the components are interchangeable. Thus regular pie pastry can be substituted for sweet, or you can use puff pastry trimmings if you have some left over. Pastry cream may take the place of a Chantilly cream or a butter cream filling. And of course flavors—coffee, chocolate, vanilla, strawberry, lemon or liqueur—can be varied to your taste. Not only is there scope for your imagination, but you can also avoid risk by trying new techniques one at a time so you gradually increase your skill.

How to Make Cakes & Pastries

In cake and pastry-making, more than any other branch of cooking, it is attention to detail that counts. Just a few techniques are used again and again in various recipes, making all the difference between sloppy and successful results. Be sure you understand the proper consistency for the mixture you are making—that you recognize the *ribbon* when beating eggs and sugar, page 145, or the way cream puff pastry just falls from a spoon when enough eggs have been added, page 163. Always preheat the oven and prepare cake pans and baking sheets ahead. Finally, acquire the habit of checking dishes while they are baking, rather than relying on stated times. Every cook's oven has its idiosyncrasies.

When making pastry, lightness of touch and the temperature at which you work are important.

To avoid overworking, the French make many of their pastry doughs directly on the table, hollowing a well in the flour, mixing the other ingredients together in the well, and then working in the flour. Speed is essential; the longer a dough is worked the more elastic it becomes, so it is hard to roll, shrinks during baking and is tough.

Many French pastries, particularly puff pastry, contain a high proportion of butter and special precautions must be taken to prevent the butter from melting. Chill the work surface by setting a tray of ice on it, and chill the rolling pin and flour in the freezer. Work fast so the dough is in contact as short a time as possible with the heat of the room and the warmth of your hands. Once in the oven, the butter must be sealed in the pastry quickly, so the richer the dough, the higher the cooking temperature. When pastry starts to brown, the heat may be reduced so cooking is completed more slowly.

How to Prepare Cakes & Pastries Ahead

Puff pastry takes most kindly to storage. It freezes well, baked or unbaked. It can be kept 24 hours in the refrigerator before baking, or two to three days in an airtight container when cooked.

Pie pastry, sweet or regular, can be baked a day or two ahead and kept tightly sealed. Unbaked dough dries out in the freezer and will lose lightness if it is refrigerated more than a few days.

Cream puff pastry is even less accommodating. Uncooked dough must be kept tightly sealed in the refrigerator and used within 8 hours. It cannot be frozen. Cooked puffs become tough after a day or so, even in an airtight container or the freezer. And once a filling has been added to any pastry, it will become soggy within a few hours.

Cakes are another matter. Those containing butter and nuts will keep well a day or two in an airtight container. In many classic recipes the cake is moistened with sugar syrup to help it keep. A cake that is filled and frosted with butter cream improves after keeping for several days, or even a week as the flavors of cake and cream will mellow. Most cakes freeze excellently, including those frosted with butter cream. Avoid freezing Chantilly or pastry cream.

How to Complete Cakes & Pastries

In France, a cake is normally baked in one piece, not in layers, and its texture is comparatively dry, though it is often moistened with liqueur or sugar syrup. A rich filling and frosting, both in generous quantities, is the rule. The simplest filling is Chantilly cream which is flavored whipped cream, but it cannot be kept more than an hour or two. Pastry cream keeps better, but it cannot be piped. Most popular of all is butter cream, used as filling and frosting, and often piped in rosettes as the crowning touch.

Decorations are always best done a short time before serving and they are a chef's pride. But this does not mean that designs must be intricate. On the contrary, the most striking touches are often very simple, such as a circle of whole strawberries or a coating of browned sliced almonds. A sprinkling of powdered sugar gives a frosty effect, while powdered chocolate will do the same for a light-colored cake. For more decorating ideas see page 169. If you learn to use a pastry bag to produce rosettes or other designs, pages 13 and 14, your cakes and pastries will look truly professional. But, don't go wild on decorations. It's up to you to know when to stop.

How to Prepare Cake Pans & Baking Sheets

Butter prevents mixtures from sticking. Cake pans and baking sheets are nearly always buttered. An exception is made for mixtures with a very high fat content such as puff pastry.

Flour used as coating on a baking sheet helps give cakes a smooth surface and discourages mixtures from spreading.

Water sprinkled on a baking sheet glues puff pastry in shape and prevents shrinkage. The steam generated also helps dough rise.

Cakes: Grease the cake pan by brushing it with very soft or melted butter. For safety, cut a waxed paper or parchment paper circle the same diameter as the pan base. Smooth the paper in the pan and grease it too. Sprinkle the pan with flour, tapping the sides to obtain an even layer of flour. Turn the pan upside down and tap it sharply to dislodge excess flour. For a crisp crust, sprinkle the pan with sugar before sprinkling with flour. Be careful not to make finger marks on the prepared pan.

Meringues & Ladyfingers: Brush a baking sheet generously with butter, especially for meringues which tend to stick. Sprinkle it with flour and tap to dislodge excess.

Yeast Doughs: Butter the pan or baking sheet but do not flour it.

Cream Puff Pastry: Rub the baking sheet very lightly with butter.

Puff Pastry: Sprinkle a little water on the baking sheet.

Pie Pastry & Sweet Pie Pastry: Plain pie pans need only be lightly buttered. However, fluted pie pans or flan rings should be well buttered.

How to Check When Cakes Are Done

When you start to *smell* a cake baking, begin checking it. When you *see* that the cake has shrunk slightly from the edges of the pan, it is probably cooked. The final verdict is given by *touch:* if you press the center gently with your finger, the cake should feel firm and the finger mark should disappear. Also, you can insert a thin skewer in the cake—if it is dry when withdrawn, the cake is done. If the cake is not ready, test again after a few minutes.

Christmas Log
Bûche de Nöel

For a snow-covered log, sprinkle with a little powdered sugar just before serving.

Meringue Mushrooms, see below
1 cup all-purpose flour
Pinch of salt
1/4 cup butter
3 whole eggs
2 egg yolks

Meringue Mushrooms:
3 egg whites
3/4 cup sugar
1/2 teaspoon vanilla extract

Sugar Syrup:
1/2 cup sugar
1/3 cup water

2/3 cup sugar
Sugar Syrup, see below
3 oz. semisweet chocolate, coarsely chopped
Butter Cream, opposite,
    made with 4 egg yolks
1 to 2 tablespoons Grand Marnier

Additional sugar
Grated chocolate or cocoa powder

Prepare Meringue Mushrooms. Preheat oven to 425°F (220°C). Grease a baking sheet and line with waxed paper. Butter and flour waxed paper. Sift flour with salt. Melt butter; cool. Beat whole eggs, egg yolks and sugar in a large bowl until combined. Beat at high speed 8 to 10 minutes until light and thick enough to leave a ribbon trail, page 145. Sift flour over batter a third at a time, folding in each third as lightly as possible. Just after last addition, add melted butter and fold in both together. Spread batter evenly on prepared baking sheet to a 15" x 10" rectangle. Bake 8 to 10 minutes until edges are browned. Do not overbake or cake will crack when rolled. Slide cake off baking sheet onto a rack by gently pulling paper with cake on top. Invert cake onto a cloth towel; remove paper. Roll up hot cake with towel and let cool. Prepare Syrup. Melt chocolate over a pan of boiling water. Cool slightly. Divide Butter Cream in 2 equal parts. Add melted chocolate to one part and Grand Marnier to the other. Unroll cooled cake. Brush with Syrup. Spread Grand Marnier Butter Cream on cake. Trim edges with a sharp knife. Roll cake trimmings into tight spirals to be attached later to log as knots. Roll up cake, removing towel as you roll. With a little butter cream, attach cake spirals to log. Use a pastry bag fitted with a medium star tube, pages 13 and 14, to pipe Chocolate Butter Cream on cake from end to end to resemble bark. If you don't have a pastry bag, spread Butter Cream on log with a spatula and mark it with a fork to resemble bark. Arrange Meringue Mushrooms on and around log. Refrigerate until ready to serve. *Christmas Log can be covered and refrigerated 1 to 2 days.* Makes 6 to 8 servings.

Meringue Mushrooms:
Preheat oven to 250°F (120°C). Butter and flour a baking sheet. In a medium bowl, whip egg whites until stiff, page 7. Add 1 tablespoon sugar and beat 30 seconds to make a light meringue. Fold in remaining sugar and vanilla. Spoon meringue into a pastry bag fitted with a 1/4-inch plain tube. Pipe mounds for mushroom caps and strips for stems. Sprinkle with sugar. Sprinkle caps with grated chocolate or cocoa powder. Bake 15 minutes then insert stems into caps. Bake 15 to 30 minutes longer until dry and crisp. If mushrooms begin to brown, reduce heat.

Sugar Syrup:
Bring sugar and water to a boil in a small saucepan. Boil 1 to 2 minutes or until clear. Cool.

1/Roll up hot cake and towel together; cool.

2/Unfrosted knots suggest sawed-off branches.

How to Make Christmas Log

Butter Cream
Crème au Beurre

Add Butter Cream to your standard layer cake and you will have a luscious gâteau.

Use These Ingredients	To Make	
	1-1/2 cups	2 cups
egg yolks	3	4
sugar	7 tablespoons	9 tablespoons
water	1/4 cup	1/3 cup
unsalted butter	3/4 cup	1 cup
flavoring according to recipe		

In a medium bowl, beat egg yolks just until mixed. In a small heavy saucepan, heat sugar with water until dissolved, then bring to a boil until syrup reaches soft-ball stage, page 146, 239°F (115°C) on a candy thermometer. Wait 20 seconds until bubbles in syrup in saucepan subside, then gradually pour the hot sugar syrup over egg yolks, beating constantly. If using an electric mixer, pour sugar syrup in a thin stream between beaters and bowl so syrup doesn't stick to either. Then beat as fast as possible until mixture is thick and cool. Cream butter and gradually beat it into yolk mixture which must be quite cool or it will melt the butter when you beat it in. Beat in flavor appropriate for chosen recipe. *Butter Cream can be prepared 3 days ahead, covered and refrigerated.*

Variations

Chocolate Butter Cream (Crème au Beurre au Chocolat): For every cup of Butter Cream, add 3 ounces semisweet chocolate which has been melted over a pan of boiling water. Cool slightly before beating into the Butter Cream.

Coffee Butter Cream (Crème au Beurre au Café): For every cup of Butter Cream, add 2 to 3 teaspoons instant coffee powder dissolved in 1 tablespoon hot water.

Walnut Cake

Biscuit aux Noix

The more walnuts you use, the richer the cake will be.

1 to 1-1/2 cups walnut halves
1/4 cup butter
1/3 cup all-purpose flour
3 egg yolks
2/3 cup sugar
1/2 teaspoon vanilla extract

1-1/2 to 2 tablespoons kirsch, if desired
4 egg whites
1/2 cup Sugar Syrup, page 140
Coffee Butter Cream, page 141, made with
   4 egg yolks
1 cup walnut halves, coarsely chopped

Prepare an 8- to 9-inch springform pan, page 139. Preheat oven to 350°F (175°C). Reserve 10 to 15 walnut halves for decoration. Grind remaining 1/2 to 1 cup walnuts to a powder a few at a time in a food processor or with a manual rotary cheese grater. Warm butter in a bowl over a pan of hot water until just soft enough to pour but still creamy. Do not let it become oily. Sift flour. Mix with ground walnuts. In a large bowl, beat egg yolks with 1/2 cup sugar 5 minutes or until mixture is light and thick enough to leave a ribbon trail, opposite. Beat in vanilla and 1 tablespoon kirsch, if desired. In a medium bowl, whip egg whites until stiff, page 7. Add remaining sugar and beat 30 seconds to make a light meringue. Gently fold flour-walnut mixture and meringue into yolk mixture, alternating a third of the flour mixture with half the meringue. Fold in butter with last addition of flour. Batter quickly loses volume after butter is added, so fold it in as quickly and gently as possible. Pour batter into prepared pan. Bake 40 to 50 minutes until cake shrinks slightly from sides of pan and cake top springs back when touched. Run a knife around sides of cake. Turn out of pan onto a rack to cool. Prepare Sugar Syrup and stir in remaining kirsch, if desired. Cut thoroughly cooled cake in 2 or 3 layers with a long serrated knife. Cut with a sawing motion, moving the knife without pressing on the cake. Gently brush cut side of each layer with Sugar Syrup. Spread bottom layer(s) with a thin layer of Coffee Butter Cream; sprinkle each layer with chopped walnuts. Stack layers. Reserve a little Coffee Butter Cream for decoration. Spread top and sides of cake with Coffee Butter Cream; press chopped walnuts around sides. Make a lattice design on top of cake with a knife point. Decorate cake edges with rosettes made by piping reserved Coffee Butter Cream from a pastry bag fitted with a medium star tube, pages 13 and 14. Top each rosette with a walnut half. *Walnut Cake can be made 2 to 3 days ahead, covered and refrigerated or kept in a cool place.* Makes 6 to 8 servings.

On the preceding pages, Apple Turnovers, page 157, are behind Lemon Pie, page 152. Rum Babas, page 165, are in front of Cream Puffs, page 160.

Coffee Roll
Biscuit Roulé au Café

Rum sprinkled over cake not only adds flavor but keeps the cake moist.

1/2 cup all-purpose flour	1/2 teaspoon vanilla extract
Pinch of salt	Coffee Butter Cream, page 141, made with
4 eggs, separated	4 egg yolks
3/4 cup sugar	2 to 3 tablespoons rum, if desired

Preheat oven to 375°F (190°C). Grease a baking sheet; line it with waxed paper. Butter and flour waxed paper. Sift flour with salt. In a large bowl, beat egg yolks with 1/2 cup sugar until light and thick enough to leave a ribbon trail, below. Beat in vanilla. In a medium bowl, whip egg whites until stiff, page 7. Add remaining 1/4 cup sugar and beat 30 seconds to make a light meringue. Gently fold flour and meringue into egg yolk mixture, alternating a third of the flour with half the meringue. Spread batter evenly on prepared baking sheet to a 15'' x 10'' rectangle. Bake 8 to 10 minutes until edges are browned. Do not overbake or cake will crack when rolled. Slide cake off baking sheet onto a rack by gently pulling paper with cake on top. Turn cake over onto a cloth towel; remove paper. Roll up hot cake with towel and let cool. Unroll cooled cake and sprinkle with rum, if desired. Trim edges of cake with a sharp knife and spread cake with half the Coffee Butter Cream. Roll up cake, removing dish towel as you roll. Spread more Coffee Butter Cream on top of cake and trim ends. Decorate roll with rosettes of Coffee Butter Cream piped from a pastry bag fitted with a medium star tube, pages 13 and 14. Refrigerate until ready to serve. *Coffee Roll can be made 2 days ahead, covered and refrigerated.* Makes 6 to 8 servings.

Ribbon Trail

Whole eggs or egg yolks and sugar are beaten together to form a *ribbon*. This means that when the whisk or beater is lifted, the batter falls slowly in a thick trail which does not sink immediately into the batter but remains on top for a few seconds. The batter will be very light and smooth with no big bubbles. It must be beaten constantly until cool and will thicken slightly.

Strawberry Cake
Gâteau Fraisier

The cake base is like a rich sponge cake and is called a génoise.

1 Génoise, see below	2-1/2 pints strawberries, hulled
1/2 cup Sugar Syrup, page 140	1/4 cup red currant jelly, melted
2 tablespoons kirsch	
Butter Cream, page 141, made with	
3 egg yolks	

Génoise:

1/2 cup all-purpose flour	3 eggs
Pinch of salt	1/2 cup sugar
3 tablespoons butter, if desired	1/2 teaspoon vanilla extract

Prepare Génoise; cool. Prepare Sugar Syrup and stir in 1 tablespoon kirsch. Prepare Butter Cream and beat in remaining 1 tablespoon kirsch. Refrigerate. Cut thoroughly cooled Génoise into 2 equal layers with a long serrated knife. Cut with a sawing motion, moving knife without pressing on cake. Gently brush cut side of each layer with Sugar Syrup. Spread about 3/4 inch Butter Cream on bottom layer. Cover with whole strawberries, pressing them into Butter Cream. Spread a little more Butter Cream over strawberries. Cut remaining strawberries in half lengthwise. Stick strawberry halves into Butter Cream around edge of cake so they stand up straight with cut side facing out. Place remaining cake layer on top. Spread a thin layer of Butter Cream on top. Decorate with remaining strawberry halves. Gently brush jelly on all strawberry halves. Spoon remaining Butter Cream into a pastry bag fitted with a medium star tube and pipe rosettes on top, pages 13 and 14. Makes 6 to 8 servings.

Génoise:

Prepare an 8- to 9-inch round cake pan, page 139. Preheat oven to 350°F (175°C). Sift flour with salt twice. Clarify butter, if using, page 7. Place eggs in a large bowl; gradually beat in sugar. Beat at high speed 8 to 10 minutes until mixture is light and thick enough to leave a ribbon trail, page 145. Add vanilla. Sift flour over batter in 3 batches, gently folding in after each addition. If using clarified butter, fold in with last flour addition. Batter quickly loses volume after butter is added, so fold it in as quickly and gently as possible. Pour into prepared pan and immediately bake 25 to 30 minutes until cake shrinks slightly from sides of pan and top springs back when touched. Run a knife around sides of cake. Turn out of pan onto a rack to cool. *Génoise can be kept several days in an airtight container or frozen.*

Soft-Ball Stage

In making candy or sweets, you can easily recognize the soft-ball stage even if you don't have a candy thermometer. The syrup will form a soft ball when a little is lowered by spoon into a cup of cold water. Immediately remove syrup from the spoon while it's still in the water and press very lightly with your fingertips to feel if it holds the soft-ball shape.

How to Make Pie Pastry

1/Combine egg yolks, salt, water and softened butter in well. Mix lightly with your fingertips.

Metz Chocolate Cake
Gâteau au Chocolat de Metz

Potato starch and ground almonds are used instead of flour, giving a rich silky texture.

8 oz. semisweet chocolate, coarsely chopped
1/3 cup milk
1/2 teaspoon vanilla extract
2/3 cup granulated sugar

3/4 cup potato starch
1/2 cup blanched almonds, ground, pages 9-10
6 eggs, separated
Chocolate Royal Icing, see below

Chocolate Royal Icing:
3 oz. semisweet chocolate, coarsely chopped
3/4 cup powdered sugar, sifted

1 egg white
1 tablespoon warm water

Prepare a 10- to 11-inch springform pan or other deep round cake pan, page 139. Preheat oven to 350°F (175°C). In a small heavy saucepan, melt chocolate in milk over low heat, stirring constantly. When mixture is smooth, remove from heat and beat in vanilla, 1/3 cup granulated sugar and potato starch. In a small bowl, mix ground almonds with egg yolks; stir into chocolate mixture. In a large bowl, whip egg whites until stiff, page 7. Add remaining 1/3 cup granulated sugar. Beat 30 seconds to make a light meringue. Stir a fourth of the egg whites into chocolate mixture. Gently fold chocolate mixture into remaining egg whites. Pour into prepared pan. Bake 45 minutes; cake center should still be slightly soft. Cool. Turn cooled cake out of pan onto a rack placed over a tray to catch drippings. *Unfrosted cake can be kept in an airtight container about 1 week.* Not more than a few hours before serving, prepare Chocolate Royal Icing. Pour warm icing over cake. Quickly spread with a spatula as the icing sets fast. Makes 8 to 10 servings.

Chocolate Royal Icing:
Melt chocolate over boiling water. Cool slightly. Beat powdered sugar and egg white with a wooden spoon until smooth. Beat mixture into chocolate, then beat in water.

2/Gradually work flour into the butter-egg mixture with your fingertips until coarse crumbs are formed.

3/Smear butter mixture into flour by pushing dough with the heel of your hand. Scrape dough from work surface with a spatula.

Pie Pastry
Pâte Brisée

One of the secrets in pastry-making is to work quickly.

Use These Ingredients	To Make	
	1 (9- to 10-inch) pie shell or 6 (3-1/2-inch) tartlet shells	1 (11- to 12-inch) pie shell or 8 (3-1/2-inch) tartlet shells
all-purpose flour	1-1/2 cups	2 cups
butter	6 tablespoons	8 tablespoons
egg yolk(s)	1	2
salt	1/2 teaspoon	3/4 teaspoon
cold water	4 to 5 tablespoons	5 to 6 tablespoons

Sift flour onto a flat surface and make a large well in the center. Pound butter with a fist or rolling pin to soften. Place butter, egg yolks, salt and smaller amount of water in well and quickly work with fingertips until partly mixed. Using fingertips of both hands, gradually work in flour to form coarse crumbs. If crumbs are dry, add more water, a few drops at a time. Press dough into a ball— it should be soft but not sticky. Lightly flour working surface and blend dough by pushing it away with the heel of your hand and gathering it up with a spatula. Dough should be smooth and pliable and should peel easily from working surface. Press into a ball. Wrap in waxed paper and refrigerate 30 minutes. *Wrapped dough can be refrigerated up to 3 days.*

Alsatian Fruit Quiche
Quiche Alsacienne aux Fruits

Preheating the baking sheet prevents pastry from becoming soggy.

Pie Pastry, pages 148-149,
    made with 2 cups flour
3 tablespoons butter
2 lbs. tart apples, peeled,
    cored, quartered
1 tablespoon sugar
2 eggs

1 egg yolk
1/2 cup sugar
4 tablespoons milk
6 tablespoons whipping cream
1/2 teaspoon vanilla extract or
    1 teaspooon kirsch
Apricot Jam Glaze, see below

Apricot Jam Glaze:
1 (12-oz.) jar apricot jam
Juice of 1/2 lemon

2 to 3 tablespoons water

Refrigerate Pie Pastry at least 30 minutes. Preheat oven to 400°F (205°C) and heat a baking sheet in it. Melt butter in a skillet. Add apples and sprinkle with 1 tablespoon sugar. Cook quickly over medium heat, shaking skillet occasionally, until apples are lightly caramelized and almost tender, page 12. In a medium bowl, beat eggs, yolk and 1/2 cup sugar until thoroughly mixed; stir in milk, cream and vanilla or kirsch. Roll out Pie Pastry dough 1/4 inch thick and line an 11- to 12-inch pie pan, pages 14 and 15. Trim. Prick base of pie shell a few times. Arrange fruit in pie shell and pour egg mixture over apples, filling shell. Place quiche on hot baking sheet on bottom rack of oven. Bake 30 to 40 minutes until egg mixture is set. Transfer to a rack to cool. Prepare Apricot Jam Glaze. Brush cooled quiche with 1/3 cup glaze. *Alsatian Fruit Quiche can be made 1 day ahead, not more because pastry tends to get soggy. If made ahead cover and refrigerate.* Makes 6 to 8 servings.

Apricot Jam Glaze:
In a small non-aluminum saucepan, melt jam with lemon juice and enough water to make a pourable glaze. Work through a strainer and store in an airtight container. Reheat glaze to melt it before using. Makes about 1-1/2 cups of glaze.

Variations
Instead of apples, use any of the following: 2 pounds pears, peeled, cored and quartered; 1 pound Bing cherries, pitted; 1-1/2 pounds Italian or Greengage plums, halved and pitted; or 1-1/2 pounds apricots, halved and pitted. Omit step of caramelizing fruit. Arrange fruit in pastry shell, placing plums and apricots cut-side up so juice does not soak pastry.

Sweet Pie Pastry
Pâte Sucrée

Chilling this delicate dough makes it much easier to roll out.

Use These Ingredients	To Make 1 (11- to 12-inch) pie shell or 8 (3-1/2-inch) tartlet shells
all-purpose flour	1-1/2 cups
salt	1/2 teaspoon
sugar	1/2 cup
egg yolks	4
vanilla	1 teaspoon
butter	1/2 cup

Sift flour onto a flat surface and make a large well in the center. Place salt, sugar, egg yolks and vanilla in the well and mix these center ingredients with your fingertips until sugar dissolves. Pound butter with your fist or a rolling pin to soften. Add butter to well and quickly work with your fingertips until partly mixed. Gradually work in flour to make coarse crumbs, scraping work surface with a spatula. When dough comes together in a ball, lightly flour work surface and blend dough by pushing it away with the heel of your hand and gathering it up with spatula. Dough should be smooth and pliable and should peel easily from work surface. Press into a ball. Wrap in waxed paper and refrigerate 30 minutes. *Wrapped dough can be refrigerated up to 3 days.*

Caramelized Apple Pie
Tarte Tatin

Named for two impoverished sisters who had to earn their living by baking their father's favorite pie.

Sweet Pie Pastry, above
5 to 6 lbs. Golden Delicious apples
Juice of 1 lemon

2 cups sugar
1 cup water

Refrigerate Sweet Pie Pastry at least 30 minutes. Peel, halve and core apples, then rub with lemon juice to prevent darkening. Preheat oven to 375°F (190°C). In a medium, heavy saucepan, cook sugar and water until sugar is dissolved, then boil to a golden brown caramel, page 11. Remove from heat and let bubbles subside. Pour hot caramel into a 12-inch heavy skillet with a metal handle; immediately turn skillet to coat bottom evenly with caramel. Pack apple halves upright and overlapping in circles on caramel, completely covering caramel. Bake uncovered on bottom shelf of oven 20 minutes. Cool slightly, allowing steam to evaporate. Roll out chilled Sweet Pie Pastry dough to a 13-inch circle, 1/4 inch thick. Refrigerate on a baking sheet 15 minutes or until firm. Place dough circle on apples to cover completely. Tuck in edges. Prick dough several times with a fork. Bake 20 minutes or until crust is light golden. If apples are not tender, cook a little longer. Cool pie to lukewarm in skillet, then place a heatproof platter over skillet and invert together. Remove skillet. If any apples stick to bottom of skillet, remove with a spatula and replace on pie. Serve at room temperature. *Caramelized Apple Pie can be baked 6 to 8 hours ahead and kept at room temperature.* Makes 8 servings.

Fruit Tartlets
Tartelettes aux Fruits

Few desserts are as tempting as a display of fresh fruit tartlets—be sure to choose contrasting colors.

Sweet Pie Pastry, page 151
1 cup Apricot Jam Glaze, page 150, or
  Red Currant Jelly Glaze, see below

2 to 3 cups fresh fruit such as
  strawberries, raspberries, black or
  green grapes, cherries and tangerines

Red Currant Jelly Glaze:
1 (12-oz.) jar red currant jelly
1 tablespoon water

Refrigerate Sweet Pie Pastry at least 30 minutes. Preheat oven to 375°F (190°C). Grease eight 3-1/2-inch tartlet molds. Roll out chilled dough 1/4 inch thick and line molds, page 14. Refrigerate until dough is firm, then bake tartlet shells blind, page 16. Cool. *Unglazed tartlet shells can be kept 3 to 4 days in an airtight container.* Prepare jam or jelly glaze. Prepare chosen fruit: Hull strawberries and halve large ones, sort raspberries, pit grapes or cherries, and peel and section tangerines. Brush tartlet shells with melted jam or jelly glaze to help prevent fruit juice from making shells soggy. Arrange fruit in shells in an attractive pattern. Brush generously with glaze, filling in all cracks. Red fruit should be coated with Red Currant Jelly Glaze and green and yellow fruits with Apricot Jam Glaze. Serve filled tartlets at room temperature within 6 to 8 hours. Makes 8 tartlets.

Red Currant Jelly Glaze:
In a small non-aluminum saucepan, melt red currant jelly with 1 tablespoon water. Stir gently but don't whisk or jelly will become cloudy. Do not cook more than 1 to 2 minutes after melting or jelly will darken. Extra glaze can be stored in an airtight container. Reheat to melt before using. Makes about 1-1/2 cups of glaze.

Lemon Pie   Photo on pages 142 and 143.
Tarte au Citron

A specialty from Provence, which is almond and citrus country.

Sweet Pie Pastry, page 151
2 eggs
1/2 cup sugar
Grated peel and juice of 1-1/2 lemons

1/2 cup unsalted butter, clarified,
  page 7
2/3 cup blanched almonds, ground, pages 9-10

Refrigerate Sweet Pie Pastry at least 30 minutes. Preheat oven to 375°F (190°C). Roll out dough 1/4 inch thick and line an 11- to 12-inch pie pan, pages 14 and 15. Refrigerate, then bake blind, page 16, 15 minutes or until pastry is set and lightly browned. Cool slightly. Reduce oven temperature to 350°F (175°C). In a large bowl, beat eggs and sugar until pale and thick enough to leave a ribbon trail, page 145. Stir in lemon peel and juice, followed by melted butter and ground almonds. Pour lemon mixture into pie shell. Bake 20 to 25 minutes until filling is golden brown and set. Cool. Serve pie at room temperature within 6 to 8 hours. Makes 6 to 8 servings.

Almond Fruit Torte
Galette d'Amandes aux Fruits

Slanted wedges of almond pastry form a pinwheel on top of this torte.

2 cups blanched almonds, ground, pages 9-10
2/3 cup sugar
1 cup all-purpose flour
1/2 teaspoon salt
2/3 cup butter

1 egg yolk
Chantilly Cream, page 157, made with
   1-1/2 cups whipping cream
1 qt. fresh strawberries

Combine ground almonds and sugar in a medium bowl. Sift flour with salt onto a flat surface and add ground almond mixture. Pound butter with your fist or a rolling pin to soften. Make a large well in center of flour mixture; add softened butter and yolk. Using your fingertips, quickly work center ingredients until partly mixed. Gradually work in flour mixture to form coarse crumbs. Lightly flour work surface and blend dough by pushing it away with the heel of your hand and gathering it up with a metal spatula. Dough should be smooth and pliable and should peel easily from work surface. Press dough into a ball. Wrap in waxed paper and refrigerate 30 minutes. Grease 2 baking sheets. Preheat oven to 375°F (190°C). Divide dough into 3 equal portions. With the heel of your hand, press each portion to an 8-inch round on a prepared baking sheet. If available, place flan rings around edge to keep dough from spreading. Bake 10 to 12 minutes until golden brown. If not using flan rings, trim rounds while still warm, using a plate or lid as a guide. Cut one round into 6 to 8 uniform wedges. Transfer wedges and 2 whole rounds to a rack to cool. *Pastry can be kept 4 to 5 days in an airtight container or frozen.* Not more than 2 hours before serving, prepare Chantilly Cream. Set aside 1/2 cup for decoration and put it in a pastry bag fitted with a medium star tube, pages 13 and 14. Hull and halve strawberries, reserving 7 or 9 whole strawberries for decoration. Place one round of pastry on a platter; spread with Chantilly Cream and top with half the cut strawberries. Cover with more Chantilly Cream. Place second round of pastry on top and spread with Chantilly Cream. Using pastry bag, pipe 6 to 8 lines of Chantilly Cream from center to edge of round, marking 6 to 8 equal sections. Arrange remaining cut strawberries between lines of Chantilly Cream. Top each section with a wedge of pastry placed at a 45° angle and supported by a line of Chantilly Cream. Pipe a rosette of Chantilly Cream on each wedge and one in the center of the torte. Place a strawberry in the center of each rosette. Makes 6 to 8 servings.

Sand Cookies
Sablés de Caen

These butter cookies come from Normandy.

Sweet Pie Pastry, page 151
Grated peel of 1 orange

Egg Glaze, page 7

Prepare Sweet Pie Pastry, adding orange peel with egg yolks. Refrigerate at least 30 minutes. Grease 2 baking sheets. Preheat oven to 375°F (190°C). Roll out dough 1/4 inch thick. Stamp out rounds with a 3-1/2- to 4-inch cookie cutter. Place rounds on prepared baking sheets. Prepare Egg Glaze and brush over cookies. Using the tines of a table fork, score each cookie with a triangular design. Refrigerate 10 to 15 minutes. Bake 7 to 10 minutes until lightly browned. Do not overbake or cookies will be bitter. Transfer to a rack to cool. Makes 8 to 10 cookies.

Puff Pastry
Pâte Feuilletée

Set a baking sheet full of ice on your working surface to cool it.

Use These Ingredients	To Make	
	1 lb.	**1-1/2 lbs.**
unsalted butter	2/3 cup	1-1/4 cups
all-purpose flour	1-1/3 cups	2 cups
cake flour	2/3 cup	1 cup
salt	1 teaspoon	1-1/2 teaspoons
lemon juice	1 teaspoon	1-1/2 teaspoons
ice water	1/2 to 2/3 cup	3/4 to 1 cup

Melt 1 tablespoon butter; refrigerate remaining butter. Sift flour onto a cool marble slab or board and make a large well in center. Place salt, lemon juice, smaller amount of water and 1 tablespoon melted butter in center of well. Mix these ingredients with your fingertips briefly. Using finger-tips of both hands, gradually work in flour to form coarse crumbs. If crumbs are dry, add more water, a few drops at a time. Cut dough several times with a metal spatula to make sure ingre-dients are blended. Take care not to knead. Press dough into a ball; it should be quite soft. Wrap in waxed paper; refrigerate 15 minutes. Lightly flour remaining chilled butter, place between 2 sheets of waxed paper and flatten with a rolling pin. Remove top sheet of waxed paper. Fold but-ter in half, replace between waxed paper and continue flattening and folding until butter is pliable but not sticky; butter should be same consistency as dough. Shape butter into a 6-inch square and lightly flour it. On a cool work surface, roll dough to a 12-inch square so it is slightly thicker in the center than at the sides. Set butter in center and fold dough around it like an envelope. Place dough, seams down, on a floured work surface and press rolling pin on top 3 to 4 times to slightly flatten dough. Roll it into a rectangle 7 to 8 inches wide and 18 to 20 inches long. Fold rectangle like a business letter into 3 equal sections. Gently press seams with a rolling pin to seal and turn dough to bring seam side to your left so dough opens like a book. This is called a *turn.* Again, roll dough to a large rectangle and fold in 3. This is the second turn. Wrap dough in waxed paper; refrigerate 15 minutes. Repeat rolling process, giving dough 6 turns all together and letting dough rest overnight in refrigerator after fourth turn. Refrigerate at least 1 hour after the last turn. *Puff Pastry that has had either 4 or 6 turns can be tightly wrapped and refrigerated up to 3 days or frozen. Thaw frozen dough in refrigerator at least 3 hours before using.*

Roll out only as much dough as you need; dough is tougher when it is rolled a second time.

1/Fold each corner of rolled-out dough over softened square of butter.

2/Bubbles in dough indicate air between layers of butter and dough. This will help the pastry rise.

How to Make Puff Pastry

3/Fold dough rectangle into thirds. The process of rolling out and folding dough is called *a turn*.

Napoleon
Mille Feuille

The French name for this flaky layered dessert means a thousand leaves.

**Puff Pastry, pages 154-155, made with
2/3 cup butter
2 to 3 tablespoons Apricot Jam Glaze,
page 150**

**Powdered Sugar Icing, see below
Chantilly Cream, opposite, made with
1 cup whipping cream
4 tablespoons raspberry jam**

Powdered Sugar Icing:
**3/4 cup powdered sugar
1 tablespoon kirsch, rum or liqueur**

1 to 2 tablespoons water

Prepare Puff Pastry, completing all 6 turns. Refrigerate at least 1 hour. Preheat oven to 425°F (220°C). Roll out dough as thin as possible to a rectangle large enough to cover a baking sheet. Sprinkle water on baking sheet and place dough rectangle on top. Prick several times with a fork. Refrigerate 10 to 15 minutes. Bake 10 minutes or until golden. Reduce oven temperature to 350°F (175°C) and bake 5 minutes longer. Loosen pastry with a metal spatula, turn it over and bake 5 minutes longer or until very crisp. Transfer to a rack to cool. *Puff Pastry can be kept 1 to 2 days in an airtight container but is best eaten the day it is baked.* Not more than 3 hours before serving, trim edges of rectangle. Crush trimmings and reserve. Cut the pastry rectangle lengthwise in 3 equal strips. Brush top layer with Apricot Jam Glaze and let stand. Prepare Powdered Sugar Icing. Glaze prevents the icing from making the pastry soggy. Spread Powdered Sugar Icing on top layer. Prepare Chantilly Cream. Spread one strip of pastry with raspberry jam, top with another strip and spread with Chantilly Cream. Set iced strip of pastry on top and press lightly. Press reserved pastry crumbs around sides of Napoleon. Chill thoroughly. Just before serving, cut Napoleon in 1-1/2-inch to 2-inch slices with a serrated knife. Makes 8 servings.

Powdered Sugar Icing:
Sift powdered sugar into a medium bowl. Beat in kirsch, rum or liqueur and 1 tablespoon water. Mix to a smooth stiff paste. Place bowl in a pan of hot water and heat icing to lukewarm; icing should be thick enough to coat the back of a spoon, page 12. If too thick, add more water. If too thin, beat in more sifted powdered sugar. Use warm. Makes about 1/2 cup of icing.

Variation

Pastry Cream Napoleon (Mille Feuille à la Crème Pâtissière): Prepare vanilla-flavored pastry cream according to Chocolate Pastry Cream, page 161, omitting chocolate and scalding milk with 1 vanilla bean split lengthwise by bringing just to a boil. Cover and let stand 15 minutes to steep vanilla flavor. Remove vanilla bean before pouring hot milk onto yolk mixture. Follow recipe for Napoleon, substituting vanilla-flavored pastry cream for Chantilly Cream.

Apple Turnovers   Photo on pages 142 and 143.
Chaussons aux Pommes

Chaussons means woolly socks—*an inelegant but vivid name for these warming apple turnovers.*

**Puff Pastry, pages 154-155, made with
  2/3 cup butter**
3 tablespoons butter
**1-1/4 lbs. Golden Delicious or McIntosh
  apples, peeled, cored, sliced**

2 to 3 tablespoons granulated sugar
Egg Glaze, page 7
1/4 cup powdered sugar

Prepare Puff Pastry, completing all 6 turns. Refrigerate at least 1 hour. Heat butter in a large skillet. Add apples. Sprinkle with granulated sugar. Cook quickly over medium heat, shaking pan occasionally, until apple slices are transparent and lightly caramelized, page 12. Cool apples, then refrigerate. Preheat oven to 425°F (220°C). Sprinkle water on a baking sheet. Roll out chilled dough 1/4 inch thick. Stamp out 4-inch rounds with a fluted cookie cutter. Put a spoonful of cold cooked apples in center of each round; do not overfill or turnovers will burst. Brush borders with Egg Glaze and fold rounds over to make half-circles. Press edges with a fork to seal. Transfer pastries to a baking sheet. Brush tops with Egg Glaze and make 3 slits on each top with a knife point to let steam escape. Refrigerate 10 to 15 minutes. Bake 20 to 25 minutes until puffed and browned. Remove from oven. Raise oven temperature to broil. Sprinkle tops with powdered sugar. Broil a few seconds to obtain a shiny glaze, being careful not to burn sugar. Serve hot or cold. Apple Turnovers are best eaten the day they are baked. *Unbaked or baked turnovers can be frozen.* Makes 20 turnovers.

Variation

Substitute 2 pounds of tart apples for 1-1/4 pounds of Golden Delicious or McIntosh apples by making apple puree: Spread a heavy saucepan with 3 tablespoons butter, add sliced apples and 3 tablespoons sugar or to taste. Press a piece of buttered foil over apples; cover with a lid. Cook over low heat 25 to 30 minutes until apples are very soft. Taste and add sugar if necessary. Cool puree before filling turnovers.

Chantilly Cream
Crème Chantilly

Try serving this with fresh strawberries or your favorite fruit pie.

Use These Ingredients	To Make			
	About 1 cup	**About 1-1/2 cups**	**About 2 cups**	**About 3 cups**
whipping cream	1/2 cup	3/4 cup	1 cup	1-1/2 cups
vanilla extract	1/3 teaspoon	1/2 teaspoon	2/3 teaspoon	1 teaspoon
sugar	1 teaspoon	1-1/2 teaspoons	2 teaspoons	1 tablespoon

Cream may be beaten by hand or with an electric mixer. Chill cream, bowl and whisk or beaters before whipping. Whip cream until it starts to thicken. Add vanilla and sugar. Continue beating until cream holds a stiff shape and sticks to whisk or beaters.

Palm Leaves
Palmiers

These pastries are golden with caramel which is formed when sugar in the dough browns in the oven.

**Puff Pastry, pages 154-155, made with
2/3 cup butter, or 1 lb.
Puff Pastry trimmings**

About 1 cup sugar

Prepare Puff Pastry, completing 4 turns. Refrigerate at least 1 hour. Do last 2 turns, sprinkling work surface with sugar instead of flour. If using Puff Pastry trimmings, give 2 extra turns, using sugar instead of flour on the work surface. Refrigerate dough at least 30 minutes. Sprinkle water on 2 baking sheets. Preheat oven to 425°F (220°C). Roll out dough to a 20" x 12" rectangle, continuing to use sugar on work surface. Trim edges. Fold one long edge over twice to reach center of dough. Repeat with other long edge. Press folded dough lightly with a rolling pin to seal. Fold one folded section of dough on top of the other. Lightly press with a rolling pin. Use a sharp knife to cut dough into 1/4-inch slices. Place on prepared baking sheets, leaving room to let leaves more than double in size. Open slices slightly to round them. Refrigerate 15 minutes. Bake 6 to 8 minutes until undersides begin to brown. Turn leaves over with a metal spatula. Bake 3 to 4 minutes longer until golden. Leaves burn quickly, so watch carefully. Makes about 30 pastries.

How to Make Palm Leaves

Work on a surface covered with granulated sugar instead of flour. Fold over each edge of the Puff Pastry rectangle twice, then fold in half. Chill the pastry if it becomes too soft to cut into slices.

Meringues with Whipped Cream
Meringues Chantilly

Instead of using a pastry bag, you can shape the meringue into ovals with 2 tablespoons.

4 egg whites
1-1/4 cups granulated sugar
1 teaspoon vanilla extract

1/4 cup powdered sugar
Chantilly Cream, page 157, made with
1 cup whipping cream

Line 2 baking sheets with non-stick silicone paper or thoroughly grease and flour baking sheets. Preheat oven to 275°F (135°C). In a large bowl, whip egg whites until stiff, page 7. Add 2 tablespoons granulated sugar and beat 30 seconds to make a light meringue. Fold in remaining granulated sugar with vanilla. Gently spoon meringue into a pastry bag fitted with a 1/2-inch plain tube and pipe mounds of meringue about 3 inches in diameter onto prepared baking sheets. Space mounds at least 1 inch apart. Generously sprinkle meringues with powdered sugar. Bake 1 hour or until firm. If meringues start to brown, reduce heat to 250°F (120°C). Remove meringues from baking sheet by pulling paper off or lifting meringues carefully with a spatula. Gently press meringue bottoms to collapse them and form a hollow. Return meringues, hollow-side up, to baking sheets. Bake 30 minutes longer or until shells are crisp. Meringues should be a pale cream color with a slightly sticky center. *Unfilled meringues can be kept 2 to 3 weeks in an airtight container.* Not more than 2 hours before serving, prepare Chantilly Cream and spoon into hollowed meringue bottoms. Place another meringue over Chantilly Cream to make a sandwich. Makes 6 filled meringues.

Variations

Almond Rocks (Rochers de Neige): Fold 1/2 cup sliced almonds into meringue mixture and spoon mixture into rough 1-1/2-inch mounds on prepared baking sheet. Sprinkle with a few more sliced almonds. Bake 1 hour or until firm on outside but soft in center. Omit Chantilly Cream. Makes about 30 individual meringues.

Raisin Rocks (Rochers aux Raisins): Follow recipe for Almond Rocks, substituting 1/2 cup raisins or dried currants for the sliced almonds.

Cream Puff Pastry
Pâte à Choux

For unusual appetizers, fill tiny cream puffs with a chicken and mayonnaise mixture.

Use These Ingredients	To Make	
	10 (3-inch) cream puffs or 8 to 10 éclairs	20 (3-inch) cream puffs or 16 to 20 éclairs
all-purpose flour	1/2 cup	1 cup
water	1/2 cup	1 cup
salt	1/4 teaspoon	3/4 teaspoon
butter	1/4 cup	1/2 cup
eggs	2 to 3	4 to 5

Sift flour onto a piece of waxed paper. In a small or medium saucepan, depending on quantities used, heat water, salt and butter until butter is melted. Bring to a boil. Remove from heat as soon as liquid boils. Prolonged boiling of the butter-and-water mixture evaporates the water and changes dough proportions. Add all the flour at once and beat vigorously with a wooden spoon until mixture is smooth and pulls away from pan to form a ball. Beat 30 seconds to 1 minute over low heat to dry mixture. Remove from heat and cool slightly. Beat 1 egg and set aside. Beat remaining eggs into warm dough, one by one, thoroughly beating after each addition. Beat enough of the reserved egg into the dough to make a very shiny mixture which just falls from the spoon. This consistency is very important. All the reserved egg may not be needed. If not using immediately, rub dough surface with butter while still warm to prevent a skin from forming, page 13. Cool. *Cream Puff Pastry can be tightly covered and refrigerated 8 hours.*

Cream Puffs   Photo on pages 142 and 143.
Choux à la Crème

Try to pipe the puffs so all are the same size to ensure even baking.

**Cream Puff Pastry, above, made with
  1 cup flour**
Egg Glaze, page 7

**Chantilly Cream, page 157, made with
  1-1/2 cups whipping cream
  1/4 cup powdered sugar**

Preheat oven to 400°F (205°C). Lightly grease 2 baking sheets. Spoon Cream Puff Pastry into a pastry bag fitted with a 1/2-inch plain tube. Pipe 1-1/2-inch mounds of pastry on prepared baking sheets. Or, drop mounds of dough onto baking sheet using 2 spoons. Leave room to let puffs double in size. Brush with Egg Glaze, smoothing surface at same time. Bake 25 to 30 minutes until firm and browned. Cracks that form as puffs bake should also be browned. Transfer puffs to a rack to cool. *Puffs can be stored overnight in an airtight container but are best eaten within a few hours of baking.* Not more than 2 hours before serving, prepare Chantilly Cream. Spoon cream into a pastry bag fitted with a 1/4-inch plain tube. Cut a slit in each puff just large enough to insert pastry tube. Fill puffs with cream. Sprinkle with powdered sugar and arrange on a serving plate. Makes twenty 3-inch Cream Puffs.

Chocolate Eclairs
Eclairs au Chocolat

Now you can enjoy fresh homemade éclairs!

**Cream Puff Pastry, opposite, made with
 1 cup flour**
Egg Glaze, page 7

Chocolate Pastry Cream, see below
Chocolate Powdered Sugar Icing, see below

Chocolate Pastry Cream:
3 oz. semisweet chocolate, coarsely chopped
2 cups milk
6 egg yolks

1/2 cup sugar
5 tablespoons all-purpose flour

Chocolate Powdered Sugar Icing:
1-1/2 cups powdered sugar
1 oz. semisweet chocolate, coarsely chopped

1 to 4 tablespoons water

Preheat oven to 400°F (205°C). Lightly grease 2 baking sheets. Spoon Cream Puff Pastry into a pastry bag fitted with a 1/2-inch plain tube. Pipe 4-inch strips of dough onto prepared baking sheets. Leave room to let éclairs double in size. Brush with Egg Glaze, smoothing surface at same time. To help rise evenly, press top of each éclair lightly with the back of a fork dipped in cold water. Bake 25 to 30 minutes until firm and browned. Cracks that form as éclairs bake should also be browned. Transfer éclairs to a rack to cool. *Eclairs can be stored overnight in an airtight container but are best eaten within a few hours of baking.* Prepare Chocolate Pastry Cream. Prepare Chocolate Powdered Sugar Icing. Dip top of each éclair in icing and let stand in a dry place. *Eclairs can be iced 4 to 5 hours before serving.* Not more than 2 hours before serving, spoon Chocolate Pastry Cream into a pastry bag fitted with a 1/4-inch plain tube. Poke 2 holes in the side of each éclair with the tube tip. Pipe pastry cream in each hole to fill éclair. Makes 16 to 20 éclairs.

Chocolate Pastry Cream:
Melt chocolate over a pan of boiling water. Cool slightly. In a medium saucepan, scald milk by bringing it just to a boil. Beat egg yolks with sugar until thick and pale. Stir in flour. Whisk in half the hot milk, then whisk mixture back into remaining hot milk in saucepan. Bring just to a boil, whisking constantly. Remove from heat and cool to lukewarm. Beat in melted chocolate. If not using immediately, rub surface with butter while still warm to prevent a skin from forming, page 13. Just before using, beat until smooth. Makes 2-1/4 cups of pastry cream.

Chocolate Powdered Sugar Icing:
Sift powdered sugar into a medium bowl. Melt chocolate over a pan of boiling water. Beat melted chocolate and 1 to 2 tablespoons water into powdered sugar. Mix to a smooth, stiff paste. Place bowl in a pan of hot water and heat icing to lukewarm; icing should be thick enough to coat the back of a spoon, page 12. If too thick, add more water. If too thin, beat in more sifted powdered sugar. Use warm. Makes about 1 cup of icing.

Cream puff pastry is always called pastry *because it acts as a container for fillings, but it is baked rather like a cake with many eggs that make it rise.*

Chantilly Swans
Cygnes Chantilly

Graceful swans are almost too pretty to eat.

**Cream Puff Pastry, page 160, made with
  1 cup flour
Egg Glaze, page 7**

**Chantilly Cream, page 157, made with
  1-1/2 cups whipping cream
1/4 cup powdered sugar**

Preheat oven to 400°F (205°C). Lightly grease 2 baking sheets. Spoon Cream Puff Pastry into a pastry bag fitted with a 3/8-inch plain tube. Pipe ten to twelve 1-1/2'' x 3'' ovals on one baking sheet for swan bodies, leaving room to let ovals double in size. Hold a 1/4-inch plain tube firmly over the 3/8-inch one and pipe fifteen S-shape necks, 3 to 4 inches long, on second baking sheet, making extra to allow for breakage. Brush necks and ovals with Egg Glaze, smoothing pastry surface at same time. To help rise evenly, press each body lightly with the back of a fork dipped in cold water. Bake necks and bodies 10 to 15 minutes until necks are firm and browned. Transfer necks to a rack to cool. Bake bodies 10 to 15 minutes longer until crisp and browned. Cracks that form as they bake should also be browned. Transfer to a rack to cool. *Swans are best eaten within a few hours of baking but necks and bodies can be stored overnight in an airtight container.* Not more than 2 hours before serving, prepare Chantilly Cream. Spoon into a pastry bag fitted with a 3/8-inch star tube, pages 13 and 14. Cut oval puffs in half horizontally, then cut each top piece in half lengthwise for the wings. Pipe in enough Chantilly Cream to fill open bottom half of each body. Insert neck at one end of body. Place wings in cream at an angle so they spread up and out from neck. Sprinkle swans with powdered sugar and arrange on a serving dish. Makes 10 to 12 swans.

Variation
Strawberry Chantilly Swans (Cygnes Chantilly aux Fraises): Fill swans with halved strawberries and top with cream.

Cats' Tongues
Langues de Chat

A wonderful crisp cookie to serve with homemade ice cream.

**1/3 cup all-purpose flour
Pinch of salt
1/4 cup butter**

**1/3 cup sugar
3 egg whites
1/2 teaspoon vanilla extract**

Grease and flour 2 baking sheets. Preheat oven to 450°F (230°C). In a large bowl, sift flour with salt. Cream butter; beat in sugar and continue beating until mixture is light and fluffy. In a small bowl, whip egg whites until soft peaks form. Stir flour, vanilla and egg whites into butter mixture, alternating a third of the flour with half the egg whites and mixing well after each addition. Spoon mixture into a pastry bag fitted with a 1/4-inch plain tube and pipe 3-inch pencils of batter onto prepared baking sheets, leaving room for cookies to spread. Bake 6 to 8 minutes until edges are golden; centers will be pale. Transfer to a rack to cool. *Cookies can be kept in an airtight container 3 to 4 days.* Makes about 40 cookies.

1/Cream Puff Pastry is the right consistency for piping when it falls thickly from the spoon.

2/Pipe Chantilly Cream into baked swan bodies. Arrange necks and wings in the cream and sprinkle with powdered sugar.

How to Make Chantilly Swans

Ladyfingers
Biscuits à la Cuiller

Ladyfingers should be firm outside, soft inside and only lightly browned.

2/3 cup all-purpose flour
Pinch of salt
4 eggs, separated

1/2 cup granulated sugar
1/2 teaspoon vanilla extract
1/2 cup powdered sugar

Grease and flour a baking sheet. Preheat oven to 350°F (175°C). Sift flour with salt. In a large bowl, beat egg yolks with 1/4 cup granulated sugar and vanilla until pale and thick enough to leave a ribbon trail, page 145. In a medium bowl, whip egg whites until stiff, page 7. Add remaining 1/4 cup granulated sugar. Beat 30 seconds longer to make a light meringue. Sift flour over egg yolk mixture. Add a fourth of the meringue and gently fold together. Fold in remaining meringue in 2 batches. Gently spoon batter into a pastry bag fitted with a 5/8-inch plain tube. Pipe uniform 3-1/2-inch Ladyfingers at least 1 inch apart on prepared baking sheet. Sprinkle with powdered sugar. Bake 15 to 18 minutes, wedging oven door ajar with a spoon so Ladyfingers dry as they bake. Remove from oven. Cool slightly on baking sheet. Transfer to a rack to cool completely. Makes about 30 Ladyfingers.

Strawberry Savarin
Savarin aux Fraises

Dough for savarin and babas is almost identical, but savarin is always baked in a ring.

2 cups strawberries
4 tablespoons sugar
1 cup all-purpose flour
2 tablespoons lukewarm water
2/3 pkg. dry yeast or
   2/3 cake compressed yeast

3 eggs
1/2 teaspoon salt
1/4 cup butter, softened
Lemon Syrup, see below
2 to 3 tablespoons rum
1/4 cup red currant jelly

Lemon Syrup:
1 cup sugar
1-1/3 cups water

Pared peel and juice of 1/2 lemon

Hull strawberries and sprinkle with 2 tablespoons sugar. Cover and refrigerate 1 to 2 hours. Sift flour into a warmed large bowl. Make a well in center of flour and pour in lukewarm water. Sprinkle yeast over water and let stand 5 minutes to dissolve yeast. Add eggs, salt and 2 tablespoons sugar. Using a mixer fitted with a dough hook, beat mixture to a smooth and elastic dough. If you do not have a dough hook, use the classic method for preparing savarin dough: Combine center ingredients with your fingertips; gradually draw in flour to make a smooth dough; beat vigorously with cupped fingers, raising it and letting it fall back into the bowl with a slap; continue beating 5 minutes or until dough is smooth and elastic. Cover bowl with a damp cloth towel. Let rise in a warm place 45 minutes to 1 hour until doubled in bulk. Grease a 1-1/2-quart savarin or ring mold. Beat butter into risen dough until smooth. Spoon into prepared mold. Cover with a damp cloth towel and let rise in a warm place 45 minutes to 1 hour until dough rises to top of mold. Preheat oven to 400°F (205°C). Bake 20 to 25 minutes until savarin is browned and shrinks from sides of pan. Remove from mold and place on a rack over a tray. *Unsoaked Savarin can be kept 2 to 3 days in an airtight container or frozen. It can be soaked with syrup up to 4 hours ahead. Warm unsoaked Savarin covered in a 250°F (120°C) oven before basting with syrup.* Not more than 4 hours ahead, prepare Lemon Syrup. Spoon hot syrup over savarin until it absorbs as much as possible. Savarin will swell and look shiny. Transfer to a platter. Just before serving, sprinkle rum over savarin and pile strawberries in center. Melt jelly in a small saucepan. Brush over strawberries and savarin to glaze.

Lemon Syrup:
Heat sugar and water in a small saucepan until dissolved. Boil and add lemon peel. Reduce heat and simmer 5 minutes. Remove from heat and stir in lemon juice. Discard peel.

Rum Babas   Photo on pages 142 and 143.
Babas au Rhum

Dariole molds for making babas are bucket-shaped. You can use any small deep molds.

2/3 cup dried currants or raisins	4 eggs
1/2 cup rum	1 teaspoon salt
1-3/4 cups all-purpose flour	1 tablespoon sugar
3 tablespoons lukewarm water	1/2 cup butter, softened
1 pkg. dry yeast or 1 cake compressed yeast	Sugar Syrup, see below

Sugar Syrup:
2-1/2 cups sugar
1 qt. water

Wash currants or raisins and soak in 1/3 cup rum. Sift flour into a warmed large bowl. Make a well in center of flour and pour in lukewarm water. Sprinkle yeast over water and let stand 5 minutes to dissolve yeast. Add eggs, salt and sugar. Using a mixer fitted with a dough hook, beat mixture to a smooth and elastic dough. If you do not have a dough hook, use the classic method for preparing baba dough: Combine center ingredients with your fingertips; gradually draw in flour to make a smooth dough; beat dough vigorously with cupped fingers, raising it and letting it fall back into the bowl with a slap; continue beating 5 minutes or until dough is smooth and elastic. Cover bowl with a damp cloth towel and let rise in a warm place 45 minutes to 1 hour until doubled in bulk. Butter eight 1-cup or sixteen 1/2-cup dariole molds. Chill molds in freezer; butter them again. Beat softened butter into risen dough until smooth. Drain currants or raisins, reserving rum, and stir them into dough. Drop dough from a spoon to fill molds one-third full. Place molds on a baking sheet. Cover with a damp cloth towel and let rise in a warm place 45 minutes to 1 hour until molds are almost full. Preheat oven to 400°F (205°C). Bake risen dough 20 to 25 minutes until babas are browned and begin to shrink from sides of molds. Immediately remove babas from molds. *Babas can be kept 2 to 3 days in an airtight container or frozen. They can be soaked 3 or 4 hours ahead. A few hours before serving, warm unsoaked babas covered in a 250°F (120°C) oven before soaking in syrup.* Not more than 4 hours ahead, prepare Sugar Syrup. Remove from heat. Place warm babas in syrup. Carefully turn them several times with a large spoon so they absorb as much syrup as possible. Babas will swell and look shiny. Using a large slotted spoon, carefully remove and place on a platter. Reserve remaining syrup. Just before serving, sprinkle a little of the rum drained from currants or raisins over babas. Add remaining rum to reserved syrup and serve separately. Decorate as desired. Makes 8 large or 16 small babas.

Sugar Syrup:
Heat sugar and water in a medium saucepan over low heat until sugar is dissolved. Boil 2 to 3 minutes until syrup is clear.

Brioche

Brioche

This rich yeast bread is perfect for brunch or afternoon tea — it's the most buttery of French yeast doughs.

2 tablespoons lukewarm water
1-1/2 pkgs. dry yeast or 1-1/2 cakes
   compressed yeast, crumbled
4 cups all-purpose flour
7 or 8 eggs

2 teaspoons salt
3 tablespoons sugar
1-1/2 cups unsalted butter
Egg Glaze, page 7

Put lukewarm water into a medium bowl. Stir in yeast, then add a little flour. Let rise 5 to 10 minutes. Sift remaining flour into a large mixer bowl. Add 7 eggs, salt and sugar to yeast mixture and mix lightly. Pour egg and yeast mixture into flour. Using a mixer fitted with a dough hook, beat mixture to a soft sticky dough. If dough is dry, beat last egg and add it little by little. Pound butter with your fist or a rolling pin to soften. Beat butter into dough using dough hook until completely mixed in. Place dough in a lightly oiled bowl. Turn dough to oil all sides. Cover bowl with a damp cloth towel and let rise at room temperature 2 hours or until nearly doubled in bulk. Place risen dough on floured work surface. Fold a third of the dough over the middle third and the remaining third over all, patting to knock out air. Return to bowl and cover with a damp towel. Let rise at room temperature until doubled in bulk or overnight in the refrigerator. Brioche dough is much easier to handle if refrigerated. Preheat oven to 425°F (220°C). Grease fifteen 3-inch brioche pans or two 6-inch brioche pans. Knead dough gently just to knock out air and divide it into 15 pieces for individual brioches or in half for large brioches. Pinch off a third of each piece of dough and shape both large and small pieces into balls. Place a large ball in each brioche pan. Cut a deep cross on top and crown it with a smaller ball of dough. An alternate method is to make holes in the larger balls and place the smaller balls on the holes. Let small brioches rise in a warm place 15 minutes and large brioches 20 to 25 minutes until pans are almost full. Brush risen dough with Egg Glaze and bake small brioches 15 to 20 minutes until browned. Baked brioches will sound hollow when tapped on bottoms. Bake large brioches 15 minutes, then reduce oven temperature to 375°F (190°C). Bake 30 to 40 minutes longer until brioches begin to pull away from sides of pans and sound hollow when tapped on bottoms. Turn out onto a rack to cool. *Brioches can be stored 1 to 2 days in an airtight container but are best eaten the day they are baked.* Makes 15 small or 2 large brioches.

Classic Method for Preparing Brioche Dough

If you don't have a dough hook, prepare Brioche dough the way French cooks have been doing for centuries: Sift flour onto a marble slab or board and make a large well in the center. Place salt and sugar in piles on one side of well, and yeast on another side of well, as far from salt and sugar as possible. Use your fingers to combine yeast with warm water. Be careful not to mix yeast with salt or sugar. Mix a little flour into yeast mixture, still keeping it separate from salt and sugar. Let rise 5 to 10 minutes. Break in 7 eggs. Briefly mix eggs with salt, sugar and yeast mixture using your fingertips. Sprinkle with some flour so it is no longer visible. Using your fingertips, quickly work flour into center ingredients forming coarse crumbs. Do not let liquid escape from well. If dough is dry, beat last egg and add it little by little. Press dough firmly together — it should be soft and sticky. Knead dough by lifting it up and slapping it down on floured work surface 5 to 10 minutes until very smooth and elastic. Pound butter with your fist or a rolling pin to soften. Mix into dough, then knead by slapping it on work surface as lightly as possible just until butter is completely mixed in. Place dough in a lightly oiled bowl and proceed according to Brioche recipe.

One method of making the Brioches is to make a hole in the center of each large ball of dough with your flour-coated finger. Press the smaller pieces of dough into pear shapes and place them on the holes.

How to Make Small Brioches

Chocolate Truffles   Photo on pages 2 and 3.
Truffes au Chocolat

Chocolate balls, roughly rolled in cocoa to resemble truffles, look like the real thing.

10 oz. semisweet chocolate, chopped	**1 teaspoon brandy or rum**
1/4 cup butter	**1 tablespoon whipping cream**
2 tablespoons strong black coffee	**1/2 cup cocoa powder, sweetened or**
1 cup powdered sugar, sifted	**unsweetened**

Melt 6 ounces chocolate with butter over a pan of boiling water. Stir in coffee, powdered sugar, brandy or rum and cream. Refrigerate 30 to 40 minutes until fairly firm. Spoon heaped teaspoons of chocolate mixture onto a sheet of waxed paper. Shape into balls and refrigerate 2 hours or until firm. Melt remaining 4 ounces chocolate in a double boiler. Put cocoa powder in a small tray with raised edges. Spear each chocolate ball with a wooden pick and dip in melted chocolate to coat lightly. Quickly transfer to cocoa powder. Spoon powder over each truffle to cover. If working with unsweetened cocoa powder, use enough to just coat truffles or they will be bitter. Let truffles harden 1 hour at room temperature. Place on a clean sheet of waxed paper. Remove toothpicks. Refrigerate truffles in an airtight container with waxed paper between layers. Because their flavor mellows with age, store truffles at least 1 week but not more than 1 month. Makes about 25 truffles.

Desserts

Hot, cold and frozen desserts cover a wide range. One group concentrates on richness as in the soufflés, creams, mousses and ice creams, laden with eggs or cream and most often flavored with chocolate, coffee, caramel or vanilla. In another approach, rich ingredients are balanced by the sharp taste of a fruit like lemon or strawberry, which we see demonstrated in Cold Lemon Soufflé and Strawberry Charlotte Malakoff. Or the fruit may stand on its own, as in fruit sherbets or Pears in Red Wine.

Just a few luxury desserts combine the best of both worlds: Pears Belle Hélène brings together poached pears, vanilla ice cream and chocolate sauce; or Pineapple Surprise, a lively mixture of fruit sherbet, fresh pineapple and kirsch concealed beneath a blanket of meringue. Compare these with the simple appeal of Apple Charlotte or Caramel Cream and you'll see something for every occasion.

Coming at the end of the meal as it does, a dessert must have impact. Take care with presentation—even simple Pears in Red Wine deserve a pretty dish. And where would Chocolate Mousse be without its rosette of whipped cream, or Peach Melba without its raspberry sauce? Pay attention to texture so your soufflés are airy and your ice creams creamy and ultrarich. Above all, emphasize flavor, adding lemon juice to develop the tartness of fruits and vanilla to enhance chocolate and coffee. Here the French often turn to liqueurs, combining rum with chocolate, Calvados with apples, and kirsch with other fruits. For a milder flavor, Cointreau and Grand Marnier blend with almost anything.

How to Make Desserts

Most desserts contain eggs, so making them can amount to an exercise in egg cookery. For soufflés and mousses that rely on egg whites for lightness, it is very important to whip the whites stiffly, page 7, and fold them as lightly as possible, pages 10 and 11. Many cold and frozen desserts are thickened with egg yolks which will curdle if overheated or cooked too long. So, when egg yolks are part of a custard mixture, as in Caramel Cream or Petits Pots de Crème, cooking is done in a water bath to control the temperature, page 9. For mousses and custard sauce, when the mixtures are cooked over direct heat, you must always keep the temperature low. And don't expect egg yolks to thicken a custard or sauce in the same way as flour does—the effect will be gradual and the finished mixture light and smooth.

There are three main types of frozen desserts: ice cream, based on custard and enriched with whipped cream; sherbet, based on fruit juice, fruit puree or wine, and sweetened with sugar syrup; and parfaits, the richest of all, based on cooked sugar and egg yolks lightened with cream. Be sure to begin with a concentrated mixture, as freezing tends to subdue flavor, but don't overdo the sugar or alcohol. Too much of either can prevent a mixture from freezing.

For the best ice cream and sherbet, constant mixing during freezing is necessary to break up ice crystals which would give the mixture a rough texture. In a traditional churn freezer, the mixture is poured into a central container surrounded by ice and salt and is beaten as it freezes with a paddle turned by a crank or by electricity. You can also get electric machines that go directly inside the freezer, saving the bother with ice and salt. Both ice cream and sherbet can be made in a regular freezer without churning, opposite and page 181, but you may be disappointed by their texture. Instead you may opt for a parfait, which is so rich it freezes smoothly without a churn.

How to Prepare Desserts Ahead

By definition, cold and frozen desserts can be made ahead; just put them in the freezer or refrigerator and they will wait for you. However, bear in mind that although ice cream will keep up to three months without spoiling, and sherbet up to four weeks, both taste best and are smoothest when freshly made. If a frozen dessert has been stored in the freezer for more than 12 hours, leave it in the refrigerator one to two hours before serving so it softens enough to make spooning easy. The flavor will be better too. Remember to chill serving spoons and bowls.

Many hot desserts can be prepared ahead and reheated, notably crepes. Unfilled, they keep well two to three days in the refrigerator or up to a month in the freezer, and when filled they can usually wait an hour or two for the final cooking or flaming. Even for soufflés a good deal of preparation can be done in advance, though it is risky to whip up the egg whites ahead. However, once in the oven, the French dictum that "a soufflé never waits for guests, it is they who must wait for the soufflé," is the unbreakable law.

How to Freeze Ice Cream & Sherbet Without a Churn Freezer

Ice cream or sherbet can be made directly in your freezer. The mixture will have good flavor, but a rougher texture than if it had been churned. Spoon the ice cream or sherbet mixture into ice-cube trays, cover with foil and freeze. Chill a bowl and whisk. When the mixture is slushy, tip it into the chilled bowl and whisk until smooth. Return it to ice-cube trays and continue freezing. For a smoother texture, repeat the whisking at least once more—or several times—until the mixture is completely frozen.

SWEET DECORATION IDEAS		
Ingredient	What to Do	Where to Use
chocolate bar	Grate or melt	Top of cakes, cold and frozen desserts
powder	Sprinkle	Top of some cakes, chocolate truffles
sprinkles	Scatter	Top and especially to cover sides of some cakes
powdered sugar	Sift and sprinkle	Top of cakes, pastries, hot soufflés, crepes
butter cream	Pipe rosettes, stars and other shapes, or spread	Top and sides of cakes
Chantilly cream	Pipe rosettes, stars and other shapes, or spread	Top and sides of cakes, pastries, cold and frozen desserts
jam glaze	Brush	Top of tarts and some cakes and pastries
fruit, fresh or poached	Leave whole if small, or cut in uniform pieces if large	Top of cakes, cold and frozen desserts
candied fruits	Halve or cut in small uniform pieces	Top and sides of cakes, pastries cold and frozen desserts
nuts whole, peeled	Toast and chop	Top and especially to cover sides of cakes, cold and frozen desserts
sliced	Toast	Top and especially to cover sides of cakes, cold and frozen desserts
small candies such as silver cake decors candied violets	Use sparingly	Top of cakes, cold and frozen desserts

Apple Charlotte
Charlotte aux Pommes

One of the traditional French desserts—delicious with vanilla Custard Sauce, see below.

3/4 cup butter
4 lbs. tart apples (10 to 12), cored,
   thinly sliced
1 vanilla bean, split lengthwise
1 thinly pared strip lemon peel
Few drops of lemon juice
Pinch of cinnamon

3/4 cup sugar
1 teaspoon Calvados or other
   apple brandy, if desired
1 tablespoon apricot jam
Additional sugar
8 to 10 slices firm white bread,
   crusts removed

Spread the bottom of a large heavy saucepan with 4 tablespoons butter; add apple slices, vanilla bean, lemon peel, lemon juice and cinnamon. Press a piece of buttered foil over apples and cover with a lid. Cook over low heat until apples are very soft, stirring occasionally. Remove vanilla bean and lemon peel. Add sugar. Stir constantly over medium heat until puree is so thick it barely falls from the spoon. If puree is too soft, the charlotte will collapse when unmolded. Add Calvados, if desired, and apricot jam. Simmer 1 minute. Add more sugar to taste. Preheat oven to 400°F (205°C). Place a round of buttered waxed paper in the bottom of a 1-quart charlotte mold. Clarify 6 tablespoons butter, page 7. Cut 14 to 16 fingers of bread 1-1/2 inches wide to line sides of mold and 4 to 6 triangular pieces for bottom of mold. Reserve 3 or 4 bread fingers for top of mold. Dip, but do not soak, one side of each piece of bread in melted butter and overlap bread fingers butter-side out in mold. Place bread triangles butter-side down in bottom of mold. Fill in any holes with small pieces of bread dipped in melted butter. Spoon apple mixture into mold and mound top slightly as it will shrink while baking. Cover with reserved bread fingers. Dot with 1 to 2 tablespoons butter. Bake 15 minutes or until bread begins to brown. Reduce heat to 350°F (175°C) and bake 40 to 50 minutes longer until charlotte is firm and sides are golden brown. Ease bread slightly away from sides of mold to check browning. To serve hot, let charlotte stand 10 to 15 minutes before unmolding onto a hot platter. To serve cold, refrigerate charlotte before unmolding. *Apple Charlotte can be prepared 12 hours ahead and refrigerated.* Unmold just before serving. Makes 6 servings.

Custard Sauce
Crème Anglaise

Serve Custard Sauce hot or cold with fresh or poached fruit, or cake.

1 cup milk
1 vanilla bean, split lengthwise or 1 to 2
   teaspoons grated lemon or orange peel

3 egg yolks
2 tablespoons sugar

In a medium saucepan, scald milk with vanilla bean by bringing it just to a boil. If using grated peel, scald milk without flavoring. Remove from heat, cover and let stand 10 to 15 minutes. Beat egg yolks with sugar until thick and pale. Strain in half the hot milk, then whisk back into remaining hot milk. Using a wooden spoon, stir constantly in a pan or double boiler over medium heat until custard thickens enough to leave a trail on spoon, page 12. Do not boil or custard will curdle. Immediately remove from heat and strain into a bowl. Add grated peel if desired. Cool completely by setting bowl in ice, then refrigerate. *Custard Sauce can be prepared 2 days ahead, covered and refrigerated.* Makes 1 cup of sauce.

Pineapple Surprise
Ananas en Surprise

A lovely version of Baked Alaska, with a pineapple shell taking the place of cake.

1 large ripe pineapple
2 tablespoons kirsch
3 to 5 tablespoons sugar

Meringue:
3 egg whites
3/4 cup sugar

Meringue, see below
1-1/2 pints Pineapple Sherbet, page 180,
   or Orange Sherbet, page 181

1 teaspoon vanilla extract

Cut pineapple in half lengthwise, including plume. With a curved grapefruit knife, cut out fruit, leaving boat-shaped shells. Cut fruit into chunks, discarding center core. Sprinkle chunks with kirsch and a few tablespoons sugar. Spoon into pineapple shells. Cover and refrigerate up to 8 hours. Preheat oven to 425°F (220°C). Prepare Meringue 15 minutes before serving. Spoon Pineapple or Orange Sherbet over pineapple chunks. Spoon Meringue into a pastry bag fitted with a medium star tube, pages 13 and 14. Pipe meringue ruffles covering sherbet completely so heat cannot penetrate to sherbet. Sprinkle with 1 tablespoon sugar. Bake 6 to 8 minutes until Meringue is browned. Serve immediately. Makes 6 servings.

Meringue:
Whip egg whites until stiff, page 7. Add 2 tablespoons sugar and continue whipping 20 seconds or until mixture forms long peaks when beaters are lifted. Fold in remaining sugar and vanilla.

How to Make Pineapple Surprise

1/Place pineapple shells over ice. Fill with pineapple chunks and sherbet.

2/Completely cover pineapple half with meringue.

Raspberry Mousse
Mousse aux Framboises

If keeping Raspberry Mousse more than one day, do not use a metal mold or mousse will darken.

1 pint fresh raspberries or 1 pkg.
   frozen raspberries, drained
1 tablespoon water
Juice of 1/2 lemon
1 envelope gelatin
3 whole eggs
2 egg yolks

3/4 cup sugar
1 cup whipping cream, whipped until
   it holds a soft shape
1 tablespoon kirsch
Chantilly Cream, page 157, made with
   3/4 cup whipping cream
6 to 8 fresh whole raspberries, if desired

Puree the raspberries in a blender. Strain to remove seeds. In a small bowl, mix 1 tablespoon water and lemon juice. Sprinkle gelatin over mixture. Let stand 5 minutes or until spongy, page 9. In a medium bowl, beat whole eggs, egg yolks and sugar until blended. Place bowl over a pan of hot but not boiling water and whisk until mixture leaves a ribbon trail, page 145. Remove from heat. Beat softened gelatin into hot egg mixture. Beat mixture until cool. Rinse a 1-1/2-quart ring mold with cold water. Stir raspberry puree into cool egg mixture and place bowl over ice. Stir until mixture starts to thicken; immediately fold in softly whipped cream and kirsch. Pour into mold. Cover and refrigerate at least 2 hours or until firm. *Raspberry Mousse can be prepared to this point 24 hours ahead and refrigerated. Let it come to room temperature before serving.* Not more than 2 hours before serving, unmold mousse by running a knife around edges and dipping bottom of mold in a pan of lukewarm water for a few seconds. Unmold onto a serving plate. Prepare Chantilly Cream. Spoon into a pastry bag fitted with a medium star tube, pages 13 and 14. Pipe Chantilly Cream around base of mousse. Top mousse with Chantilly Cream rosettes. If desired, place a raspberry on each rosette. Serve at room temperature. Makes 6 to 8 servings.

Chocolate Mousse
Mousse au Chocolat

An unbeatable favorite!

6 oz. semisweet chocolate, coarsely chopped
1/4 cup strong black coffee
4 eggs, separated
1 tablespoon butter

1 tablespoon rum or 1/2
   teaspoon vanilla extract
Chantilly Cream, page 157, made with
   1/2 cup cream

In a medium, heavy saucepan, melt chocolate in coffee over low heat. Cook, stirring constantly, until chocolate is thick and creamy but still falls easily from a spoon. Remove from heat and beat in egg yolks one by one to thicken mixture. Beat in butter and rum or vanilla. Cool slightly. Whip egg whites until stiff, page 7. Heat chocolate mixture until hot to the touch. Gently fold into egg whites, pages 10 and 11. Pour into 4 mousse pots or parfait glasses. Cover and refrigerate at least 6 hours for flavors to blend. *Chocolate Mousse can be prepared to this point 2 days ahead and refrigerated.* Not more than 2 hours before serving, prepare Chantilly Cream. Spoon into a pastry bag fitted with a medium star tube, pages 13 and 14. Pipe a large rosette on each mousse to cover top completely. Serve cold. Makes 4 servings.

Grand Marnier Soufflé
Soufflé Grand Marnier

Before making the soufflé, look at whipping egg whites, page 7, and folding mixtures, pages 10 and 11.

1 cup milk	2-1/2 tablespoons all-purpose flour
3 egg yolks	2 to 3 tablespoons Grand Marnier
Grated peel of 2 oranges	5 egg whites
1/4 cup granulated sugar	1 tablespoon powdered sugar

Preheat oven to 425°F (220°C). Thickly butter a 1-quart soufflé dish, being sure edge is buttered well so mixture won't stick. Sprinkle buttered dish with granulated sugar, tapping sides to distribute evenly; pour out excess. In a medium saucepan, scald milk by bringing it just to a boil. Beat egg yolks with orange peel and 2 tablespoons granulated sugar until thick and pale. Stir in flour. Whisk in half the hot milk, then whisk back into remaining hot milk. Bring to a boil, whisking constantly until mixture thickens. Cook over low heat 2 minutes, whisking constantly. Mixture will thin slightly, indicating the flour is completely cooked. Cool to lukewarm. Stir in Grand Marnier. *Grand Marnier Soufflé can be prepared to this point 3 to 4 hours ahead. Rub surface of mixture with butter to prevent a skin forming, page 13. If made ahead, cover and refrigerate. Preheat oven to 425°F (220°C) 30 minutes before serving.* Whip egg whites until stiff, page 7. Add remaining 2 tablespoons granulated sugar; beat 20 seconds longer to make a light meringue. Heat Grand Marnier mixture until hot to the touch. Remove from heat and stir in a fourth of the meringue. Add mixture to remaining meringue and fold together as lightly as possible, pages 10 and 11. Spoon into prepared mold. Bake 12 to 15 minutes until puffed and browned. Sprinkle with powdered sugar and serve immediately. Makes 4 servings.

Chocolate Soufflé
Soufflé au Chocolat

Baked as directed, the top of the soufflé will be crusty and the center will be a creamy chocolate sauce.

4 oz. semisweet chocolate, coarsely chopped	1-1/2 teaspoons brandy
1/2 cup whipping cream	5 egg whites
3 egg yolks	3 tablespoons granulated sugar
1/2 teaspoon vanilla extract	1 tablespoon powdered sugar

Preheat oven to 425°F (220°C). Thickly butter a 1-quart soufflé dish, being sure edge is buttered well so mixture won't stick. Sprinkle buttered dish with granulated sugar, tapping sides to distribute evenly; pour out excess. In a heavy saucepan, melt chocolate in cream over low heat, stirring constantly. Cook, stirring constantly, until mixture is thick and will just fall from the spoon. Remove from heat and beat egg yolks into the hot mixture to thicken it. Stir in vanilla and brandy. *Chocolate Soufflé can be prepared to this point 3 to 4 hours ahead. If made ahead, cover and refrigerate. Preheat oven to 425°F (220°C) 30 minutes before serving.* Whip egg whites until stiff, page 7. Add granulated sugar. Beat 20 seconds longer to make a light meringue. Heat chocolate mixture until hot to the touch. Remove from heat and stir in a fourth of the meringue. Add mixture to remaining meringue and fold together as lightly as possible, pages 10 and 11. Spoon into prepared mold. Bake 12 to 15 minutes until puffed and a crust has formed on top. Sprinkle with powdered sugar and serve immediately. Makes 4 servings.

Crepes Suzette
Crêpes Suzette

A classic dessert, supposedly created to honor a lady friend of Edward VII when he was Prince of Wales.

1/2 cup butter	**3 to 4 tablespoons Grand Marnier**
1/4 cup sugar	**14 to 16 Crepes, page 18**
Grated peel of 1 orange	**2 to 3 tablespoons brandy**

Cream 1/4 cup butter with sugar and orange peel until soft and light. Beat in 1 tablespoon Grand Marnier. Spread butter mixture on underside, or spotted side, of each crepe, stacking crepes on top of each other. Keep covered at room temperature. Heat 1 to 2 tablespoons butter in a chafing dish. Place a crepe butter-side down in chafing dish. Heat 30 seconds or until very hot. Fold in half twice, underside folded to the inside, making a triangle. Leave at the side of chafing dish. Repeat with remaining crepes. When all the crepes are heated and folded, the butter should have caramelized in bottom of chafing dish, adding flavor to crepes. In a small saucepan, heat brandy and remaining 2 to 3 tablespoons Grand Marnier. Pour over crepes and carefully ignite, page 11. Serve immediately. Makes 4 servings.

Apple Crepes
Crêpes Normande

Calvados is apple brandy—an ideal flavoring for apple desserts.

3 to 4 tablespoons butter	**Calvados Sauce, see below**
3 to 4 tart apples, peeled, cored, thinly sliced	**14 to 16 Crepes, page 18**
2 to 3 tablespoons sugar	**1/4 cup Calvados or other apple brandy**
3 to 4 tablespoons whipping cream, if desired	

Calvados Sauce:

2/3 cup whipping cream	**2 tablespoons Calvados or**
1 tablespoon sugar	**other apple brandy**

Melt butter in a medium skillet. Add apple slices. Sauté 2 to 3 minutes. Sprinkle with sugar; toss to coat. Cook 1 to 2 minutes longer until caramelized, page 12, tossing occasionally. Apples should be tender but not soft. Stir in cream, if desired. Prepare Calvados Sauce. Grease a 2-quart baking dish. Not more than 2 to 3 hours before serving, spoon 2 tablespoons apple mixture on each crepe and roll into cigar shapes. Arrange diagonally in prepared baking dish. Preheat oven to 400°F (205°C) 30 minutes before serving. Bake Crepes 8 to 10 minutes until very hot. Reheat Calvados Sauce. Flame crepes with Calvados, page 11. Serve immediately; serve sauce separately. Makes 4 servings.

Calvados Sauce:
In a small saucepan, boil cream until reduced by half. Stir in sugar and Calvados. Boil 1 minute longer. *Calvados Sauce can be made 1 to 2 days ahead, covered and refrigerated.*

Petits Pots de Crème
Petits Pots de Crème

A specialty of Maxim's in Paris. They come in three flavors so each guest can choose two or three.

3 oz. semisweet chocolate, coarsely chopped	3/4 cup sugar
1 qt. milk	2 teaspoons instant coffee powder
1 vanilla bean, split lengthwise	1 teaspoon hot water
12 egg yolks	

Preheat oven to 325°F (165°C). Melt chocolate over boiling water. Cool. In a medium saucepan, scald milk with vanilla bean by bringing it just to a boil. Cover; remove from heat and let stand 10 to 15 minutes. Remove vanilla bean. In a medium bowl, beat egg yolks with sugar until pale and slightly thickened. Whisk in hot milk. Strain mixture into a pitcher. Pour a third of the mixture equally into 4 mousse pots or custard cups. Dissolve coffee powder in 1 teaspoon hot water and stir into pitcher of remaining custard. Pour half this custard equally into 4 more mousse pots. Stir cool melted chocolate into remaining custard. Fill last 4 mousse pots. Although the last custard mixture combines vanilla, coffee and chocolate, chocolate will predominate. Skim off surface bubbles with a spoon. Cover mousse pots with lids or foil and place in a water bath, page 9. Bring just to a boil, transfer mousse pots in water bath to oven. Bake 25 to 30 minutes until almost set and a knife inserted in center comes out clean. Reduce oven temperature if water starts to boil or custard may curdle. Do not overbake. Remove pots from water bath. Cool. *Petits Pots de Crème can be made 24 hours ahead, covered and refrigerated.* Serve at room temperature. Makes 12 individual pots or 4 to 6 servings.

Strawberry Charlotte Malakoff
Charlotte Malakoff aux Fraises

Ground almonds give body and richness to this fruit charlotte.

12 to 14 Ladyfingers, page 163	1 tablespoon kirsch
3 tablespoons kirsch	1/2 cup whipping cream, whipped until
1 pint fresh strawberries, hulled	it holds a soft shape
1/2 cup unsalted butter	Chantilly Cream, page 157, made with
2/3 cup sugar	1/2 cup cream
1 cup whole blanched almonds, ground,	Melba Sauce, opposite
pages 9 and 10	

Butter a 6-cup charlotte mold or soufflé dish. Line bottom of mold with a circle of waxed paper. Line sides with Ladyfingers, trimming so they fit tightly. Sprinkle remaining Ladyfingers with 2 tablespoons kirsch. Slice strawberries, reserving 6 whole ones for decoration. Cream butter, gradually adding sugar. Continue beating until mixture is light and fluffy. Stir in ground almonds, 1 tablespoon kirsch and sliced strawberries. Do not beat mixture or oil will be drawn out of almonds. Fold in whipped cream. Spoon half the mixture into prepared mold. Cover with kirsch-soaked Ladyfingers. Spread remaining almond mixture evenly on top. Cover and refrigerate charlotte at least 4 hours or until firmly set. *Strawberry Charlotte Malakoff can be prepared to this point 3 to 4 days ahead and refrigerated.* Not more than 2 hours before serving, make Chantilly Cream and spoon into a pastry bag fitted with a medium star tube, pages 13 and 14. Trim tops of Ladyfingers level with almond mixture. Unmold charlotte onto a platter. Decorate top and base with rosettes of whipped cream and reserved strawberries. Serve Melba Sauce separately. Makes 6 servings.

Caramel Cream
Crème Caramel

Molds are lined with caramel which becomes a sauce when unmolded.

Caramel Topping, see below
2 cups milk
1 vanilla bean, split lengthwise

1/3 cup sugar
2 eggs
2 egg yolks

Caramel Topping:
1/2 cup sugar
1/4 cup water

Prepare Caramel Topping. Pour hot caramel into a 4-cup soufflé dish or 8 custard cups. Immediately turn dish or custard cups to coat base and sides evenly with caramel. Cool. Preheat oven to 350°F (175°C). In a medium saucepan, scald milk with vanilla bean by bringing it just to a boil. Remove from heat. Cover and let stand 10 to 15 minutes. Remove vanilla bean. Add sugar and stir until dissolved. In a medium bowl, beat eggs with egg yolks until blended. Stir in hot milk. Cool slightly and strain into prepared dish or cups. Place in a water bath, page 9. Boil water. Transfer dish or cups in water bath to oven. Bake 40 to 50 minutes in soufflé dish or 20 to 25 minutes in custard cups. Reduce oven temperature if water starts to boil or custard may curdle. Do not overbake. Cream is done when it is set and a knife inserted in center comes out clean. Remove dish or cups from water bath. Cool. *Caramel Cream can be made 24 hours ahead, covered and refrigerated.* Not more than 1 hour before serving, run a knife around edge of cream and turn out onto a deep platter or serving plates. Makes 8 servings.

Caramel Topping:
In a small heavy saucepan, heat sugar and water until sugar is dissolved. Boil until caramelized, page 11. Remove from heat and let bubbles subside.

Melba Sauce
Sauce Melba

Pour this over your favorite ice cream to create a special dessert.

1 pint fresh raspberries or 1 pkg.
    frozen raspberries, thawed
1 tablespoon kirsch

3 to 4 tablespoons powdered sugar,
    if desired

Puree raspberries in a blender. Strain to remove seeds. Add kirsch and powdered sugar to taste. If using frozen raspberries, powdered sugar may not be needed.

Pears Belle Hélène
Poires Belle Hélène

Homemade ice cream can be replaced by ready-made, but do make the chocolate sauce!

1/2 cup sugar	4 ripe pears
2 cups water	Juice of 1 lemon
Pared peel of 1 lemon	Rich Chocolate Sauce, see below
1 vanilla bean, split lengthwise	1 pint Vanilla Ice Cream, page 182

Rich Chocolate Sauce:

4 oz. semisweet chocolate, chopped	1/2 teaspoon vanilla extract or
1/3 cup whipping cream	1 tablespoon rum
2 tablespoons butter, cut in pieces	

Choose a saucepan that just fits pears standing upright. Heat sugar and water in saucepan until sugar is dissolved. Add lemon peel and vanilla bean. Simmer 5 minutes. Peel pears, leaving stems on. Rub lemon juice over pears to prevent discoloration. Carefully remove core through bottom of each pear. Cut thin slice from bottom so pears stand upright. Immerse pears in syrup. If needed, add more water to cover. Gently simmer pears in sugar syrup 20 to 25 minutes until tender. Remove from heat. Cool pears to lukewarm in sugar syrup. Drain and refrigerate. Chill 4 dessert dishes in freezer. Prepare Rich Chocolate Sauce. Just before serving, reheat chocolate sauce. Flatten a scoop of Vanilla Ice Cream in each dessert dish. Place a pear on top. Cover with hot chocolate sauce. Serve immediately. Makes 4 servings.

Rich Chocolate Sauce:
In a small heavy saucepan over low heat, melt chocolate with cream, stirring often. When mixture is smooth, remove from heat and add butter, piece by piece. Stir in vanilla or rum.

Pears in Red Wine
Poires au Vin Rouge

Poaching pears in red wine gives them a pretty pink color.

1/2 cup sugar	Lemon juice, if desired
4 cups red wine	Additional sugar, if desired
1 strip of lemon peel	Chantilly Cream, page 157, made with
1 (2-inch) cinnamon stick	3/4 cup cream
6 firm pears (about 3 lbs.)	

Choose a saucepan that just fits pears standing upright. In the saucepan, heat sugar, wine, lemon peel and cinnamon stick until sugar is dissolved. Boil syrup 5 minutes; cool slightly. Peel pears. Carefully core from base, leaving stem on top. Cut a thin slice off bottom so pears stand upright. Immerse pears in syrup. Add more wine to cover if needed. Cover saucepan and gently simmer pears 20 to 45 minutes until tender. Cooking time depends on variety and ripeness of pears, but 20 minutes is minimum to prevent discoloration around cores. Cool pears to lukewarm in syrup. Drain, reserving syrup. Arrange pears in a shallow dish. Strain syrup into saucepan and gently simmer until thick enough to coat a spoon; do not let syrup caramelize. Taste, adding lemon juice or sugar if desired. Cool slightly and spoon over pears. Refrigerate. *Pears in Red Wine can be cooked 24 hours ahead, covered and refrigerated.* Not more than 2 hours before serving, prepare Chantilly Cream. Serve cold pears and Chantilly Cream separately. Makes 6 servings.

Pineapple Sherbet
Sorbet à l'Ananas

Choose a very ripe pineapple for maximum flavor.

1 large pineapple	**3 to 4 tablespoons kirsch**
1 cup water	**1 cup Sugar Syrup for Sherbet,**
Juice of 1 lemon	**opposite, cooled**

Chill 6 sherbet glasses in freezer. Cut the plume and bottom from 1 large pineapple. Cut into slices. Remove peel and core. Pull pineapple into shreds with 2 forks. Stir shredded pineapple, water, lemon juice and 1 tablespoon kirsch into 2/3 cup sugar syrup. Taste and add more sugar syrup if needed. Freeze in a churn freezer until firm. Pile sherbet in chilled glasses and sprinkle each with a little kirsch just before serving. Makes about 1-1/2 quarts of sherbet.

Variation

Iced Pineapple (Ananas Givré): Halve pineapple lengthwise, including plume, and scoop out fruit. Reserve fruit for another use. Refrigerate pineapple shells. Just before serving, scoop sherbet into balls with an ice cream scoop and pile in chilled pineapple shells.

Lemon Sherbet
Sorbet au Citron

This sherbet can be sweet or tart, according to your taste.

Grated peel of 4 lemons	**2 cups Sugar Syrup for Sherbet,**
1 cup fresh lemon juice (5 to 6 lemons)	**opposite, cooled**
3 cups water	

Chill 6 sherbet glasses in freezer. Stir lemon peel, juice and water into 1-1/2 cups sugar syrup. Taste and add more sugar syrup if needed. Freeze in a churn freezer until firm. Pile in chilled sherbet glasses. Makes about 1-1/2 quarts of sherbet.

Variation

Iced Lemons (Citrons Givrés): Halve 5 or 6 lemons and scoop out all the pulp, being careful not to pierce the skin. Reserve pulp for another use. Pack the sherbet in hollowed lemon shells. Cover with the lemon shell lid and top each lemon with a bay leaf just before serving.

To ensure freshness, pack ice cream or sherbet into chilled bowls or metal molds and cover tightly with foil or freezer wrap before storing in the freezer.

1/If using an ice cream maker, churn orange juice mixture until it sets and holds its shape on a spoon.

2/Without an ice cream maker, place mixture in freezer. Stir occasionally with a wire whisk to break up lumps so mixture will freeze evenly.

How to Make Orange Sherbet

Orange Sherbet
Sorbet à l'Orange

Like Lemon Sherbet, this mixture can be packed in hollowed orange shells for a pretty presentation.

Grated peel of 2 oranges	**1/3 cup water**
3 cups fresh orange juice	**1 cup Sugar Syrup for Sherbet,**
Juice of 1/2 lemon	**see below, cooled**

Chill 4 sherbet glasses in freezer. Stir orange peel, orange juice, lemon juice and water into 2/3 cup sugar syrup. Taste and add more sugar syrup, if needed. Freeze in a churn freezer until firm. Pile in chilled sherbet glasses. Makes about 1 quart of sherbet.

Sugar Syrup for Sherbet
Sirop pour les Sorbets

Use this simple syrup whenever you make sherbet.

3/4 cup sugar	**2 teaspoons lemon juice**
1/2 cup water	

In a small heavy saucepan, heat sugar with water and lemon juice over low heat until dissolved. Boil just until the syrup is clear, 2 to 3 minutes. Makes 1 cup of syrup.

Strawberries Romanoff
Fraises Romanoff

Just right for serving in summer with cake or Ladyfingers, page 163.

1 qt. fresh strawberries
Juice and grated peel of 1 orange
3 tablespoons Grand Marnier

1 tablespoon brandy
3 to 4 tablespoons sugar
1 cup whipping cream, whipped until stiff

Wash strawberries. Reserve 4 whole strawberries for decoration. Hull remaining strawberries, cut in half and put in a medium bowl. Add orange juice, peel, Grand Marnier, brandy and sugar to taste. Stir to dissolve sugar. Let stand 10 to 15 minutes. Stir whipped cream into mixture and spoon it into a glass bowl. It will thicken slightly. Tightly cover and refrigerate at least 6 hours for flavors to blend. *Strawberries Romanoff can be prepared 24 hours ahead and refrigerated.* Just before serving, decorate with whole strawberries. Makes 4 servings.

Vanilla Ice Cream
Glace à la Vanille

Little black dots in vanilla ice cream are vanilla-bean seeds—a sign of authenticity.

2/3 cup Vanilla Sugar, see below, or
   plain sugar
2 cups milk
1 vanilla bean, split lengthwise

5 egg yolks
1 cup whipping cream, whipped until
   it holds a soft shape

Vanilla Sugar:
1 vanilla bean
2/3 cup sugar

Prepare Vanilla Sugar. In a medium saucepan, scald milk with vanilla bean by bringing it just to a boil. Cover, remove from heat and let stand 10 to 15 minutes. In a medium bowl, beat egg yolks with Vanilla Sugar until light and slightly thickened. Whisk half the hot milk into egg-yolk mixture. Whisk mixture back into remaining milk. Stir constantly with a wooden spoon over low heat until custard thickens slightly, page 184. Do not overcook custard or it will curdle. Immediately remove from heat and strain into a medium bowl, removing vanilla bean. Cool custard. Freeze in a churn freezer until slushy. Add softly whipped cream to mixture and continue freezing until firm. Makes about 1 quart of ice cream.

Vanilla Sugar:
Insert vanilla bean in sugar, cover and let stand 1 week.

Variations

Chocolate Ice Cream (Glace au Chocolat): Omit vanilla bean. Melt 7 ounces semisweet chocolate, coarsely chopped, over boiling water. Beat into custard before straining.
Coffee Ice Cream (Glace au Café): Omit vanilla bean. Add 1-1/2 tablespoons dry instant coffee to scalded milk before whisking into egg yolk mixture.

Peach Melba
Pêches Melba

This is the real Peach Melba, created by the famous chef Escoffier to honor singer Dame Nellie Melba.

1/4 cup sugar
1 cup water
Pared peel of 1 lemon
1 vanilla bean, split lengthwise
4 ripe peaches, halved

Chantilly Cream, page 157, made with
   1/2 cup cream
1 pint Vanilla Ice Cream, opposite
Melba Sauce, page 177

In a small heavy saucepan, heat sugar and water until sugar dissolves. Add lemon peel and vanilla bean. Completely immerse peach halves cut-side up in sugar mixture. Gently poach 8 to 12 minutes until just tender. Remove from heat. Cool peaches in syrup to lukewarm. Peel peaches and refrigerate in syrup. Chill 4 sherbet glasses in freezer. Not more than 2 hours before serving, prepare Chantilly Cream and spoon it into a pastry bag fitted with a medium star tube, pages 13 and 14. Just before serving, place a scoop of Vanilla Ice Cream in each sherbet glass and arrange 2 drained peach halves on each side of ice cream. Coat peaches with Melba Sauce and top with a rosette of Chantilly Cream. Makes 4 servings.

Cold Lemon Soufflé
Soufflé Froid au Citron

This cold soufflé is set in a paper collar. When the collar is removed, the mixture looks as if it has risen.

1-1/2 envelopes gelatin
1/4 cup cold water
6 eggs, separated
1-1/2 cups sugar
Juice of 4 lemons (2/3 cup)
Grated peel of 4 lemons (2 tablespoons)

1-1/3 cups whipping cream, whipped until
   it holds a soft shape
Chantilly Cream, page 157, made with
   3/4 cup cream
3 tablespoons pistachios, blanched,
   chopped, if desired

Wrap a strip of waxed paper or a double thickness of foil around a 6-cup soufflé dish so it extends 2 to 3 inches above edge of dish. Fasten with scotch tape or string. Sprinkle gelatin over 1/4 cup cold water in a small pan and let stand 5 minutes until spongy, page 9. In a large bowl, beat egg yolks, 1 cup sugar, lemon juice and peel until blended. Place bowl over a pan of hot but not boiling water. Whisk until mixture is light and thick enough to leave a ribbon trail, page 145. Remove from heat. Melt softened gelatin over low heat; beat into lemon mixture. Continue beating until mixture is cool. Whip egg whites until stiff, page 7. Add remaining 1/2 cup sugar and beat 20 seconds to make a light meringue. Place bowl of lemon mixture over ice and stir mixture constantly until it starts to thicken. Remove bowl from ice and fold in softly whipped cream, pages 10 and 11, then fold in meringue. Fill prepared soufflé dish. Mixture should be 1 to 2 inches above top of dish. Refrigerate 2 hours or until firm. Not more than 2 hours before serving, prepare Chantilly Cream. Trim paper collar level with soufflé mixture. Spread top of soufflé with Chantilly Cream and mark a diamond pattern with a knife point. Spoon remaining Chantilly Cream into a pastry bag fitted with a medium star tube, pages 13 and 14. Pipe rosettes around edge of soufflé; refrigerate. *Cold Lemon Soufflé can be refrigerated 24 hours.* Let it come to room temperature before serving. Remove paper collar just before serving and press pistachios around sides of soufflé, if desired. Makes 8 servings.

Iced Praline Parfait
Parfait Praliné

Praline is a mixture of caramel and toasted almonds. It is ground and used to flavor desserts.

3/4 cup sugar
1/2 cup whole unblanched almonds
1/4 cup water

4 egg yolks
1-1/2 cups whipping cream, whipped until
    it holds a soft shape

Grease a baking sheet. Chill 4 parfait glasses in freezer. Combine 1/4 cup sugar and almonds in a small heavy saucepan. Heat over low heat, stirring occasionally, until sugar dissolves and starts to brown. Continue stirring over low heat until mixture is deep brown and almonds pop, indicating they are toasted. Do not burn the caramel, page 11. Immediately pour hot praline onto prepared baking sheet. Cool. When hard, break into pieces. Grind a few pieces at a time in blender or food processor to a fine powder. In a small heavy saucepan, heat remaining 1/2 cup sugar and 1/4 cup water until sugar dissolves. Bring to a boil. Boil to soft ball stage, 239°F (115°C) on a candy thermometer. At this temperature, syrup will form a soft ball when a little is lowered by spoon into a cup of cold water and is immediately removed from spoon while under water. Beat egg yolks in a medium bowl until slightly thickened. Let bubbles in the hot sugar mixture subside. Gradually pour hot sugar syrup over egg yolks, beating constantly. If using an electric beater, pour syrup in a thin stream between beaters and bowl so syrup doesn't stick to either. Increase speed to high and continue beating until mixture is thick and cool. Stir in praline powder, reserving a little for decoration. Fold in softly whipped cream, pages 10 and 11. Spoon mixture into chilled parfait glasses. Sprinkle with reserved praline powder and freeze at least 4 hours. Makes 4 servings.

Variations

Iced Chocolate Parfait (Parfait au Chocolat): Omit praline. Melt 5 ounces semisweet chocolate, coarsely chopped, over boiling water. Cool but do not allow to set before adding to cool yolk mixture. Continue beating until completely cool before folding in whipped cream. Top parfait with a candied violet or a rosette of Chantilly Cream, page 157.

Iced Coffee Parfait (Parfait au Café): Omit praline. Dissolve 1 tablespoon instant coffee powder in 3 tablespoons hot water; beat into cool yolk mixture. Sprinkle parfait with a little powdered coffee or top with a rosette of Chantilly Cream, page 157.

How to Cook Custard Until a Trail Is Left on the Spoon

When ready, egg custard thickens only slightly. If overcooked, it will curdle because the egg yolks coagulate, in effect forming sweet scrambled eggs. Custard is close to thickening point when most of the white foam on top disappears, leaving the surface an even yellow color. Remove sauce from heat and lift out wooden spoon. Always use a wooden spoon for stirring—not a whisk. Custard should coat the spoon lightly. Draw a finger across the back of the spoon: It should leave a clear trail in the custard. If the trail quickly disappears, the custard is not thick enough and should be cooked about half a minute more before testing again.

Caramel Bavarian Cream
Bavarois au Caramel

Bavarian cream is a custard with gelatin added.

Caramel Syrup, see below
1 envelope gelatin
3/4 cup water
6 egg yolks
6 tablespoons sugar

Caramel Syrup:
1 cup sugar
1/3 cup cold water

1-1/2 cups milk
1/2 cup whipping cream, whipped until
 it holds a soft shape
Chantilly Cream, page 157, made with
 1/2 cup cream

1/2 cup hot water

Prepare Caramel Syrup. In a small bowl, sprinkle gelatin over 1/2 cup water. Let stand 5 minutes or until spongy, page 9. Rinse a 1-quart mold with cold water. In a medium bowl, beat egg yolks and sugar until pale and slightly thickened. In a medium saucepan, scald milk by bringing it just to a boil. Whisk half of the hot milk into egg yolk mixture. Whisk mixture back into remaining hot milk. Stir constantly with a wooden spoon over low heat until custard thickens slightly, opposite. Do not overcook custard or it will curdle. Immediately remove from heat and strain into a medium bowl. Add softened gelatin; stir until completely dissolved. Add half the Caramel Syrup. Cool, stirring occasionally. Place cooled custard over a bowl of ice and stir constantly until it starts to thicken. Fold in softly whipped cream, pages 10 and 11, and pour mixture into prepared mold. Cover and refrigerate at least 2 hours or until firm. *Caramel Bavarian Cream can be prepared to this point 24 hours ahead and refrigerated. Let it come to room temperature before serving.* Heat remaining half of the Caramel Syrup with remaining 1/4 cup water; let cool for sauce. Not more than 2 hours before serving, unmold cream by carefully running a knife around edges and dipping bottom of mold in a pan of lukewarm water for a few seconds. Unmold onto a serving plate. Prepare Chantilly Cream and spoon it into a pastry bag fitted with a medium star tube, pages 13 and 14. Pipe Chantilly Cream rosettes around base of mold. Serve at room temperature. Serve sauce separately. Makes 6 to 8 servings.

Caramel Syrup:
In a small heavy saucepan, heat sugar with 1/3 cup cold water until sugar dissolves. Boil until syrup caramelizes, page 11. Remove from heat and immediately add 1/2 cup hot water. **Stand back as caramel will spatter.** Heat over low heat until caramel dissolves. Use half of this caramel syrup to prepare Bavarian cream. Reserve remaining half to prepare sauce.

Variation

Caramel Charlotte (Charlotte au Caramel): Line a 1-1/2-quart mold with Ladyfingers, page 163, trimming so they fit tightly. Pour in Caramel Bavarian Cream mixture and cover with Ladyfingers. Cover and refrigerate at least 2 hours. Trim tops of Ladyfingers level with caramel mixture and unmold onto a platter.

French Recipe Titles

Index

Index

Index

Index

Index

A-6.83391421101239-90